Quinlan

Prices 50% higher
in 1991

Go
South Inside

OTHER BOOKS BY CARL D. LANE

Go South Inside

Cruising the Inland Waterway

By
Carl D. Lane

With Drawings by the Author

International Marine Publishing Company
Camden, Maine

To Jim and Liz Emmett
of the
M.V. *Chinook*

... whose only home these many years
has been their beloved "Intracoastal."

Copyright © 1977 by Carl D. Lane
Library of Congress Catalog Card Number 77-82090
International Standard Book Number 0-87742-070-X
Typeset by A & B Typesetters, Inc., Concord, N.H.
Printed by Alpine Press, South Braintree, Massachusetts
Bound by New Hampshire Bindery, Concord, N.H.

Contents

Preface

Way back in the Dirty Thirties, when the Great Depression was supposed to be over but wasn't—at least not for aspiring writers—I loaded my family in a Model A Ford station wagon, drew my pitiful all from the bank and headed for Florida to live and write as economically as possible. The cheapest domicile that we could find was an ancient power cruiser, an Elco, sans engine, lashed to a rickety dock hard by a beautiful South Seas beach and close to a fragrant citrus grove, and we lived on this vessel all winter. From it my son went to school and on it I wrote and prospered mildly and my wife did the household chores, just as we did in the cold northern winters of our native Maine. Our living costs went down by half and we lived, mostly outdoors, an idyllic, almost lazy life in the soft tropical winter of Florida. It would have been even nicer if we could have moved the boat. However, there was a little skiff with a sail on the after trunk, and in this craft we did our local cruising. The next year the owner installed a used Red Wing engine and jacked the rent to 25 bucks a month and we were able, if there happened to be a slight surplus in the kitty for fuel, to cruise, and so we discovered the Everglades and the Bahamas and the endless pleasant gunkholes of the long Florida coastlines.

It was a great and happy way of winter life, and we have been doing it ever since. To be sure, we now do it in our own boats and we usually leave from and return to Maine. We still love it, still enjoy the tropical winters at a fairly modest budget, truly get away from the crowds and frustrations of an over-populated shore life, and, I suspect, live longer—for that first winter was a long time ago.

Of course, we are no longer alone. Literally thousands of "live-aboards" so spend happy winters in the warmer climates of the East Coast. They no longer need moor to rickety docks. There are scores and scores of fine marinas with every amenity, and state and national parks, and many nautical clubs and numerous anchoring-out areas where one can still winter in the sun in luxury and at bargain prices. All you need is a boat: canoe, kayak, sloop, mini-cruiser, fisherman, sloop, trawler, or a 200-footer with a crew of 20. Each October and November, a watcher at any port on the Intracoastal Waterway could count a hundred boats a day winging southward—and the same number returning in April and May.

The purpose of this work is to acquaint the reader with the current facts of life afloat; in a boat that follows the sun down the East Coast in winter; the do's, don'ts, the special techniques, the costs, the rewards, and the dangers. In various boats, both sail and power, our family has spent some 26 winters in the South, in the islands of the Caribbean and the Leeward chain; we have made the round-trip passage through the "Ditch" 22 of those times. We are far from record holders: a retired admiral from Rhode Island made the trip 42 times, and probably many a professional skipper has bested that record. We have had vacations and experiences and memories that we could have obtained in no other way, and that we could otherwise probably not have afforded. Further, we have, unlike the average seasonal boatman, reaped a hundred percent return from our nautical investment, because we use the boat the full 12 months of the year. Like the tortoise, we carry our home with us always and need no other. Every moment of the life is precious, unique, and utterly satisfying . . . even if, for contrast, we take to a shore cottage on our Maine island each summer. We have a life of rich values indeed. Perhaps the greatest value of all is the host of very special friends we have made and treasured over the years. I do believe that seafaring friends, above all others, are the best friends.

You, too, can join this special society, especially if you already have a boat, however modest. You do not need great baskets of money, or millionaire yachts, or upper-crust club connections. You just join 'em in some pleasant marina or friendly boat yard or palm-shaded lagoon, and be yourself. You have joined. Few members resign. We know one fine gentleman, still operating his own vessel after over 50 years afloat, who just answered to the age of 93! It is a rare privilege indeed to be counted a "member."

It is my hope that this book will see you on your way to joining this unique brotherhood, that it will answer some of the questions, smooth out some of the rough spots, instruct and guide, and that we will soon have the pleasure of another happy "live-aboard" in the ever-growing fleet that annually enjoys America's many watery winter hideaways.

Carl D. Lane
M. V. PENOBSCOT

Cranberry Island, Maine
and
Fort Myers, Florida

Maps of the Waterway

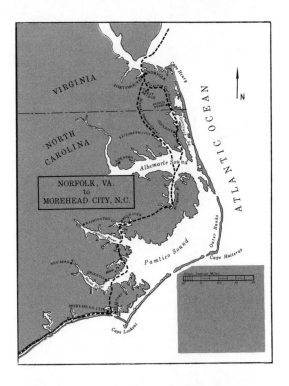

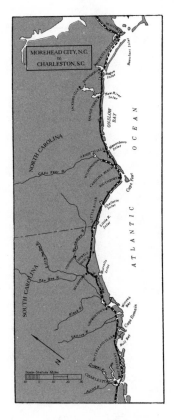

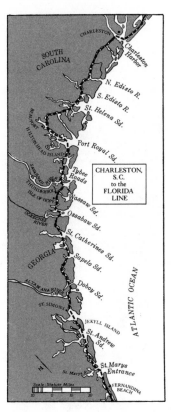

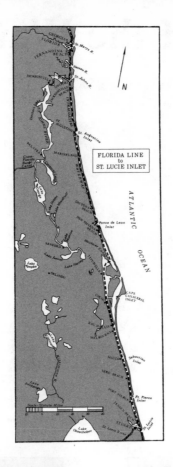

FLORIDA LINE to ST. LUCIE INLET

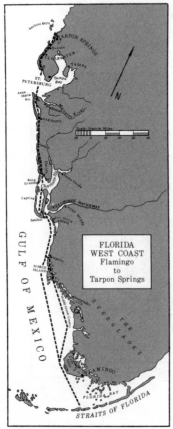

FLORIDA WEST COAST Flamingo to Tarpon Springs

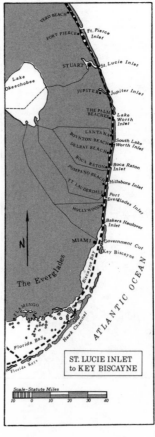

ST. LUCIE INLET to KEY BISCAYNE

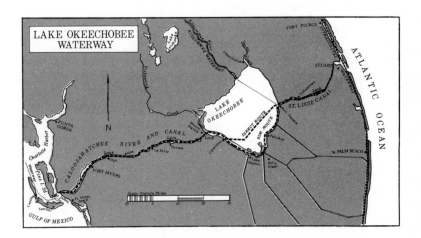

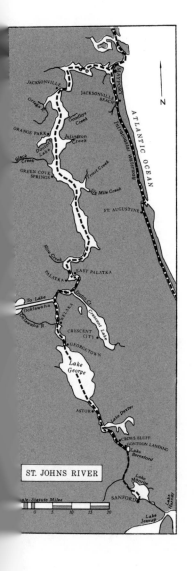

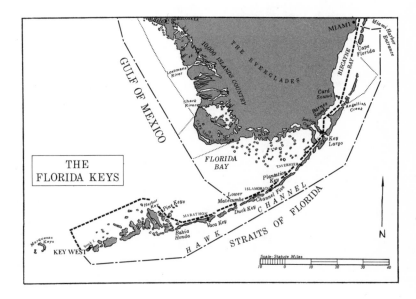

(Maps: *Waterway Guide*)

Chapter 1
The Atlantic Intracoastal Waterway
or the Great Ditch

To most of us, the way "south to the sun" is by superhighway, by swift wings through the sky, or, even in these modern days, by rails of steel. There are no longer coastal steamship services, nor could a man find a safe route for horse and buggy. But ... lying calm and beckoning in the warm sun ... yet another route is there for all to use; to many, it is the very best route of all. This is simply a great, long ribbon of blue water, threading the coastal marshes and the base of the Piedmont, from winter to summer, from storm skies to almost eternal sunshine, from Virginia to the very southern tip of the United States at Key West (and beyond), open to all, free to all. It embraces natural rivers and sounds and bays, tiny creeks and broad estuaries, man-made canals and cuts, winding marsh sloughs and inlets beyond which the sea rolls and heaves. It is known, officially, as the Atlantic Intracoastal Waterway, and to thousands of small-boat travelers simply and affectionately as "The Ditch."

To these many it is an alternate, delightful, and challenging road to the warmest winter climate in the United States: to Florida and the fabulous Keys and the Bahamas and the lower Caribbean islands. They have learned, as have their compatriots in travel trailers and motor homes and campers, the few special techniques required, and they go on to enjoy and value the very special life possible on this watery road to the sun.

The Waterway is an ancient concept; only recently have its many parts, both natural and man-made, been joined into a single, continuous water route of over 2,000 miles. Actually, it begins at Cape Ann, in Massachusetts, follows the coast behind several natural sea barriers, enters the Delaware and

1

Chesapeake Bays, and, finally, at Norfolk, Virginia, at the southern end of Chesapeake Bay, becomes truly an "inland" waterway. Originally (and still officially) commencing at Trenton, New Jersey, it is entirely protected for its length of 1,400 miles to Miami, Florida. From there it continues to Key West or, via a cross-Florida waterway through Lake Okeechobee, to the Gulf Coast; then it follows the coast, more or less protected behind barrier islands and in dug canals, through the states of panhandle Florida, Alabama, Mississippi, Louisiana, and Texas, to the Mexican border at Brownsville. It is owned in its entirety by the federal government, which only recently acquired state and private rights and assumed responsibility for its operation and maintenance through the Army Corps of Engineers. Not only did George Washington himself survey an original link through the Dismal Swamp back in pre-Revolutionary times, but he also owned much of the land through which the Ditch traversed. Not long ago, too, sections of improved waterway (dug canals or dredged creeks and rivers) were operated by private ownership, with passage tolls similar to those in effect on toll roads of colonial times.

The motivation of the federal government was national security; vast bulk cargoes, especially of oil, were moved through the Waterway during World War II, safe from the marauding submarines that operated along the Atlantic seaboard. A secondary motivation was the encouragement of commercial barge lines and the development of industrial and heavy storage plants along one of the least developed of America's frontiers. This alone has caused the incredible growth of many once-small southern communities, such as Norfolk, Morehead City, Wilmington, Charleston, Jacksonville, Fort Lauderdale, and Miami. It has provided increased tax bases, which assist all the states and cities involved. While recreational use is a side result, it is most definitely recognized by the government as a legitimate and important use, and recreational boating is in no way frowned upon or curbed. Indeed, those states that depend upon winter visitors, and have built huge sections of their economies upon them in the form of hotels, marinas, and leisure industries, themselves contribute to this aspect of the Ditch by participation and cooperation. The Ditch is entirely free for all users; *entirely*. There are no charges of any kind by either federal or state governments. The passage rate, or "toll," for a three-story Willis pusher tug shoving a few 400-foot "flats" through the Waterway is exactly the same as for a 16-foot canoe or a family cruiser: nothing.

The passage is, further, far more scenic than, say, parallel Route 1 or I-95, and it is very much a sail through American and Indian history. Whole areas are identified with the early explorations of numerous Europeans seeking riches, trade passages, and territory, and with our own history from pioneer days, through the wars with England and our own Civil War. The original Americans called this their homeland. Before them were the Caloosas and many other early Americans. It is no trick for the traveler through these areas to research the past in modern libraries or, for that matter, in the proud publicity of many a coastal town or state. Of particular interest to cruisers, because they were written by cruisers, are the following books: *America's Inland Waterway* by Allan C. Fisher, Jr. (National Geographic Society, Washington, D. C., 1973) and *The Inside Passage* by Anthony Bailey (The Macmillan Company, New York, 1965).

The province of this work is to instruct and guide in the special arts and techniques required to traverse and "live" on the Waterway. Nevertheless, I am making a plea that you enhance your enjoyment and understanding of the subject with some historical background reading. Almost any local Chamber of Commerce will provide sources for such reading.

The Waterway leads to that land of the sun, Florida, to which all the glamorous winter vacations, "roads south," air flights from winter, lead. The Ditch leads substantially to the very same places and cities, and even to inland glamour areas, such as Disney World, Miami (often referred to as "Baghdad on the Waterway"), the orange groves and cattle ranches and tropical lakes, to which the roads and railbeds lead. The Waterway traveler misses nothing of the sunny land he seeks. Once there, the sailor has innumerable choices as to where he spends his winter life, or to where he cruises. He pays no penalty whatever for arriving "by boat," or living on a boat. Once there, he will find

Miami, sometimes called "Baghdad on the Waterway," casts a spectacular reflection on the waters of Biscayne Bay. (Miami-Metro Department of Publicity and Tourism)

land travel no problem, thanks to modern car rental services, public transportation, and the oft-seen "bike" or small "scooter" that many boats carry.

But let us start this adventure where it should start, at Mile Number 1, which is one mile south of Norfolk, Virginia. The passage from your home port is not logically part of the Ditch passage, for it requires no special techniques, no skills that the skipper does not already have if he can operate a vessel at all. The Ditch requires many special techniques (in anchoring, locking through, passing, and maintenance, for example) and does *not* require some techniques the skipper already has (navigation by compass or RDF, sailing, for example . . . although *some* boats have sailed all the way!). The "snow birds" come from many ports: sometimes from distant Canada via the Trent-Severn Waterway, or from Georgian Bay, into the Erie Canal and the Hudson River and down the coast (already in the official waterway at New York but hardly in the protected ditch it becomes below Norfolk), or from Nova Scotia and Maine, and occasionally from England or Norway. Standard, basic practices, learned from experience and research (including research in my own several manuals on the subject*), will take you to Mile 1. From there, this book will smooth out the rough spots and answer the many queries the first-time skipper is bound to have as he sails southward.

All the charts that you will need from Norfolk to Miami are now contained in a single compact "set" of strip charts, the small-craft series, numbered from 829-SC (12206) to 847-SC (11467).

NOTE: The National Ocean Survey has recently begun changing its chart numbering system so that all charts will bear five-digit numbers. Both old numbers and new numbers will be carried on the charts during the transition period. In this book, the old number is listed first, with the new number following in parentheses.

If you plan to depart from the Waterway, say, up a river, you will require additional charts. These often *cross* the Waterway charts and give information from an inlet or the sea to an upriver port. Such a chart would be needed, say, to leave the Ditch and visit Wilmington, North Carolina, or Jacksonville, Florida.

In the Keys, you will need further small-craft charts (Miami to Key West with all connecting keys shown in full, all shores). A general concept of the area here is desirable, so use the coast or (at much less cost) the single ocean chart numbered 1112 (11460) or 1002 (11013), which shows *both* Florida coasts, the Bahamas, Cuba, and the Dry Tortugas. It is helpful to have a

---

The Boatman's Manual, by Carl D. Lane, W.W. Norton, New York, 1962 (4th edition, 1978).
Navigation the Easy Way, by Carl D. Lane and John Montgomery, W. W. Norton, New York, 1949.
The Cruiser's Manual, by Carl D. Lane, Funk & Wagnalls, New York, 1969.

"picture" of the entire coast and area and then relate the small-craft charts to it. This is done, for the navigator, by shipping charts numbered 1000 (13003), 1001 (11009), and 1002 (11013). A satisfactory dodge is to carry a set of the free charts issued by oil companies, as these readily relate the small-craft charts not only to the adjacent ocean shore (which is seldom more than a few miles from the Ditch) but also to inland towns and navigable waters. Do not use these oil company charts to navigate. While accurate, they are not detailed sufficiently for safe navigation, which is not *my* warning but that of the oil companies themselves.

Charts are obtainable from most marinas, from many inland booksellers, or by mail from: National Ocean Survey, Distribution Division C44, Riverdale, Maryland 20840. This last source, as well as authorized private distributors, will supply, free of charge, a complete catalog on request. In it are listed *all* the published Atlantic Coast charts, ocean charts and tide tables, Coast Pilots, etc., together with prices of each. An order to the NOS, with a check, will be promptly forwarded postage paid. Your local chart outlet, unless it is in the coastal area and near or on the Waterway, is unlikely to stock Waterway and ocean charts. However, they, too, can place an order for you and deliver promptly.

As you read this book, it will be helpful to refer to the charts on pages viii-xi. Even on an oil company road map, or in a modern atlas, the Waterway is shown by a red line approximately parallel to the coastline. Later in this work, when we become more specific and locate a place by name or buoy number (such as for anchorage locations, shallows, cross currents, etc.), the small-craft charts are a must. Incidentally, many coastal public libraries have these charts on file (for in-house reading), and the local Coast Guard facility, the U.S. Army Corps of Engineers, and the local U.S. Power Squadron officers have such material available for inspection and research.

The Great Ditch itself, from the deck of a yacht, is a path of ever-changing beauty equal to, but quite different from, any scenic auto highway on this continent. The greater part of it is natural, formed ages ago when the ancient seas receded and left pools and creeks, many fed by melting snows from the Appalachian range as it emerged from the Ice Age. As still occurs today, the lapping seas on the coastline created offshore sand bars, inshore of which swash channels formed. At one time quite deep, these channels gradually filled, or partially filled, with sediment from the Piedmont, yet they maintained runoff creeks to each other and to the sea. Thus today we have a series of connected pools. Many of these pools overflow to the sea in the form of "inlets," and all form a long chain stretching the entire length of the soft coast (the sand or sediment coast, rather than the rock coasts of the northern shores, which extend to the base of the great mountains of ancient times). Improved by dredging and by canal building to accommodate vessels drawing up to 12 feet, this is essentially the Atlantic Intracoastal Waterway today.

Utilizing these natural waterways, the Ditch is a series of salt ponds, creeks, rivers, sounds, bays, "thorofares," lakes, canals, and "cuts." It is by no means a straight line between north and south but dips and dodges in all directions (including north when you are heading south!), taking advantage of the waters that are *naturally* there. The man-made portions, the canals, make up less than 18 percent of the total mileage, and even they have the beauty and charm of the original waters. Great sections of the Ditch run through heavily timbered land, through gray cypress forests and pitch pine and oak and nut trees. Only a few years ago, it was necessary to carry a saw to remove hindering tree limbs. The vines of the South—the moonvine, the Confederate jasmine, the scuppernong grape—cover much of the northern land. In October, you can draw to the bank of the Dismal Swamp Canal and pick grapes from your foredeck!

Nearing the coast, the Ditch, now in tidal sand and rich muckland, traverses vast, level plains of soft, waving marsh grasses, studded by lush "berms" of deciduous trees. (A berm is a small, half-acre copse of trees found throughout these marshlands.) Near the coast, the wind-sculptured cedars take over and, in time, the first palm trees ... sabals these, growing in beds of Spanish bayonet ... join the scene. The rolling blue Atlantic is frequently to be seen, just over the outer bar or breaking over the bars at the inlets. The Deep South, now pure sand and supporting yet other types of greenery, has its own beauty: the lovely mangroves and coconut palms and seagrape.

Very little of this scenery is adulterated. An occasional highway crossing over a bridge, a settlement of fishermen or beach cottages, a shrimper fleet at dockside, quick passage along the waterfront of a small community, distant beach resorts, a tall lighthouse, a cozy marina. These civilized things are there but bear no relation to the scene or to you; they are remote, quiet, another world there to join only if you wish. It is entirely possible to anchor out every night of the passage out of sight of a habitation or even a light. Yet it is possible to find a telephone or fuel within any 10-mile stretch of the Waterway.

The cuts (one of them is over 40 miles long) are straight, steep-banked canals, about 300 feet wide, barren of habitation and cutting through wild, often timbered country, alive with songbirds, with raccoon and deer and wild hog and, below Charleston, an occasional alligator or manatee. They are anything but monotonous: wonderful "breaks" in the passage to loaf and read and let the autopilot do the work. In the Deep South, these connecting cuts often utilize original creek beds and thus twist through the salt marshes for miles of ever-changing vistas. Indeed, many cruisers consider the salt marshes of Georgia the most unique part of the passage.

But ... back to Mile 1 ... or, the real beginning, Mile ZERO.

This occurs at the confluence of the Elizabeth River and the Eastern Branch, exactly at the U.S. Naval Hospital, in Portsmouth, Virginia, and the base of the U.S. Coast & Geodetic Survey. It moves through the heavily industrialized Norfolk-Portsmouth areas and immediately presents the cruiser with a choice: to proceed south via the usual Virginia Cut route or the

Buoy 36, with Norfolk (Va.) Harbor's Portsmouth Naval Hospital in the background, is the official starting point of the Intracoastal Waterway. (Waterway Guide)

Above: *Coinjock swing bridge over North Carolina cut, 50 miles south of Norfolk.*
Below: *The Dismal Swamp Canal, before drought struck the region. (U.S. Army Corps of Engineers)*

alternate route through the Dismal Swamp Canal. The distance is about the same, the beauty equal though different. The Dismal Swamp Canal will accommodate drafts to five feet maximum, even though there is more depth than that. However, this is an ancient canal (circa 1780), originally with wooden retaining banks, and these soggy planks now lie on the bottom of the canal waiting for passing propellers, especially twins. It is a beautiful passage, through lush farming country, inside two locks, and it eventually joins the Pasquotank River, a natural stream of rare beauty in October and April . . . and so to Elizabeth City, North Carolina. This, like Great Bridge on the Virginia Cut route, is a staging port and an excellent port in which to fit out, stock up, and take departure. The Elizabeth Iron Works, no longer a builder of seagoing vessels, has been turned over to yachtsmen, and there is no more friendly and obliging marina, even in friendly North Carolina. It is highly recommended for an auspicious start of the long hitch southward or, in the spring, the passage up the Chesapeake.*

At Great Bridge, behind the only lock on this route, is another famous marina that understands yachtsmen and their needs. Outfitting here is easy and pleasant. A car is not required, but if it is, the store and market keepers offer a free lift back to the boat. This route, through the Virginia Cut and into a wide, winding river that flows into lovely coastal marshland, is also beautiful and leads to the same place: to Albemarle Sound.

This great sound has a nasty reputation. Shallow and with huge fetches to the eastward, it quickly "rages" under even a moderate breeze. While the crossing is only about 15 nautical miles, it can be rough if the seas are on either beam. Seasoned cruisers avoid it if rough and wait until sundown or dawn to cross, anchoring meanwhile in the North Landing River (north) or the Alligator River (south). Similar conditions prevail in the lower reaches of the Pungo River, the Pamlico and Neuse Rivers, and sometimes in the Bay River. Happily, these are the *only* waters of any extent that "kick up" on occasion to the point of forbidding passage. The only port of refuge supporting a marina in this area is Belhaven, an antebellum community well worth a stopover.

Through some of the wildest remaining land in the East (still noted for bear, wild hog, wolf, and varmint hunting, as well as outstanding bird shooting), the Ditch trends toward the coast, again offering a good stopover port, the village of Oriental on the Neuse River. The coast is joined at bustling Morehead City, a deep-water port, sportfishing center, and yacht refitting area. Only a few years ago, it was necessary for all boats to exit to the sea here and coast offshore to a more southerly inlet. Now the Waterway enters huge Bogue Sound, which it traverses via a dug channel on the western edge into the natural coastal marshes of North Carolina. This is wide open country. Views are miles long. Habitation again becomes sparse and takes on a quiet

*Drought conditions caused the closing of the Dismal Swamp Canal in late 1976, and rumors fly about whether or not it will again be open to yacht traffic. Be sure to check the status of the Canal before you reach the junction.

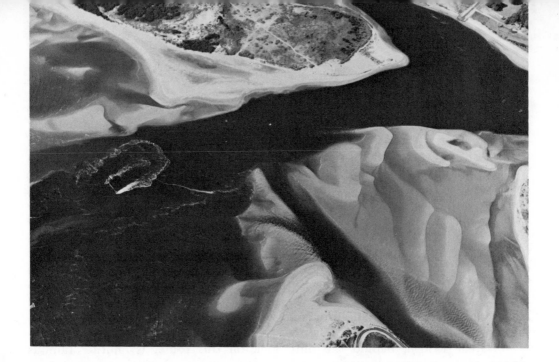

Above: *Aerial view of Lockwoods Folly Inlet, N.C. (U.S. Army Corps of Engineers)*
Below: *USS North Carolina, World War II battleship open to the public in Wilmington, N.C. (Greater Wilmington Chamber of Commerce)*

resort character. For the next several days, the Ditch closely follows the coastline, through wooded salt marsh, ever winding and twisting. It is crossed here by innumerable creeks from the inland prairie, many of which have broken through to the sea and created inlets. Unfortunately, most are too shallow to use. This is the coast along which the blockade runners operated, trying . . . and often failing, as at Lockwoods Folly Inlet . . . to reach Wilmington, the last open port of the Confederacy. At Carolina Beach, just before the Ditch enters the mighty Cape Fear River, there is today a museum commemorating the daring of these very blockade-runner masters. This coast is also the locale of several pirates of renown, Edward Teach (Blackbeard) being the most famous, for he lurked behind the beach in these very inlets to swoop upon his prey. This, too, is well-known oyster country. Natural oyster bars are everywhere, and not a few cruisers stop over at low tide and hack out a bushel of the tasty bivalves.

A side trip up the Cape Fear to Wilmington is a pleasant passage diversion. Wilmington is a happy, easy-paced city of southern beauty that offers many vacation pleasures, not the least of which is a tour of the great World War II battleship USS *North Carolina*, forever open to the public. From here south to Charleston, there are numerous marinas and boatyards, most hard by the Waterway and, as you may well imagine, adequately advertised. The passage ends at Snows Cut, a short canal that affords entrance to the Cape Fear River, about 10 miles from the sea inlet.

Directly west of the cut, across the river, are the ruins of Old Brunswick (now called Anderson's Landing), a precolonial settlement and fortification well worth exploring. It is a public park, free, but unhappily has no proper

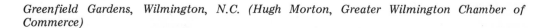

Greenfield Gardens, Wilmington, N.C. (Hugh Morton, Greater Wilmington Chamber of Commerce)

Old Baldhead Light, Smith Island, near Southport, N.C. (Department of Conservation and Development, Raleigh, N.C.)

landing. The cruiser must anchor off, and not too close because of the ruins of a submerged wharf, and dinghy in. Swift currents in the river sometimes make it prudent to await a fair tide to Southport, another fine yacht stopover operated by the state of North Carolina. Facilities for extensive repairs, engine work and parts, and sportfishing are available here. One of the last of the lightships is operated here as a public museum, this one the famous Frying Pan Shoals vessel. South of here, at Howell's Point, may be observed the first palm trees; they are rather ragged and winter-beaten, but nevertheless a sure sign of the upcoming tropics.

There are numerous opportunities along this coast to purchase big market shrimp running as much as 24 to the pound (dressed), as well as fresh local fish (shad, spot, striped bass, flounder, bluefish, grouper, and mackerel). Blue crabs are abundant and may readily be trapped off the boat in 'most any anchorage. (No license is required to fish, crab, or oyster for noncommercial use.)

Frying Pan Shoals lightship, near Southport, N.C., leaving her station to a light tower. (U.S. Coast Guard)

This type of coast ceases south of Little River, South Carolina, and soon the Ditch becomes the man-made Pine Island Cut, 27 miles of canal through a high, sandy plateau, well treed and with creepers, myrtle, and Spanish moss entwined. The walls of this earth cut are spiced with ancient shells, certain evidence that the whole area was formerly sea bottom. The cut parallels a region that is a playland of the South—just a mile east, yet invisible and inaudible—where some 20 resort communities offer fun in the sun to all comers.

Upcoming is the best-loved stretch of the entire Waterway to many: the beautiful Waccamaw River, highway to dozens of bordering plantations that supplied the indigo and rice and yams in colonial days. This river winds like a serpent through forested land to Georgetown, on Winyah Bay, some 25 miles downriver. It is fed by numerous streams, which originate back in the Blue Ridge and Smoky Mountains, some 350 miles inland; several of these streams are navigable for vessels drawing up to six feet. These creeks border ancient rice paddies, which may still be seen, and sometimes boast small, rural cross-road villages of the storybook variety. Any or all are well worth a few days of exploration. There are many lovely, quiet anchorages off the river, in tree-shaded lagoons and river loops and deep creeks. Brookgreen Gardens (accessible by road from the Wachesaw Landing area) has a nationally famous open-air horticultural display well worth a visit in the early spring. While the estate was populated for 300 years, hardly a structure can now be seen; all is peace and quiet and simple beauty. The only landing for fuel or yacht service is at a sleepy little village called Bucksport, which also has . . . glory be! . . .a fine gourmet restaurant famous for shad and shad roe and barbecued wild pork. You can secure your bow line to your chair in the restaurant.

Georgetown, below, is a truly historic, graceful, colonial town, quite as lovely as Williamsburg and well aware of its charm. It has limited yacht facilities, and for diesel at commercial prices, stop *only* at the first fuel station on the starboard hand when entering. Unhappily, Georgetown traded its birthright for progress and permitted, practically in town, the erection of a gaseous, noisy paper mill and a raucous, sprawling steel operation. A charming, one-of-a-kind colonial showplace has become a place for a quick look only. The harbor is dirty and polluted, the docks ancient and untidy, and the acrid stink of acid bleach pervades all. Yet it is difficult to forget the pure beauty of Georgetown's old buildings, its churches and plantation homes, its ancient live oaks and azaleas and rhododendron.

Coming up is Charleston, also an old, old city, happily one that is well protected by being located entirely upon a wide peninsula that permits modernization and expansion only in a single direction—*away* from the old city. The Waterway to it is again through coastal marshland, through country where cable ferries still operate and mules pull hay ricks in the marsh grass. Shrimper fleets hide up the entering creeks, nestled against crude wharves that front small clusters of houses bordering the ever-present menhaden factory. The factories have long since been converted to process oysters, clams, and shrimp, for the menhaden have left these waters.

Charleston is heralded by slowly increasing "civilization" and the appearance of a road, at last, between the Waterway and the sea. Palms are everywhere now; indeed, on the port hand is the lush Isle of Palms, where Charleston's beaches are located. Into the harbor, with Fort Sumter hard by, and up the Ashley River, skirting the old city and its unique architecture, is the Municipal Marina, the only yacht facility. This is the heart of boating in Charleston. While the city has a deep-water port and a naval and submarine base, it sadly lacks yacht facilities. There is a huge marina with hundreds of berths but, alas, there is little space for transients. Usually it is necessary to "raft" with another boat: a very unpleasant situation and one that permits the city to collect two or three times the dockage for a single berth. Nevertheless, most boats remain for a day or two, so attractive is this unusual city. It is "walkable," probably the best way to see the original city of the 1700s and savor the architecture, the great manor houses with their ornamental iron gates and polished brass door knockers, the old slave market, the gaol, the famous battery, and, with luck, to meet some of the kindly, friendly people of South Carolina.

Gourmet dining is readily available in Charleston. There are tours, some to

Fort Sumter, famous Civil War site, has a commanding view of the harbor at Charleston, S.C. It is a National Monument open to the public year round. A yacht landing provides free tie-ups during visits. (Charleston Trident Chamber of Commerce)

outlying plantation gardens well worthwhile in season. A cab ride or dinghy trip upriver to Olde Charles Towne Landing, site of the original settlement, is a most pleasant way to spend a day. Here are frequent outdoor symphony concerts, lawn dances, a nature walk, and an outstanding zoological park.

From here, the Waterway changes character somewhat. While still in the coastal marshland, this area is cut by many large sounds and rivers trending in an east-west direction. They twine and wind and intertwine—like a basket of basking snakes—and the Army Engineers have cut short canals between them at their closest points, often a great loop or direction change. Thus the Ditch here is a series of great open reaches, seldom rough because there is little heavy current save near an inlet, laced with canals. The land here is less sandy and tends toward black, rich mud. Again there are few or no roads between the Waterway and the seacoast, and therefore no habitations . . . or very, very few. Thus in one of these links, this one natural but dredged, the cruiser comes to another unique southern city, Beaufort, South Carolina. (There is a Beaufort, North Carolina, also. It is pronounced *Bo-fort;* this one is *Bu-fort.* Yankees, take note.)

There are two yacht facilities here: one on the strand before the town and the other a half mile up Factory Creek. Anchoring out is no problem, of course. Beaufort is an historic city with many stately plantation homes, old churches, a colonial military cemetery, and a fine, modern shopping area. Nearby is Port Royal (where she-crab soup is made and canned) and, beyond, Parris Island, boot camp of the U.S. Marine Corps. The creeks and sounds in this general area twist to such an extent that great parcels of land, quite inland from the sea, are, in fact, islands, and are so called. Thus Ladies Island and Fripp Island are in no way related to islands in the usual sense; or as one would refer to Long Island, New York, or Tangier Island in the Chesapeake. But technically they are surrounded by water and are therefore islands. From here southward, there are hundreds of such land parcels, for this pattern of connecting rivers and sounds continues almost to the Florida line.

One of the most charming of these sounds is Port Royal Sound, leading away from Beaufort, past famous Hilton Head Island (home of endless condominiums, tracts of private homes, and at least three PGA golf courses). A modern marina offers an opportunity for you to live it up for an evening, along with fine restaurants and branches of big-city stores. From here to the next "stop," St. Simons Island, is a long day's haul, and most boats anchor out at least one night. This, too, is river-sound country, quite wooded, yet with surprising vistas of many miles. At times you can glimpse a boat ahead, winding in and out of the coils of the creeks—only a mile as the eagle flies, yet 10 miles by Waterway. Many, many feeder creeks enter the route, creeks with colorful names like Rockdedundy and Teakettle and Burnt Store. Over the savannahs, now becoming broad and lush, rise innumerable "hammocks," which are berms of several acres, green with trees, often myrtle entwined, and alive with bird life. Most are named, a few have fisher or hunter shacks, and all command a vista of a vast sea prairie with the distant surf a white line on the horizon. Through this land the Waterway trends ever southward and, now, ever westward as well, for the days are noticeably longer . . . or seem so, since sunset is later.

An interesting alternate route in this section is to enter the Frederica River, near the southern end of Buttermilk Sound, and proceed to the chart notation, "Fort Frederica National Monument, Oglethorpe Barracks." This is the site of an ancient British outpost and, later, settlement of immigrants from England. The National Park Service has done its usual splendid job of restoration and exhibition. Unhappily, they have not provided a boat landing, but this may be effected by dinghy to the rip-rap bank or to the tottering dock of the adjacent, now-abandoned hotel. There is good anchorage off the fort and many boats use it. The creek is deep and safe and makes a natural exit into the Waterway proper a few miles south. The stop at St. Simons is tricky, for in this area there are suddenly extremely high tidal differences, as

Florida's broad Indian River offers ample opportunities for cruising under power or sail. (Florida Department of Commerce)

much as nine feet at times. This makes for swift currents and difficult dockage, partly because the stop has a most clumsy system of finger docks from which there is no safe departure against the tide. (The local marina keeps a powerful tug handy to haul boats into the stream.)

This is the Brunswick, Georgia, area—known so well for its play islands of St. Simons, Sea Island, Jekyll Island, Amelia and Cumberland Islands. These are genuine islands, set in broad waters, and most are private plantations recently divided into vacation and resort facilities. Cumberland Island, a Rockefeller holding, has become, in large part, a state oceanside park. Its southern tip is the last land in Georgia; the Florida line bisects the inlet between it and Fernandina, the first of the many Florida coastal cities.

We are now in Florida, our destination, and any port from Fernandina south is worthy of consideration for a winter base. We have passed other possibilities, of course (Charleston, South Carolina, and Beaufort, Hilton Head Island, the plush Savannah area), and many snow birds prefer these areas to the deeper tropics. At the Georgia-Florida line, the nature of the Waterway changes rapidly and soon, after a short passage through a dug canal south of the St. Johns River, the marshland becomes a recognizable sandy reef between the Waterway and the sea. For the most part, the route is now in the old swash channel . . . improved and dredged, of course . . . and shortly enters the headwaters of the long and lovely Indian River. At its confluence with the St.

St. George Street in St. Augustine, Fla., oldest city in the continental United States. (Florida Department of Commerce)

Lucie and exit into the ocean, a short, sandy marsh cut is the Ditch and then, again, the dry outer bar and swash channel pattern takes over all the way to Miami and Biscayne Bay, the beginning of the Keys area.

The land here is flat, well wooded, and very tropical. Florida as a state is less than 10 feet above sea level, and none of its several inland named "mountains" is over 300 feet high. A mile beneath it is the granite spine of the Appalachian system, long since sunk and covered by successive layers of sea-deposited coral and limestone. On this flat sand spit has been built modern Florida, evidence of which commences immediately along the Waterway as the cruiser fetches up near the Moorish skyline architecture of St. Augustine, just beyond the first of the many inlets on this coast. From here south, there is no doubt that you are in Vacationland. Nestled on both banks are ever-increasing small communities, sometimes within range of a tossed shell; others are distant and remote across wide, blue waters. Periodically, large cities appear—Daytona and New Smyrna and Titusville and Eau Gallie and Stuart

Above: *Fort Matanzas, near St. Augustine, is a National Monument. (Florida Department of Commerce)* Below: *A diver feeds porpoises underwater at Marineland, the popular oceanarium south of St. Augustine. (State of Florida Development Commission)*

Lighthouse Military Museum, Key West Light Station, Fla.
(Florida Department of Commerce)

and West Palm Beach—and, suddenly, there is no more shoreline. There is nothing save a serpentine border of concrete seawalls, pierced by entering canals, each rich in moored yachts and lush homes, and the very sun is eclipsed by mighty, endless jungles of high-rise apartment structures. Happily, there is but 50 miles of this when, just below the very heart of the City of Miami, the "Gold Coast" abruptly ends and the waters widen and the trade winds blow untainted and the sea becomes green and translucent and there is yet another vast wonderland of beauty and charm ahead . . . and nary another city to the very last key!

While the visible Florida seems to cease just south of Miami, it is still there, just a scant fathom below the tropical waters that surround the chain of keys. It is a vast underwater plateau with a few tiny bits of its original oolite backbone rising above the surface. These are the Keys . . . Elliott and Largo and Vaca and Sugarloaf and Duck and Big Pine and, finally, Cayo Hueso, which we call Key West. Through these bits of exposed plateau, most now richly populated, winds the Waterway, sometimes far offshore in clear, emerald-green waters, sometimes close aboard islands alive with roseate spoonbills and fish-hawks nested in ancient mahogany and lignum-vitae trees.

Here officially ends the Waterway, or one branch of it. The other has branched off far north, at Stuart, Florida, in the form of the Okeechobee Waterway, which crosses the state and continues, in the Gulf of Mexico, following the shoreline, all the long, long miles to the Mexican border in Texas.

This branch utilizes the canalized St. Lucie River to a lock, raising the waterway 14 feet to a wide, deep canal dug into the vast inland prairie. Orange groves line the canal and sugar cane fields. On the natural land, huge herds of beef cattle graze. This land, with scarcely a habitation in sight, nevertheless supports a cattle industry larger than that of Texas, and many of the little hamlets are completely western in character. It is not at all unusual to spy a genuine mounted cowboy along the Ditch. Huge, shallow Lake Okeechobee forms a link in the cross-state waterway; then it gives into another prairie canal, which enters the canalized Caloosahatchee River, past

Above: *Orange groves line the Waterway along Florida's central Atlantic coast.* Below: *Lake Okeechobee is a link in the cross-Florida waterway. (Florida Department of Commerce)*

A palm-lined street on the resort island of Boca Grande, Fla. (Florida Department of Commerce)

bustling Fort Myers, into the Gulf and thence up the coast. A new lock at Port Myakka will raise the lake level slightly and provide a still greater water storage capacity.

The west coast of Florida bears no relation to the east coast. Its character is entirely different. It is shallow, sandy, rather sparsely settled, and, for most of its length, protected by beautiful, natural offshore barrier islands. Some are resorts: Marco, Sanibel (Santa Ybel), Boca Grande, and Casey and Siesta Keys. Some are as wild as when Gasparilla pirated in these water only 150 years ago: the Ten Thousand Islands, Cape Romano, Captiva, Cayo Costa, Palm, Caladesi. Cruising here is more like cruising in the North. The water is open and seldom restricted by canals. There are many anchorages, many small communities offering dockage. Vegetation, 'longshore, is apt to be mangrove and seagrape, with hard pine and palm inland where the elevation is at least four feet. There are many beaches, excellent shelling, superior pan-fishing (as opposed to the dramatic game fishing of the Gulf Stream), and, quite noticeably, a leisurely, *mañana* type of life. Many snow birds prefer the west coast to the east coast, for it is undeniably more rural, less artificial, and less expensive.

We passed, when crossing the St. Johns River, yet another major area of Florida cruising. This is the St. Johns River system. Leaving the sea at Mayport, this unique river trends due west and passes the huge city of Jacksonville, Florida (a metropolis comparable to Cleveland, Ohio, or Rochester, New York). Growing, industrialized, not at all tropical, it is the distribution point for much of the southeast, and hardly a place to winter.

Above: *Sponge boats tied up at Tarpon Springs, Fla.* Below: *The St. Johns River stretches southward from Jacksonville. (Florida Department of Commerce)*

Inlets off the St. Johns River are often clogged with water plants, which make tasty meals for manatees and alligators. (Florida Department of Commerce)

A few miles farther, the river turns abruptly southward and continues so for several hundred miles, to a point almost within the city of Daytona Beach, on the Atlantic Coast. Its course is a wide, natural, tropical river, with many large lakes, winding, narrow passages, and lush, overwhelming deciduous growth overhanging the water almost everywhere. Its southerly trend carries the cruiser into warmer latitudes and unique country. This is the honeycombed limestone land of northern Florida, with many remote, lagoon-like anchorages, which are frequently in deep, clear springs that are the homes of schools of fish and manatees and alligators. There are just enough small, waterside communities to provide services, never the hustle of the resort cities of lower Florida. The waters are the very best for fishermen, the land roundabout the best for game hunters and bird-shooters. The St. Johns land is utterly different from the rest of Florida and is receiving increasing attention from winter visitors. It is entirely possible to live safely and well on a boat in these waters.

This has been a brief, overall "picture" of the passage from the North to the sun . . . a sort of "what-it's-like" presentation. It has been necessarily brief. The next step in obtaining an impression, short of an actual passage down the Ditch, is to study the appropriate charts. It's not all good. It's not all bad. Few people will agree as to what is good and what is bad. But thousands come to the Land of the Sun each year, and some eventually make it their home. Many of us feel that the "bad" is readily found when arriving by automobile over crowded, inadequate roads, or expensive plane flights, or dirty, poorly serviced railroads; when dependent upon seasonally inflated hotel and restaurant charges; waiting in line for everything from a haircut to a gourmet dinner; overcharging by an economy well adjusted to "northern visitors"—and all excused by the Chamber of Commerce cry of: "Why complain? The sun's out, isn't it?" And many of us, too, feel that all this can be avoided. The trick is to become independent of the worst of the abuses, and that's a difficult trick for the short-term visitor. One way, obviously, is to carry your own house, like the turtle ... and there is no more pleasant manner in which to do so than to have that house be a boat.

And that's what this book is about. . . .

Chapter 2
Life on the Waterway

By far the majority of those who take to the Waterway life each winter are boatmen of some experience, even though such experience may not be in the semitropical waters of our land. These people are finally able, in terms of money and leisure time (though not *always* money!), to extend the dream that motivated them in the first place to expand their time afloat from a few summer months to include some or all of the winter months. This . . . this live-aboard life . . . is really what they originally acquired a boat for. Suddenly the summer cruise does not end on Sunday evening or at the end of the annual two-week vacation but goes on and on until there is little memory left of life ashore, and shipboard life has become the "normal" life. Frequently, the convert divests himself of his shoreside home, his summer camp, his golf club membership, and even his automobile. Most certainly he no longer keeps a snowmobile or a smelt shanty or a deer rifle, because these are the tools of cold weather and the first thought he ever had about living on a boat year 'round was to get away from winter. As soon as it became economically possible, he became the complete convert in whatever vessel he owned, could borrow, charter, or build. And like his forebears who tried the slimy life ashore in the Age of Lizards, he returned happily to the sea. All the dreams he dreamt while skippering his boat in his early days have now come true, and he joyously embraces the new, nautical way of life.

Of course, many who lead the life afloat are newcomers to the yachting scene. They buy a boat that seems to meet their needs and just move aboard. Amazingly, especially if a dealer with heart and compassion is involved, it often works! I know a couple from Denver who had never been away from their mountain playland. Upon retirement, they took a trip to Florida, saw the ocean for the first time, and a boat dealer ditto, and bought a boat. They lived on it most successfully for years. Indeed, they never went back to Colorado. Lots of folks live on boats that should have been retired years ago, secure in the knowledge that little will be demanded from the boat save that it remain afloat. Others, having the boat, make the few simple adjustments necessary to meet the winter climate of the South, give their skis to the Salvation Army, and take off. People with jobs often have the boat taken down or up by the professionals or friends and manage a few steal-away vacations during the winter. There are many techniques for the live-aboards (which is the recognized term for the boating fraternity to whom this work is directed), and getting there, for most, is a big part of the fun.

A popular and practical way to try out the life is to charter, especially for brief stays. It's expensive, but quite trouble-free. There are many charter fleets, offering boats, usually sailers, complete down to food, fuel, ice, and rum, ready to take off on arrival. They are advertised in many boating periodicals. In 1977 they averaged about $100 a day, but that cost divided among four or six persons isn't too bad for a few weeks. For those without a boat or cruising experience, it is an excellent way to test the life. The following ports (going south) can turn up such charters, often via a yacht broker or active yacht yard: Great Bridge, Virginia (Norfolk); Wrightsville Beach and Charleston, South Carolina; Savannah, Georgia; Jacksonville Beach, Florida; and, of course, West Palm Beach, Fort Lauderdale, Miami, Naples, St. Petersburg, and Tampa. All the major islands of the Caribbean have such charter services. It is essential to select a port with ready access to air service.

I know several old-timers who have found the time, if not the money, who find their live-aboard dreams realized by skippering boats up and down the coast, usually for fuel, dockage, subsistence, and the fare home. They do not demand pay, merely a flexible schedule rather than a timetable and daily mileage quotas. Sometimes ads will appear in yachting journals, or in the classified and/or "Boat Services" columns of daily newspapers (such as the yacht-oriented *Miami Herald*), seeking such services or offering them. The deal is made, certainly in writing. It should include an acceptable timetable; rights to also ship the Mrs. or others; insurance by the owner; a clear understanding of who pays the fuel, dockage, subsistence, service, and repairs; and the return fare home (and for a specified number of persons). Such services on a pay basis cost about $50 a day for the skipper, plus, if the boat is 45 feet or thereabouts, another $40 a day for a mate, plus $10 subsistence per day each, plus laundry, plus fare home, including meals, cabs, motels, etc. So it is easy for any owner to save himself up to $1,000 by using a no-pay nonprofessional, and it is easy for the nonprofessional to get a free ride to the South and enjoy a live-aboard life. It is not necessary to have commercial papers (license) for this service, since it is not your boat, and, further, you are not carrying passengers for hire. It is best to agree upon a contract price or a per diem rate, and so avoid the labor laws that may, in some situations, apply.

To be sure, this service is also available through yacht brokers and delivery pools, on an hourly or daily pay basis, but there is little advantage in this if the talents and experience of the skippers are equal. In either case, normal insurance, endorsed for extended seasonal use and operation in the hurricane season, possibly foreign (as when cruising the Bahamas), covers in full.

By far the majority of those who opt for this life move and live on their own boats, often family yachts many years old or products of the used boat market. They vary from tiny pocket cruisers to huge luxury yachts, both power and sail. They include every imaginable type of vessel: catamarans, Chinese junks, trawlers, sportfishermen, motorsailers, trimarans, sleek sailing sloops and schooners and heavy offshore coasters, small brigs and ultramodern plastic wonders with four engines, three decks, and two bars. Most are adequate, some are dangerous, a few start and do not make it. They are crewed by families more often than not, sometimes by lone skippers bound for Tahiti and other dream ports, and, of late, by many younger people with long, golden hair, whether their bikinis have tops or not. A few have professional crews. Some engage a paid skipper to "take them down." There are plenty of sailing vessels, most apt to be too deep and quite unhandy in the Waterway. And it is not unusual to see a lone canoe or Foldboat wending its way south under paddles.

Few of these navigators are ever called upon to face up to the "perils of the sea." There is no need to go to sea, save in very special cases, such as extreme draft or extreme mast height. The great majority of the southbound fleet is seldom in more than 12 feet of water once the Great Ditch has been reached. The Waterway is maintained at a uniform 12 feet to the Florida line; the region beyond, maintained at eight feet for many years, is gradually being deepened to a two-fathom control depth. Moreover, the bottom in all but a very few areas (so noted on the charts) is soft, usually mud with a thin overlay of sand or silt, and a grounding at sane speeds is no great matter. The Coast Guard will heed genuine distress calls, of course, but most boats can slide clear of a grounding by appropriate propeller work in a passing wake, or wait for the tide (if there *is* tide at that location). Other yachts are generous in assisting and readily understand the display of a rope's end from the taffrail. (It means: "Please tow me off.") There is constant shoaling, especially at junctures or crossings, and it is usual to discover dredges working year 'round the entire length of the passage. In general, the standard rule applies: stay on the outside of curves and bends. However, the Waterway is exceptionally well marked and very easy to follow, with seldom a stretch wherein two to six markers are not in view, the key ones lighted at night. Some passages are further marked by ranges, clearly shown on the small-craft charts, and they should be carefully followed by any vessel drawing over four feet.

There is considerable commercial traffic on the Ditch, especially around Norfolk; Wilmington, North Carolina; Southport, North Carolina; Bucksport on the Waccamaw; Georgetown, Charleston, Fernandina, and Jacksonville. For the most part, the cargoes are bulk, both dry and liquid (oil, turpentine, fertilizer, shell, sand, grain), carried in huge "flats" pushed by powerful twin-screw, tunnel-stern diesel "tugs." These units draw eight feet loaded and, when moving at top speed, average about eight knots. They are skippered 24 hours a day by seasoned pilots who fully understand the problems of the yacht meeting or passing and cooperate fully in making the meeting easy and safe.

These vessels *cannot* navigate in waters shallower than 10 or 12 feet, and it behooves the yacht to give way, no matter who has any situation rights. The tug will yield as far as it can, slow or stop, signal, and expect you to "work" around it in narrow channels. On the sounds and bays they are no problem, of course. Other commercial traffic includes many small "tows," often special cargoes such as huge nuclear reactor casings, Army and Navy ordnance and knocked-down highway bridges, concrete and steel girders, and dredged materials. In the northern waters there are many crab trawlers, inshore shrimpers, and local ferries; in southern waters, large shrimpers (fishing off-shore from Hatteras to the Yucatan), menhaden or porgy boats, and a few regular-run cruise vessels (these having shallow draft and being up to 150 feet overall). By far the most traffic will be in yacht form . . . none of which should be dismissed lightly. The great majority is well and safely handled, but you never know which wheelhouse contains one of those dangerous "cow-

Shrimp boats are a frequent sight for cruisers in Florida waters. (Florida Department of Commerce)

boys" bent on endangering everything he sees. More about these idiots later . . . .

Vessels of more than nine-foot draft should not plan to use the Waterway substantially, especially in the run between Norfolk and Morehead City, North Carolina. They will be dangerously close to bottom and will lack the power of the tugs to dig themselves out. Many miles of the Ditch are without tide, so rising water cannot be depended upon. Likewise, masted vessels with spars of more than 52 feet must go "outside," for 52 feet is the controlling clearance for all fixed bridges on the Ditch. Trimarans in the 30-foot-beam class, too, might expect some tight squeezes between the fenders of opening bridges, especially in the presence of strong currents or wind. All of these vessels might better take outside routes, "stitching" along the coast by entering deep inlets, some only a day or two apart, and entering a port for layovers. This is the way the professionals move the big boats, unhindered by speed limits and the courtesy slow-downs required by safety and good manners when meeting other boats in the Waterway.

The Waterway weather generally works out as *fine*, partly because most boats move south (toward warmer weather) in the fall and north (toward cooler weather) in the spring. An ideal time to leave Mile Zero is during the month of October: it's usually just right—not too hot, not yet chilly—and the identical weather is apt to prevail right down to Key West. And leave the South, say the Miami area, for the return trip, during late April or early May. The fair weather pattern may be broken up, of course, but hardly by the sudden advent of deep winter or stifling summer. You can expect some 80-degree weather in October, even in the Norfolk area, possibly some rainy days near the coast, and Florida will be cooling off with 80- to 90-degree days. And the pattern is just about the reverse coming north in May. A November departure from Mile Zero is by no means risky, weatherwise. Some folks like cool weather and the lovely colors of fall along the Ditch and in the salt marshes. You can then expect occasional ice on the decks as far down as Charleston, especially after a night of heavy coastal fog. Northerly winds might well prevail, but they are not of great moment, since they are at your back and diminishing as you head south. We have made the passage in all months. December was not at all bad, January a little rough until the South Carolina line. Snow . . . henceforth a dirty word . . . may be expected in light falls clear to Jacksonville, Florida, and winter frost on the coast as far south as Fort Pierce, Tampa, and the upper Everglades.

There are few "pea-soup" fogs south of Norfolk during the cruising months. There are, however, occasional coastal fogs, seldom long-lived, and, over the inland marshes and creeks of South Carolina and Georgia, sometimes "morning fog." This soon burns off, and by 10 A.M., normal navigation may proceed. It is folly to try to run compass courses on the Ditch in fog; just wait a few hours and it will clear.

Thunderstorms are, of course, possible at most any time. However, the storm months in the South are limited to about May to October, so chances of thunder squalls or "rainy spells" going south are scant. Going north in the spring, you are leaving them astern. Northeasters are possible in the Hatteras-Cape Fear segment, but to the Waterway cruiser, this means only dirty weather and rain; the passage may continue, and frequently a day's run will beat the weather.

The great fear is the West Indian hurricane. October is the very height of the hurricane season, and it behooves all skippers to keep an eye peeled for possible trouble. Fortunately, hurricanes do not occur every year, and there is an excellent warning system, giving every vessel ample opportunity to seek shelter. Radio, television, marinas, marine police, and the Coast Guard all have coverage and hourly reports that should leave no boat unwarned. The prudent skipper will pay attention and play it safe . . . lay over. Select a location (advised by locals) where the storm damage could be the least, and prepare . . . and don't move until advised that the threat positively has passed. Local watermen usually try to get away from other boats, from docks and wharves, from open stretches of water, from nearby structures, from trees, overhead wires, and microwave towers. This takes them up a creek more often than not, deep in the marshes, in narrow waters: good holding ground and the right place for the ultimate defense if necessary . . . to pull the plug and let 'er sink to safety. To be sure, we don't want to do that with our sleek yachts; nor will we have to, if plenty of time is taken to plan ahead. By all means, if at all possible, depend upon many stout lines or chain run to immovable objects ashore rather than depend upon your anchor(s). High water will surely come, and anchors seldom hold against the seas then built up by increased wind fetch. Fortunately, the Waterway is generously laced with creeks and bayous that can be entered with caution and that might provide the safety needed . . . first from the hurricane, then from other boats, then from wreckage, and finally from high water.

Most marinas will evacuate all boats when a hurricane is due (to protect their own docks and equipment). They will sometimes offer to haul you out (although they usually are quite limited in space), which, on the proper sort of land, is an excellent defense. Boatyards may also do this. Protected marinas, up creeks and not overly exposed, will take you in—usually at a month's dockage fee. However, take heart . . . a real hurricane occurs on the average only once in 11 years, and the hurricane scares you can live with.

Year 'round in the South is not as idyllic as the Chamber of Commerce would have us believe. It's warmer, far warmer, than the North, but the South *does* have winter. The great life-saver is the sun. It makes for warm days (since few days are cloudy), but the nights sometimes get right down to chilly, to the frost range and not much higher, directly on the 72-degree water itself. You may expect from 10 to 25 days annually when you need a sweater to help combat the 58-degree temperature, bright sun notwithstanding. These spells occur when the northers come down—cold fronts spawned in Alaska. Whenever you note headlines in the local newspapers like, "Midwest Staggers Under Fierce Winter Storm," put on some heating fuel: the tail end of that storm—much tempered, of course—will be on you within a week or less. The tropics are said to commence at about Vero Beach, just above West Palm

Bahia Mar Yacht Basin, Fort Lauderdale. (Florida Department of Commerce)

Beach, in Florida, and it's a pretty safe bet that south of that point you can depend upon tropical sunny weather such as we associate with the Bahamas, the Virgin Islands, and the Mexican Quintana Roo coast. The northers will still find you, but not often and not violently, and they will hardly alter the characterization of "tropical."

Heat is quite as much concern. The South stays genuinely hot until almost Christmas, relents slightly and spasmodically during January and February, then commences to build up to those 100-degree days of the summer months. By April you feel that it's time to move north. But it isn't. The solution is to cruise slowly, loafing along at an average of 25 miles a day (with layovers at interesting places, fishing areas, yard work periods), and "follow the season." The early and late seasonal heat is much tempered by the southeasterly trade winds, which render many a stifling day bearable, even pleasant. The rains and humidity do not begin until mid-May, an excellent time to be halfway home.

The Waterway is literally peppered with marinas—large and small, good and bad. There are only two stretches when one is farther than 20 miles from a marina. These are: Between Elizabeth City (or Coinjock) and Belhaven—though there is a tiny marina at the bridge across the Alligator River—and between Isle of Hope (Savannah) and St. Simons Island (Brunswick). These are long day's runs, and slow boats usually plan to anchor out in one of the many snug berths in the area. As you approach the vacation land, the marinas increase by the square and cube until, in Florida, they border each other. Here, the marinas are no longer entirely geared to transients. Their clients usually remain—sometimes for the entire winter—and it is necessary to make

City of Miami's Miamarina.
(Miami-Metro Department of
Publicity and Tourism)

Bud 'n' Mary's Marina is on
the Hawk Channel (ocean)
side of Upper Matecumbe
Key. (Florida Department of
Commerce)

reservations well ahead. However, even these marinas hold a few berths open for transients (mostly to sell fuel), and overnight stays are not difficult to find. Many of the Waterway communities operate municipal marinas, often of quite a capacity, and these, too, afford excellent targets when cruising. They are usually well-crowded, popular, often quite inexpensive, near the town (so you can spend your money with their merchants even if you do not have a car), and glad to have you . . . if there's space! In recent years, the city marinas have been increasingly under pressure from their own boat-owning citizens to provide berths, and the transient or winter visitor is less apt to find accommodations. Perhaps this is as it should be, but it does often drive the visitor to the more expensive commercial marinas.

For those who plan to tie up each evening, it is wise to plan well ahead and space the passage by marinas rather than ports. To get a berth (because the professionals, who get out at dawn, usually tie up around 3 P.M.), it is essential to get in by 4 P.M. or call or radio ahead. Most commercial marinas monitor a CB or VHF channel and will hold a berth until 6 P.M. Marinas are listed not only on the small-craft charts (together with description, fuel available, depth of approach and dockside, facilities, services, etc.) but also in the excellent annual, *Waterway Guide*, Mid-Atlantic and Southern editions. (Any marina or chandlery, at $5.95 each in 1977 or from the publisher, by mail: Marine Annuals, Inc., 238 West St., Annapolis, Maryland 21404.)

While there is an abundance of anchorages on the Waterway, they have not been extensively used until recent years. This change is due, of course, to ever-rising marina costs. Only a few years ago, we bought a few gallons of fuel at a handy dock or boatyard, or a bucket of bait or a beer, and were welcome to tie up at no charge. After a few years, we asked, timidly, if we could plug into the dock light and listen to Fred Allen or the Happiness Boys on the radio, or fill the water tank at the well, and the answer was a cheerful "yes." A few years more, and more boats appeared twice each season with the same and many more demands and . . . voilà . . . the marina business as distinguished from a fuel stop was born. It has gone to dizzy heights since, as yachts demanded and were willing to pay for more and more: 220 volts, dockside water, security service, courtesy cars, floating docks, parking, mail ports, dockside

Fort Pierce to Stuart	LONGEST BERTH (in Feet)	APPROACH	ALONGSIDE	FUEL BRAND	GAS ★ DIESEL ● BOTH ▲	RAILWAY LIFT-RAMP	ENGINE REPAIRS	PROPELLER	MARINE - HULL	PROPANE GAS ★ / GAS ★ DIESEL ● BOTH ▲	MARINE SUPPLIES	GROCERIES	ELECTRICITY - ICE	SHOWERS 110/220/BOTH	PUMP-OUT STATION LAUNDROMAT	RESTAURANT - SNACK BAR
FORT PIERCE																
1. Pelican Yacht Club	75	5	5	AME	▲		R							▲	S	R
2. Marina at Fort Pierce	100	5	5	66	▲		L	★		PH	●	I		110	S	R
3. The Captain's Galley	100	5	5			RESTAURANT DOCK										
4. Fort Pierce Marina	100	5	5	TEX	▲		R					I		▲	SL	R
JENSEN BEACH																
5. Bailey Boat Co.	60	6	5	EX	★	●	L		★	PH	●			110		
6. Frances Langford's Outrigger Resort	100+	6			▲							I		▲	SL	R
MANATEE POCKET																
7. Sailfish Marina	100		6	GUL			L									
8. Mariner ...								E								
9. La...		6	6	CHE	▲				★		●	I		110	SL	●
10. ...ey River Houseboats / ...Cay Marina (Fish-N-Hol)	70	6	6	COMP...TION PROJECTED 1975												
				SALES AND RENTALS												
Mariner Cay Marina (Buckhead)	90	6	6	COMPLETION PROJECTED 1975												
11. David Lowe's Boatyard	60	6	8				L		▲	PH	●			▲	S	
12. Pirate's Cove	100	6	5	GUL	▲							I	●	▲	SL	R
13. Manatee Marina Resort	40	5	5	AME	▲						●	I		▲	S	R
14. Johnson Boatyard	40	6	6			●	LR	▲		PH	DRY STORAGE & TOWING					
ST. LUCIE RIVER																
15. Whiticar Boat Works					BUILDING & REPAIRS											
16. Bay Harbor Club	100	10	5	CHE	▲							I		▲	S	R
17. Anchorage Marina	80	6	6	TEX	▲		R				●	I		▲	S	R
18. Casa Rio Boat & Motor Sales	40	8	5	CHE	★	●	LR	★			●			110		
19. St. Lucie Marine	50	6	6	AME	★		L	▲		PH	●	I		110		
20. Lydia Yachts	100	7	7	GUL	●	BUILDING & REPAIRS										
NORTH FORK																
21. St. Lucie Hilton Country Club Resort	70	7	7	CHE	▲		R				●	I	●	▲	SL	R
SOUTH FORK																
22. Stuart Town Dock					TOWN DOCK											
23. Martin Marine Center	40	6	6	GUL	★		L	▲			●			110		
24. Wood's Cove Marina	60	6	6	AME	★	●		★		PH	●			▲		
25. Intracoastal Boatel-Motel	60	6	4									I		▲	S	

Waterway Guide is an invaluable handbook for full descriptions of marina facilities along the North-South route (shown here reduced in size). A similar listing appears on the jacket flap of small-craft charts.

lights, swimming pool, telephones *on board*, ship chandlery, engine service, weather reports, and now . . . cable TV!

It cost the dockmaster hard cash to provide these services, and he had little trouble reaping it as the boating explosion brought ever-increasing numbers of boats to his dock each year. The marina business today is a highly specialized business with investments in the millions; it is the target of eager local tax assessors and the ever-increasing demands of the yachting public . . . much of which today is composed of corporation owners who care little for the tax-deductible dollars the marinas charge. A "good" marina now has dock carts, a bar, a kiddie pool, a nine-hole golf course, and babysitter service. Many cost, like Miami and Fort Lauderdale, 50 cents and up per foot per night. That, with the face-saving piddling discount, is $725 plus sales tax for a 50-footer for a month! A marina in the Keys charges 35 cents per foot per day *after* you have joined the "club" via a $250 initiation fee *and* annual dues of $250 more!

Thus, these conditions, present in all marinas no matter what their basic rates, have slowly driven many cruisers to more and more anchoring. It is common to find, at sundown, a dozen boats snugged into some popular anchorage in the remote marshes of the coastal plain, where a dozen years ago some people considered it dangerous to anchor out. The new attitude is due

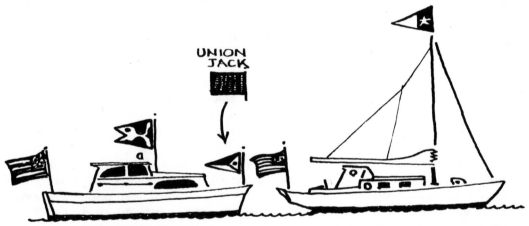

THE FLAGS TO FLY AT ANCHOR OR AT A MARINA OR CLUB

The U.S. Ensign (not the yacht ensign). From a staff on the taffrail on all yachts, power or sail, and in no other place.

The Private Signal. From the single mast of a powerboat or the aftermost mast of a two-masted vessel. Replaced during tenure of office by officer's flags of club officers. A sloop flies this signal at her masthead when not underway.

The Burgee. From the bow staff of a powerboat or the forward mast of a schooner, yawl, or ketch.

The Union Jack. Flown from the bow staff only at anchor or docked, and only on Sundays and holidays, never underway.

All flags fly from 8 a.m. until sundown, taking time from the host marina, club, or senior officer present. Never fly advertising banners or coded signal flags. Never dress ship while underway. Flags are raised in the following order: ensign, burgee, and private signal, and lowered in the reverse order. Even though moored or docked for extended periods, flags are flown every day, rain or shine.

to both the high cost of fuel and marinas, plus a certain indifference of marina dockmasters to small boats, sailboats, and multihull boats, especially if they do not need or want fuel. By and large, anchoring out is a healthy trend and relates boating to what boating is all about . . . a minor, innocent adventure quite away from the shore life and the need to display at least *some* independence and self-reliance. So look for something like 50 percent of your Waterway companions in an anchorage rather than in a marina.

For perhaps the first time in any publication, this work will, in Chapter 5, list *all* the anchorages available to the cruiser, together with depth, holding ground, and special notes. Many cruising people know these spots, but few annuals or monthlies have listed them for fear of advertiser objection: after all, marinas don't want their advertising outlets recommending free anchorages! In preparing a cruise itinerary, it is best to mark anchorages on the charts concerned.

There are no problems in obtaining fuel, gas or diesel, anywhere along the Ditch. Many marinas will grant a slight price break for quantity gallonage, say, 250 gallons or more. Smart diesel users seek out distributors, usually at a dock, near commercial or fishing interests, and get very bottom prices. In 1977, diesel fuel that cost 48 cents and up at marinas and boatyards could be bought at any distributor's for 33 to 36 cents a gallon. No minimum was required. Such distributors can be found in all ports larger than a village or hamlet. If there are shrimpers, there's usually a distributor. Or a distributor will send his truck for 200 gallons or more. Easily spotted from the channel, oil distributors are located in the following ports at least: Norfolk, Belhaven, Morehead City, Southport, Georgetown, McClellanville, Charleston, Savannah, (Thunderbolt), Fernandina, Jacksonville, New Smyrna, Daytona, Fort Pierce, Fort Lauderdale, Miami (in Government Cut), Key West, Fort Myers Beach (through bridge), St. Petersburg, and Tampa. All will accept credit cards of their company brand.

Engine work and repair, parts, fish bait, chandlery, fresh seafood, dockside telephones, rental cars (at the larger marinas), propeller and hull work are all handy to the waterfront, and well advertised, in the larger ports. The small-craft charts list such services along with the marina listings; so do the *Waterway Guide* and the service manuals for your own engine and accessories, appliances, and electronics. Supermarkets are a little more difficult to find directly on the waterside. Some marinas have free courtesy cars that you may use for shopping; others will carry you, or you can always call a taxi. The following ports have large supermarkets within a half-mile walk of the waterfront: Great Bridge, Belhaven, Morehead City, Southport, Georgetown, Beaufort, St. Augustine, Daytona Beach, Eau Gallie, Manatee Pocket (Salerno), West Palm Beach, Fort Myers Beach, Fort Myers, Labelle, Boca Grande, St. Petersburg, and Clearwater Beach. There are numerous small convenience stores, some part of a marina complex. The Gold Coast is loaded with markets, many visible from the Ditch, but dockage is difficult in most cases. In some ports, a market can be found by threading toward a visible shopping center *off* the Waterway . . . usually near a canal, liberally sprinkled with homes, yet often having a dock at the inshore end. The biggies (like Fort Lauderdale and Miami) are the most difficult to shop, though at Dinner Key (south Miami) there is a supermarket close in.

It is a bit more difficult to find the grog shops, though a visit to a shopping plaza will often turn one up. Marina bars will sell bottled liquors, of course, but at greatly padded prices. The cheapest liquor prices are found in Maryland (especially Annapolis) and in Florida. North Carolina has stark, state-run stores (a nice one is at Morehead City, right on Main Street); South Carolina hides state licensed outlets in tiny, mean, rural shacks, as if ashamed of them; they are identified by a red ball. Virginia just recently opened a store (state operated) in the shopping center at Great Bridge, seconds from the docks, perhaps half a mile away. In Florida, where the competition is intense, there are many, many chain liquor outlets in every city, and most have reasonable prices.

There is one Waterway shopping "must" that experienced cruisers seldom miss—this at the very center of the famous low-country dining. At Charleston, take a cab to the largest supermarket in the world, a giant Piggly-Wiggly on Meeting Street, about two miles from the city marina. Here is a true international provisioner, with dozens of small national shops and the famous Harold's Cabin now occupying a huge store-within-a-store. It has all the specialties from all over the world: baklava, fried ants, chitlins, poi, chicle leaves, curried goat, smoked robalo; you name it, Harold will have it. This store also has the best imported wine cellar in the country, for Charlestonians depend much upon sherry, port, and Madeira for both table use and cooking. The Piggly-Wiggly is an experience, and we seldom miss it, or fail to be relieved of a few hundred bucks on every passage.

The Waterway route through tidewater Dixie has nothing to do with the major north-south highways and their sterile, stereotyped motels and standard menus and "tourist trap" attractions. Life here, near the coast, has a timeless quality about it. History is understood and revered; tradition is respected. One can still find old-time hotels and "boarding houses," general stores, fine dining, and uncompromised low-country cooking. One of the most enjoyable features of travel through the tidewater is the superb dining available, frequently directly on the waterfront, and most cruisers avail themselves of the opportunity to spice the cruise days with gourmet and near-gourmet dining. Following is a list of the best-loved restaurants and hostelries, all save a few on or adjacent to the marina docks. Most feature low-country cooking, with a special accent on seafood (crab, oyster, flounder, shrimp, turtle, snapper). Each listing gives location, name, specialty, cost range, an indication of whether there is a bar (but beer and wine are usually available), and special notes. Of course, there are other dining places, and almost any landing will turn up some sort of restaurant. On the next page are those best loved by old-time Ditch crawlers:

Belhaven (N.C.)	The River Forest Manor	Southern seafood, ribs, chicken buffet. Oyster fritters, soft-shell crabs, game. Bar. Medium prices. Dockside. Outstanding.
Morehead City (N.C.)	Capt. Bill's and Sanitary Fish Market	Both seafood only, but fresh. No bar. Low prices. Both dockside.
Bucksport (S.C.)	Bucksport Farm Bell Restaurant	Shad, shad roe. Bar. Medium prices. Dockside.
Charleston (S.C.)	Perdito's Old Colony The Scarlet O'Hara	Gourmet low-country cuisine. Bars. High prices. Not dockside. (Call cab and house will pay one-way fare.)
Hilton Head Island (S.C.)	Sea Pines Plantation (Harbour Town)	Excellent. Bar. Medium prices. Dockside.
Thunderbolt (Ga.)	Tassey's Pier	International cuisine. Bar. Medium prices. Dockside.
St. Augustine (Fla.)	Menendez	Gourmet Spanish. Paella. Bar. High prices. On waterfront strand.
Jensen Beach (Fla.)	Frances Langford's Outrigger Restaurant	Gourmet Polynesian. Bar. High prices. Dockside.

South of this area, the Gold Coast offers many and varied gourmet dining establishments. Directly on the water are: Creighton's, on the west bank of the canal, at Lauderdale-by-the-Sea; at the bridge immediately north of Lettuce Lake, in Pompano, is the famous Polynesian buffet at Imperial House. Near Port Everglades, at Bahia Mar, is Patricia Murphy's Starlight Restaurant; at Pier 66, also in Fort Lauderdale, is another famous gourmet restaurant. In Miami there are endless choices. We especially like the Jamaica Inn, on Key Biscayne, and its unique "Pub," and the Candlelight Inn in Coconut Grove (Dinner Key Marina). The Keys are literally loaded with outstanding dining rooms. Try one of the several restaurants of the Ocean Reef Club or the Anglers Club; all are super. A real "fun place" (green turtle steak, stone crab claws, dolphin, conch chowder) is the Green Turtle Inn, in the Plantation Key area and not far from several marinas. Key West has quite a foreign atmosphere and the dining to go with it.

We have heard, here and there, of private home dining rooms that offer the genuine article in tidewater cooking. Marina operators, possibly Chambers of Commerce, might turn one up for you. In this manner we found two:

At Masonboro, North Carolina, just south of Wrightsville Beach, Uncle Henry Kirkham provides a genuine Ca'lina oyster roast: bushels of delicious roasted oysters, hush puppies, perhaps a stuffed flounder and black beer, with black coffee, pecan, sweet potato, or peanut pie as a chaser. A fun place; hardly accepted gourmet dining in the common meaning, yet outstanding. Check with a marina dockmaster; Uncle Henry provides only when he feels like it.

At Beaufort, South Carolina, a charming woman in old lace and puffed sleeves opened her old Federalist plantation home, hard on the river marsh in the antebellum section of Beaufort, to a small group of us cruisers. We enjoyed a traditional half-hour in the lovely old parlor, were served sherry or Madeira (because "there were ladies present"), and sat down amid antique mahogany and old family silver and linen napery to the kind of a meal the "master" himself must have enjoyed back in the 1850s. Clear turtle broth, "garden sass" salad, a huge jambalaya (shrimp, crabmeat, chicken, ham chips, and strips of roast port, laid upon a steaming bed of long-grain and wild rice, all richly spiced and laced with a dash of sherry), spoon bread, a decorous sliver of syllabub, with strawberry and cream gently blending with the delicate almond flavor; then espresso in the parlor and a discreet touch of Bourbon for the men in the trophy room. It was . . . and is . . . an occasion to remember and treasure. This was in 1973. Quite possibly it is no longer available, but it is cited to inspire you to seek out other places—for of this sort of experience are some of the great Waterway moments composed.

So this has been a broad look at "Life on the Waterway," the "what" of that life. Quite as important is the "who" of that life.

Life afloat is a very special way of life. It does not draw ordinary types, and the composition of the group is highly specialized in its interests, experience, state in life, even age. They are quite apt to be people *exactly the same as you are.* To be sure, there are great variations and reactions, yet they—all having about the same objectives, problems, and talents—react within defined and even narrow bounds. It is easy to "crash" this special social order. You may correctly assume that all are, essentially, boating people, and that those who have other deep interests are not present in the group. It's akin to joining a golf club because you like to play golf; you probably will not meet there the polo player or the skeet shooter or the scuba buff, and you can be reasonably sure that those you meet will have golf as a first interest and will talk golf and play golf. And so it is on the Waterway. People on boats like boats (even if they do occasionally play golf or shoot skeet), yet they still have interesting and appealing facets to their characters that make for normal association and socializing. Just as on shore, you all, as a group, share similar experiences and problems, situations, and objectives, and this, per se, creates a social system into which or from which one can go as far as he wishes. The very uniqueness of this specialized life seems to strain out some of the personalities we find uninteresting in shore life. Undoubtedly this is because boatmen, as all others, fall into a basic pattern and type. Yet it is a comfortable pattern to which we need make no great adjustments and so can feel happy and secure.

To be sure, we have a responsibility to society and must observe the basic standards and values of society. Later chapters will acquaint you with some of these codes. Oh, there is nothing difficult or overly codified about them, but it will truly ease the path of a newcomer as he traverses the Ditch for the first time . . . and, incidentally, make some of the friendships that most of us on the circuit value above all else. Believe me, the tyro is truly welcome. There are no closed doors, no entrance fees. Just be the same person you are ashore in your relationships with your fellow man. Apply the same rules you use ashore, stir in a small dash of humility (since you *are* a tyro), and you will do all right.

Your first contact with the life will be in terms of your boat, for, like your home ashore, this is what strangers see first. You will be judged in terms of your boat; the judgment will be modified, confirmed, and finally fixed when they get to know you personally. This alone is a sound reason to keep your boat in clean, orderly condition, to polish your seamanship and develop safe and sane steaming habits. People you would like to know are apt to own boats that you would like to own, and vice versa, of course.

Formal membership in clubs and "squadrons" is not at all necessary. Nothing wrong with it, of course, but the real fellowship of the Waterway is a club that is entirely unorganized, entirely without formality; it is just based on friendship and the happy security of the group. Yet this club can, when required, violently reject the intrusion of some idiot who lacks both courtesy and knowledge in his thoughtless operation of his vessel. The passing violations are an example. A few years ago an overtaken vessel, violently tossed about by a speed jockey in a narrow channel, shot out the windshield of the offender, and not a witness could be found to testify for the offender. The club has blackballed greedy marinas and dishonest engine-repair services. It has loudly applauded kindly and concerned dockmasters, marine patrol sheriffs who applied the law to locals as well as transients, and skippers who displayed understanding of the problems of smaller, slower boats. It is a good club to belong to; indeed, life afloat could be lonely and meaningless without membership.

After over 20 round trips on the Great Ditch, it becomes as familiar as a street in the old home town. The look that this chapter has provided is an evaluating glance . . . better than nothing, and at least from a longstanding member of "the club." It is a point from which to take off, a point from which to make initial preparations for the first voyage, possibly to avoid some of the mistakes of the newcomer. If it also whets the appetite for more of this fascinating way of life, for more of this unique and charming tidewater, that is all to the good. Welcome aboard.

Chapter 3
The Economics of Living Afloat

Of all the shoals, of all the rocks shown on the charts that you will consult in this exciting new life afloat, the most dangerous, and the one on which more vessels founder than any other, is an invisible one. It is the shoal of costs and the rocks of dollars and cents—which might possibly be spelled *sense* and lose no meaning. These dangers lurk on every course. Only a wise and realistic yacht master can avoid them, for they won't go away, and they become more dangerous the more you ignore them. Of supreme importance, of paramount consideration are the basic, simple questions: How much will it cost? and, Can I afford it?

If you already have a boat, you know the annual cost of her operation; or you certainly should know. This chapter will concern itself with the "extras," the additional costs that you will face by reason of extending your season and your cruising waters. It will assume that you start at Mile Zero on the Intracoastal Waterway.

For the man who acquires a boat for this life, the newcomer, let him understand that boat ownership and operation are composed of at least the following items. He must put a price on each item by realistically estimating or searching his own and others' records. This price must be adjusted for current costs and purchasing power of the dollar and, preferably, a generous "bounce" factor should be added.

41

BOAT OWNERSHIP COSTS

In Cash

Fuel	Replacement costs
Oil	Maintenance, repair costs
Dockage	Local taxes
Seasonal storage	Licenses
Yard work, hauls	Insurance
Utilities (dockside)	Interest and payments (if mortgaged)
Materials for self-work	

In Accruals

Major replacements, such as sails, batteries, engine
    (annualized in a capital account)
Depreciation
Selling costs (brokerage, advertising, dead storage)

There are some pluses to year-round living aboard. You will have no need for the winter haulout for storage, or a winter cover, or a northern yacht club, and you may well avoid local taxes. On the other hand, the insurance must be endorsed (and the additional premium paid) for 12 months' active coverage and, possibly, for foreign cruising. The cost of your domicile, or rental, probably your automobile, food and drink budgets, clothing, medical, and other normal family costs will continue in whole or in part and must be considered. Plus the cost of getting from where you are to Mile Zero.

Some neophytes have gone into a dreamlike trance and sold everything "up North." This is a vast mistake. Try it first by whatever means you can, for a short time the first time, via boat rental or charter, and only then, if you are sure that you like it and can afford it, cut the shore ties. To buy a boat as a trial is folly. You seldom make money on a used boat (only the broker does), and selling from original ownership could easily lose the cost of a winter charter three times over.

MARINAS, DOCKS, AND ANCHORAGES

Marina costs, a large part of life afloat, have risen steadily during the last five years. This is due, in great part, to the basic change in the purpose of a marina, for it is no longer a temporary tie-up for the night or a fuel stop. It has taken on the character of a resort and must supply just about what a good motel would supply, and reasonably be entitled to payment for same. Added to this is the fact that there just aren't enough docks to meet the demand. So small, poorly run fuel stops try to charge as much as their big sisters that *are* worth it. The tiny sloop using no fuel, and the trimaran needing *two* dock spaces, are discouraged. The marina excesses are mostly in the Gold Coast area, where there is glamour and excitement merely by location, with the marina having to provide little of it. Fortunately, there are many other areas of reasonable marina costs, and it is hardly necessary to pay the 35 to 60 cents per foot per night charges. There are still many 15-cents-a-foot marinas, a few 10-cent ones, and not many in the 25-cent class. These latter usually offer substantial term discounts of up to 70 percent over the day rates. The municipal or "city" marinas are the least expensive . . . and the most crowded, of course.

A sound practice when steaming is to fuel up, anchor out for three or five nights, then duck into a marina for a refuel, a shore excursion, showers, and a break in pace. This was not considered status a few years ago; now you find $100,000 yachts anchored out and the expensive marinas patronized in great part by corporation-owned boats and the professional delivery crews, neither of which spend their own dollars.

There is no cost to anchoring. Many communities have designated free anchorage areas, and frequently the Coast Guard has marked them with anchorage buoys (white nuns, usually four in number, one at each corner of the anchorage area). A few marinas have "moorings," which are heavy anchors, with buoys, to which you may tie up for a dollar or two a night. This gives you dinghy landing privileges, sometimes a desirable matter. The City of Fort Lauderdale, in its only yacht anchorage, has such a system at $2 a night (It is in the lovely lagoon at Las Olas Bridge. Pick up a mooring, tie up, and a marine patrolman will arrive to collect sometime.) In the natural bends, coves, and offshoots of the Waterway, you may anchor wherever you wish, but always out of the channel and in no way affecting the passage of other vessels or the pursuits of fishermen.

Transient dockage is a large expense in the more populous cities of Florida, in the Keys, and in some west coast cities. Yet a cruise in Florida waters must be largely by "marina"; there are very few anchorages in glamour areas, and no "cheap" marinas. Be prepared to pay an average of 25 cents per foot per night (which includes utilities). Look out for two snide devices to glean an extra buck from the yachtsman. These are: (1) The addition of the length of overhangs, such as a bowsprit or Swedestay bumpkin, a stern swim platform, or dinghy davits, to the length of the boat. (2) An additional charge for electricity at heavily inflated meter rates, seldom adjusted to the small cruiser, which does not require air conditioning, electric heat and cooking, two TVs, two refrigerators, and a deepfreeze. An obvious answer is to stay away from such marinas, but, believe me, they could not care less at the moment.

Municipal marinas, some of the overhead of which is borne by the local taxpayer, are often very reasonable, usually close to 15 cents a foot per night, including electricity, water, parking, mail service, and security. They usually offer substantial seasonal discounts and as much as a 70 percent discount by the year. Naturally, local boatowners subscribe to many docks in these marinas and local pressures have drawn many a long way from their original purpose of attracting northern winter visitors. But there still is space, dockmasters are apt to

Dinner Key Marina is operated by the City of Miami. (Miami-Metro Department of Publicity and Tourism)

be relaxed and friendly and the great waterway society flourishes in them. (See the Table of Dockage Rates at the end of this chapter.)

Here are the current rates of two typical city marinas, the first on the east coast of Florida, the second on the west coast.

(1) Per day   15 cents per foot deck measurement

Per month   5 cents per foot per day times the number of days in month.
For both rates, add 4 percent sales tax. Includes electricity, water, parking, mail port, watchman, picnic area with fireplace, snack bar.

(2) Per day   25 cents per foot, deck measurement, to 6 days
15 cents per foot, deck measurement, 7 to 29 days
10 cents per foot, deck measurement, 30 to 59 days.
Plus 4 percent sales tax, electricity as metered (except for first 6 days), and parking (if required) at $2 per week in reserved space. Includes water, watchman, mail port, raft (for hull work while afloat), and library.

Further, this latter marina offers attractive long-term rates as follows:

Term	Nov 1 to April 30	May 1 to October 31
2 to 3 mos.	7 cents per foot per day	5 cents per foot per day
4 to 5 mos.	6 cents per foot per day	5 cents per foot per day
6 mos.	5 cents per foot per day	4 cents per foot per day

Thus, a 40-foot vessel could berth here, year 'round, for an annual rent of $656 plus, say, $200 for electricity (heat, light, air, TV, refrigeration, and Constavolt or the equivalent). The agreement is that, should you depart temporarily (as on a cruise), the dock may be rented and the proceeds go to the marina. The average winter stay of four months, for a 40-footer, would be a modest $72 a month dock rental. Where can you beat it?

Marinas expect, in all fairness, that you buy your fuel from them, and possibly also paint and chandlery, and that you abide by their rules—generally sane codes for living in harmony with others. The "rules" are usually aimed at loud radios and TV; use of generators; engine tuning after noon; noisy parties; use of docks for painting, construction, etc.; washdowns only in calm weather; and use of outboards belonging to the boat within the marina.

All marinas expect you to leave—fast!—when so advised upon a hurricane alert. For this, you are obligated to have your engines operative at all times during the storm months of October to June. You run *inland* to a pre-determined berth, or to a boatyard that will haul you out, where you are protected from the greatest hazard, not the wind but high water. The Coast Guard will advise you, or the local U.S. Power Squadron, or the marina management. You are advised to *get off the boat* . . . take a motel room or move in with Uncle Dave. Don't try to "ride it out" unless you are an old hurricane hand, understand the nature of hurricanes, and have a vessel that can take it. Very few modern yachts can take a hurricane, so why try?

If you skipper a catamaran or trimaran, be prepared to be turned away or to pay for two or more dockage spaces. Generally, small sailing boats and pocket cruisers . . . neither of which uses much fuel if any, and both of which "use" a dock capable of bringing in more dollars from a larger boat . . . are often turned away; or they are tucked into some unhandy corner (at full rates, of course). Beware of the dockmaster who wants to raft a boat against you *after* you have checked in. He usually collects full dockage from both . . . or from 3 or 4! . . . and has no legal right to do so unless it is clearly agreed upon at the time of checking in. It is your dock, and you are in no way bound to have strangers stamping over your decks at all hours. If you suspect a rafting policy, tie your dinghy 'longside and dare anybody to move it! However, rafting is almost a necessity in such popular ports as Charleston, South Carolina, which has only one marina in the city proper. And it is crowded with locally owned boats, commercial craft, "tour" and head boats, and a miserable six transient berths allowed by the city fathers. An effort should be made to organize any necessary raft. The boat planning to leave first should be outside, the layover boat inside. Hard shoes should be warned off your decks, especially if they are worn by a party of drunks at 2 A.M. of a hot night. And allow only clean, scrubbed fenders and clean lines.

However, in spite of this mild bitching, it wouldn't hurt at all to be co-operative as a yachtsman. At least invite a friendly boat to share your berth, and see if you can't convince the dockmaster that he can't collect twice for the same berth. Who knows, the next time you may be the one who arrives late and must be rafted or turned away.

About reservations: in season, and from about Southport, North Carolina, down the coast to the Keys in Florida, and especially during weekends, holidays, and the snow-bird migration, do make advance reservations. Phone ahead before leaving the overnight stop. While many marinas monitor VHF and CB channels, these seldom reach far ahead, so even with luck, you might bridge only an hour's run. When calling, give the name of the boat and her length and draft. Specify whether she is sail or power, private or commercial, and whether you require 110-volt AC service or 220. Then give your ETA (estimated time of arrival). Most marinas will hold a reservation until 6 P.M., and later if you are known to them.

It is usual (to save a morning crush at the fuel pumps) to top tanks upon arrival, before proceeding to the assigned dock. Pay the entire bill at this time. Credit cards are welcome and dockage may be charged to fuel company cards. Personal checks are usually acceptable upon identification (driver's license, voter's card, etc.) because, in the South, offering an uncovered check is prima facie evidence of fraud, and arrest and charges are automatic. It is not necessary to tip dockmasters unless you ask for a special service.

Marinas all have means of disposing of trash and garbage. Some have tanks for disposal of used engine oil. A very few attempt to make a sewerage hookup, which you shouldn't do if you have empty holding tanks. All will hold mail for you, call you to the phone (via loudhailer), order LP gas bottles of appropriate size for you, arrange for engine and other services, or haulouts, sell you paint and ice . . . and if they make a dollar on it, so what? Fewer and fewer have ice; it is usually in vending machines and in bagged cube form (marked up to about 85 cents a bag). Some have bait, fresh fish and shrimp, and a little mini-bar or snack market. Most have at least local charts and a rack of the excellent *Waterway Guide*, the *Yachtsman's Guide to the Bahamas*, and the local Chamber of Commerce material. The larger marinas will have a weather wire and a bulletin board with the tapes displayed. A few have fences but will lend you a pass key. Larger marinas may have car rental desks, scuba diver propeller changing and cleaning services, possibly a Travelift for quick haulouts. In the Deep South, there might well be a swimming pool, miniature golf, tennis courts, and a happy hour bar . . . all (save the bar) included in the per-foot-per-day price.

An alternative to the marina is the local boatyard. Often it will have a few docks set aside for transient boats who simply want to tie up for the night, possibly to top the tanks. These tie-ups usually are modestly priced (like $3 a night). Surely they lack the glamour, but they do offer a simple, uncomplicated relationship with the shore and usually quite human, interesting characters. Some of these boatyards have become popular winter bases and rival the formal marinas. They are to be found, even on the Gold Coast, up the creeks and rivers, and they are highly recommended for the budget-minded. Look for them at Jacksonville Beach, Daytona Beach, Eau Gallie, Jensen Beach, Manatee Pocket, up the New River and the Miami River, and, on the west coast, at Fort Myers, Sarasota, Bradenton, and St. Petersburg. En route, such yards are also at Great Bridge, Virginia; Elizabeth City, North Carolina; Morehead City; Swansboro; in the Wrightsville area, both north and south of the bridge; Holden Beach; Briarcliff; Georgetown; McClellanville; in the Charleston area (not in the city itself); Thunderbolt, Georgia; and Fernandina, Florida.

The day has long since gone when the visiting yachtsman could tie up at the local yacht club, break out a burgee or membership card from his northern yacht club, and receive exchange courtesies. The yacht clubs of the South couldn't afford it. Most are closed to visiting yachts unless sponsored by a local member. A very few accept visiting yachts only if they are members of clubs listed in Lloyd's Registry of American Yachts and Yacht Clubs. And they charge about the same as a good marina. Do not count on this; most clubs are full up all winter, and you must have a strong IN even to be noticed.

Here is still another docking technique. Much of the residential areas of plush communities on both coasts are entwined by a system of navigable canals. Almost every house on the canal has a dock, but not every house has a boat. So, in order to help cover taxes and carrying costs, some of these homeowners offer their docks for rent on a seasonal basis. They frequently offer addresses of prestige, with quiet, palm-shaded streets, and they are surrounded by lush landscaping. They are equal . . . indeed, superior . . . to most marinas and clubs.

You will find the offerings in the local papers, in the classified sections under "Boats for Sale" or "Marine Services." (*Miami Herald*, daily and Sunday, is the best source). Depending upon the community and the neighborhood, the dockage will run from $100 to $250 a month, usually with electricity, water, parking, and sometimes use of a pool or a garden patio. A frequent objection to this practice is that of sewerage disposal. Unless you have holding tanks (not merely a chlorinator), you must not dock and live aboard on a canal with a closed end. Check to see that the canal is open, i.e., connected on *both* ends to other water so that there is a tidal flow through the canal.

Also check the delivery capacity of the electrical conduit to the dock, too often engineered for a simple dock light only. Check, too, the parking space for your car (if you have one) as well as for your guests' cars. Many northerners have discovered a very pleasant and reasonable winter by using private docks . . . and have made some happy friendships as well. If you must remain in the high-cost areas (and who can deny their excitement and color?), this is probably the best way to achieve it. We once lived so, less than half a mile from the famous Bahia Mar (marina plus) for $125 a month, saving, over Bahia Mar, a neat $600 a month. It is wise to make arrangements months before arrival, even for the *next* season, for the most desirable docks go quickly or are leased year after year to the same boat.

CRUISING COSTS

The actual costs of the passage to and fro can be forecast only in terms of your own boat. Fuel, of course, is the big expense. Displacement boats, limited to about 10 knots for efficient running, use less fuel than planing boats (up to 30 knots), but they go more slowly and so use less fuel for a longer time. Displacement boats have a slight edge on efficiency, because planing boats cannot move at their most efficient speeds through much of the Waterway, or shouldn't. The figure of gallons per hour (GPH) times hours run times fuel cost equals the passage cost, a pretty penny at today's fuel prices. Gasoline sold on the waterside suddenly has become worth 10 to 12 cents a gallon more than roadside gas. Diesel, which does not carry a road tax when sold to a boat, seems to remain about the same as roadside costs. The least expensive outfit, yet one that is entirely satisfactory for Waterway travel and winter living aboard, is a single-screw, medium-power diesel boat; this because it is the most efficient. High-powered twin-screw boats may be required for fishing, or simply for dash and status, but the cost rises to excessive figures (like 32 gallons of gasoline an hour for a 30-foot, 26-knot cruiser; that's a cost of $20 an hour, or almost a dollar a mile).

To be sure, the entire Ditch may be sailed, and has been by many a hardy soul, but time, then, must be of no consideration. In the fall, there are frequent periods of bright, crisp weather, with northerly winds that often grant genuinely large daily mileages. I once came down, in late October, in a 44-foot ketch with a total fuel bill, Mile Zero to Jupiter, Florida, of $24. The winds were kind and the time my own. The free wind is not to be counted on unless you are offshore.

Chapter 2 has given a few hints on quantity buying of fuel and where it may best be obtained.

Oil changes cost little, if one does it himself and has bought the oil, by the case, from a distributor. (It is easy to save 50 percent over retail prices with a five-gallon pail or one-quart cans.) Carry a five-gallon drum (or buy your oil in one) and a small battery-driven exchange pump, and you can save as much as $35 an engine over "marina service."

Some marinas have LP gas in 20-, 40-, and 100-pound cylinders. Local distributors will usually deliver if you have the time, but insist that they fill your own tanks. Exchange bottles, to transients, all seem to be rusty, battered, and ready to collapse. The gas runs about 15 cents a pound. Partly exhausted bottles will be filled. If you need LP gas fast, hire a cab and head for the nearest travel trailer park that handles LP.

These voyage costs, in the islands or in Mexico, seem to expand beyond all reason. Diesel in the Bahamas runs near a dollar a gallon, gas sometimes as high as $1.20. LP gas, if you can find it, will reach $10 for a bottle of 20 pounds. Water, which is very scarce on some islands, goes for three to 10 cents a gallon, and it's often not very good drinking water. Dockage costs at the swank clubs will rival those of the Gold Coast. The Bahamas are most definitely anchoring-out islands for most of us, with an occasional splurge, dockside, at special places such as Nassau, West End, Chub Key, Bimini, and Spanish Wells. In Mexico, the yacht is still a strange animal. One must call a fuel truck, just like the commercial boats do. Premium gasoline, about equal to our regular, is in the dollar-a-gallon area. Diesel is a little less expensive and inclined toward a "bunker" grade. Like the Bahama tour, this is a sailboat passage for most of us.

Water, stateside, is free at the fuel or marina dock. Test it before filling your tanks; some water in the South has a decided sulfur content (it smells like rotten eggs), and other local water is heavily overtreated with chlorine. If you must have it, boil it to remove some of the obnoxious odors and tastes. Don't drink raw water in any Mexican port: Montezuma's Curse will surely be lurking in it, however clear it seems. In the Bahamas, while the water is usually quite safe, it is often roof-collected and therefore given to queer tastes and color. Best, if you can, drink rum, the least expensive liquid in the islands.

HAULS, SERVICE, REPAIRS

Maintenance, as everywhere else, runs into big money these days. The going wage, starting in Virginia, is about $14 an hour for a skilled mechanic, which is okay if *you* decide whether he's skilled or not. A good man is probably worth that. But too many yards send you a trainee, or a "team" (often both trainees) at twice the cost, and they seem to encourage frequent coffee breaks, long periods of waiting at the stock room, and mysterious disappearances . . . all on your time. There is a strong feeling that repair work, to transient boats, is a big ripoff. It's pretty difficult to prove, of course, so most of us avoid the big yards and seek out the lesser ones, or those that permit owner labor. These are present in all large ports, usually yards geared to commercial work. They charge to haul (for a Travelift, about $1.50 per foot in and out), plus a daily charge of a dollar or so while "on blocks." For a brief job, such as a transducer replacement or a check, they charge only in and out. If at all possible, obtain not only an estimate (which means nothing to some yard operators) but a contract price as well. Get it in writing, signed. If the nature of the repair permits, try to get dockside service (as at a marina) and deal directly with the service firm. TV repairs, refrigeration, electronics, engine tuning, etc., can thus be done . . . and at substantial savings.

Local marina operators who do not own a yard can turn up do-it-yourself yards where you can do any and all work yourself. These are located mostly in populated areas. There are several up the New River in Fort Lauderdale, up the Miami River in Miami, on the Caloosahatchee River west of Fort Myers, one about 10 miles east of it (called 107 Marina), and another south of

West Palm Beach, at Lantana. Local Newspapers also list these yards in the classifieds or sports pages. While not seeking large-boat business, many out-board marinas have Travelifts with latch headers, which can handle masted boats up to eight or 10 tons. Try them by phone.

You can seldom avoid a haul in the South if you are there for the winter, for if the bottom is wood, it must be done twice a year in the tropics; a glass hull might need work every eight or nine months. This is also the time to do work on the topsides, shaft, prop, and transom, and any recaulking or re-fastening of planks. So seek out, well in advance, commercial yards, self-service yards, and yards of obvious low overhead, and stay away, far away, from the Gold Coast if at all possible.

Once settled in for the winter, with some self-work coming into focus, it becomes important to discover sources for the paint, parts, chandlery, equipment, and gear you may need. Of course, you can refer to the fancy so-called marine catalogs—filled with nautical gifts and useless gadgets and pot-metal chandlery—and pay through the nose. It is wise to remember that southern Florida is unlike any other area in America. In no other place is there such a concentration of yachts, such a market for nautical items ... and such a dogfight for the business generated. The public is the gainer. There are marine discount houses, marine flea markets, columns in the daily press offering gear: new, used, surplus, and assemble-it-yourself. You can actually buy name-brand paints (for example) for close to the 50 percent discount the dealer gets. There is sharp competitive pricing in the fields of marine electronics, optics, air conditioning and refrigeration, epoxies and fiberglass, deck chairs, dinghies. Prices firm up a little (but there are still discounts) for heavy castings, anchors, chain, aluminum findings, galvanized ware, and metal items that have little or no machining. Outboard motors, replacement parts, radars and RDF, and compasses are apt to remain high. (This must be where the money is. I once had to pay $55 for a transducer replacement for a depth sounder that cost $89.50 including the original transducer.) There is a constant price battle on rope, life preservers, fishing tackle, reels, water skis, and rubber rafts (which dry out and become useless in stock).

Here is where to look, via the yellow pages, your dockmates, and the classified columns: up the Miami River; in Coconut Grove (south Miami, near Dinner Key) is a fabulous marine discount house; in Fort Lauderdale, around S. Andrews Avenue and the New River; in Pompano Beach. In most any Florida yachting center that supports *several* ship chandlerers, one will surely be a price-cutter. In the Norfolk area, check especially the so-called Navy surplus outlets; in Morehead City, North Carolina, on Main Street, due west of the waterfront. I heard there was a place in Tampa, Florida; ask around.

Marina dockmasters often have "wholesale" connections and can readily order needed items. Their discounts vary from 33 percent (hard goods, parts) to 50 percent (paint, rope), and they don't really expect to make it all, but they'll try. There is nothing wrong with trying to make a deal with them, split the discount, or make a counter-offer to a quotation. They have nothing at stake but a telephone call and will usually deal. Don't feel cheap or bad about it. Nobody feels sorry for a man with a yacht, least of all the chandlerers, and their line is grossly overpriced anyway.

TAXES

In general, the states in which you will winter will offer a 90-day visitor's period during which your own license or registration (or document) will be valid and acceptable. After that it is a matter of chance. Some dockmasters report you to local tax assessors after 90 days. Other communities don't bother you; their merchants are glad to have the extra transient income. In Florida the registration fee (about $30 a year for a 40-foot boat, about $40 a year for a 50-footer) is also the property tax, and there are *no other taxes on a boat*. Most boats move about so often that the tax men do not catch up with them. Documentation (licensing by the federal government) does not take the place of state registration; it merely keeps the tax man off your back for a while. In Florida the local tax collector is responsible for gathering in the boat taxes, and he usually is understaffed and unequipped to run down this slight source of additional tax revenue. When police, marine patrols, and the Coast Guard check licenses, they accept the license of your own state, or a federal document, and indicate no interest in enforcing tax regulations. Most northern boats that I know do not pay Florida taxes.

If you want to send a child to school, you must immediately pay the boat tax for the full year, or the child will not be enrolled.

In Florida there is a sales tax on almost everything but food. This includes dockage and fuel that has not already been plastered with a state road tax. Present tampering would indicate higher percentages in the near future. Florida also has a new and very nasty law: a full four percent sales tax on used boats. The state gets a four percent cut off the top of every boat sale, even of the same boat and even if it is sold every few days! Think twice before buying a used boat in Florida. As an out-of-stater, you can avoid this tax by removing the boat immediately from Florida waters ... but that's not what most of us intend to do. Brokers, who have been placed in the impossible position of also being considered dealers, know the loopholes, and they will happily advise on the legal ones in order to continue making sales.

Your federal income tax is due no matter where you are. If the boat is your true home and you substantially live on it, wherever, you may claim the standard home-oriented deductions (taxes, interest, etc.). Be prepared to prove your contention with signed logs, docking and other local receipts, paid voyage bills, and a photo of your boat, with license number showing, in the surroundings you claim that she is in. Left over from the days when anybody could claim boat expenses as business and business entertainment expenses is a strong feeling of doubt by the IRS when handling boat deduction claims. You are on solid legal ground, but you might have to prove it.

If you earn income on your boat and are self-employed (as a writer, artist, craftsman, marine surveyor, yacht broker, etc.), you may claim as a business deduction the cost of maintaining the area or quarters in which you work. Cost may be all or part of proportioned cost needed to produce the income you report and are about to be taxed on. (Schedule E and Form 1040 from the IRS.) These costs may include heat, light, insurance, taxes, depreciation, maintenance, dockage in just proportion, as well as costs of any materials used, supplies, stationery, postage, etc. Moving the boat (fuel, oil, etc.) cannot be deducted unless the moving is required by your profession (such as photographer or writer for a boating magazine, travel for income purposes, or change of location incidental to job or assignment relocation). It can very seldom now satisfy tax examiners if you claim the boat is needed for business entertainment. That dodge, even for corporations, must be indisputably proven.

You in no way lose any Social Security, pensions, state benefits by living on a boat. You become a little hard to find, but that is readily solved by having your income sent to your principal bank and drawing from it, by mail, into a temporary winter bank. Vacationland banks are used to this, and they will happily carry small or temporary accounts. Should you need medical aid during a southern vacation, your insurance or Medicare cards will produce it.

Your legal residence is where you reside for more than six months of each year or where your principal residence is located, whether occupied or not. If a boat is your *only* home, you can consider it so, paying any state taxes in whichever state you spend the most time, obviously selecting the one that has the least, or no, state income tax. You should get on the voter's list in this state, and use it as an official address (for federal tax purposes, insurance, etc.). It is not necessary to have the boat registration, a car registration, driver's license, banking facilities, broker, etc., match the state of residence; these do not prove residence.

MARINE INSURANCE

Marine insurance is expensive and will continue to become more so as the speed, power, sophistication, and number of boats increase. Someday we may have a realistic differentiation between the slow, small cruiser or sloop and the huge crewed mass of gleaming chrome and expensive tonnage that zooms down the Waterway and is an obvious menace to itself and all life within a thousand yards. We, in our little slow boats, pay for the four sets of props these giants smash up on every passage; for the docks they wash away and the boats they capsize ... and sometimes the people they kill. Meanwhile, we slog along at nine knots, with hardly a wake, a danger to nobody and no thing, and pay the same high rates as the speed demons do.

There is no present cure save to go without insurance. Some boats do just that. The happy medium is to develop prudent habits and insure only against complete loss of the vessel, either by policy or policy "deductibles." This means *you* pay to replace the damaged rudder that may occur or the paint that is scraped off against a spike-studded wharf, but you are covered against a large loss such as a fire or complete vessel loss in a storm. In addition, and even if you carry no other insurance, you should definitely carry coverage against liability—losses *you* or *your boat* may cause to others. Marine insurers will write such coverage, as will your own local agency, for it is not a strange coverage once the tag "marine" is removed from it.

With only liability insurance, it becomes essential that you become truly a prudent and skilled navigator, with mature judgment and respect for the sea. Let someone qualified to judge make the judgment. Go through the free courses offered by the U.S. Power Squadron and the U.S. Coast Guard Auxiliary; they turn out highly qualified small boatmen.

Mutual insurance companies, rather than "stock" companies, offer some rate relief, and they should be investigated. Your local agency would rather sell you a stock policy (higher commissions), but talk them down. Be aware that an extra premium is demanded for extending coverage beyond seasonal or lay-up periods, for navigating in a hurricane belt, for sailing to some foreign ports (Bahamas excluded), and for navigating a full 12 months. Some policies grant credit in the form of refunds for "lay days," or periods during which the boat is in commission but not moved. This peculiarly suits the live-aboard winter cruiser. There are also credits for completing Squadron or Auxiliary courses (about five percent credit), for having diesel power, for a good personal record, and for superior and automatic fire suppression equipment. A personal survey by insurance inspectors is often required, especially for wooden boats, sailing boats, and all boats over 10 years of age. Some companies refuse to insure "old" boats, ferrocement boats, home-built craft, and foreign-flag vessels. Dinghies are considered "equipment" of the parent vessel and do not require separate coverage, even if equipped with power or sail.

A very rough cost guide . . . very rough . . . is: a vessel with a *replacement* cost of $35,000, diesel-powered, single screw, cruiser, wooden construction, say, five years old, would cost, for 12 months' operation ($500 deductible), in the area of $700 annual premium. That would be in a stock company, AA rated. In a lesser company, or a mutual, it would cost about 20 percent less.

A very smart trick is to buy your insurance in Florida, in the Fort Lauderdale-Miami area. There are thousands of boats there, and insurers must compete for their business . . . and do! You will get a better deal and better service where the boat action is than from your local agent in some inland town.

HOUSEHOLD COSTS

Food costs will be about the same as ashore. Supermarket prices are about the same all over the nation, and all mark prices *up* in the season. Winter is the Florida season, and prices are definitely *up;* not much, but the increase probably averages five percent. Fish and shellfish will be less expensive along the Waterway, at fishermen's outlets, and *will be fresh.* Local produce—eggs, milk, oranges, and vegetables—at a "stand" will be the same as in a market, for the radio daily tells these low-overhead operators the going retail price ranges of all commodities. You seldom save money; you can only hope for garden-fresh produce.

In some areas, in season, a price break occurs if you pick your own produce. This applies especially to citrus fruits, strawberries, tomatoes, peaches, apples, beans, kale, turnips, and corn. Huge farms and groves are located below Miami (Homestead area), in the lower Everglades, the Lake Okeechobee area, the St. Johns River area, the lower Caloosahatchee River, and east of Tampa (strawberries, citrus). At Wabasso, in the famous Indian River country, the cruiser may pull up to a dock on the Ditch and stock up with citrus fruits in season at packing-house prices. Watch for a sign about one mile south of the highway bridge.

A deep freeze helps the budget very much. You can stock up at any large port (where the competition is keen) or go to a custom-butcher for quantity cuts of beef, chicken, lamb, and pork. A lucky catch of fish can be stretched out to serve for months. It is especially economical to buy shrimp (Yucatan shrimp, 28 to 36 to a pound, heads off) in quantity and freeze them. Treats like stone crab claws, Key West lobster, pompano, shad and shad roe, snook, red snapper, turtle steak, conch, coon oysters . . . available only in the South . . . freeze and keep well.

You can afford to buy canned goods in quantity for the average boat because most boats have truly huge storage spaces below the cabin sole—cool and accessible. So take advantage of the market specials and stock up. To protect yourself against possible loss of the paper label in the moist bilge atmosphere, mark the cans as to content with a grease pencil.

Liquor, wines, and beers are available everywhere, and the prices are as low as anywhere in the country. There are quite a few Florida-bottled brands of liquor, especially rum, that offer real value. (State tax is low.) State law makes cash or personal check the only legal payment; no credit cards for liquor. The state supports huge liquor chains in high competition with each other. Each runs weekly "specials," which seem to be everything in the store at discount prices. Watch them closely and shop by the case or half-case, going to the store that has the best price for the brand you want. Several chains advertise that they will match the lowest price for the brand in the press ads of that day; just clip the lowest price from your morning paper and present it at the nearest such store. All liquor in Florida is subject to the state tax of four percent.

The chain stores usually have the best selections of both domestic and imported wines in the city. They run impressive "specials" on the California wines, have good selections of Bahamian and Jamaica rums, Mexican tequilas and sangrias, even sake and Swiss schnapps.

STILL MORE MONEY CONSIDERATIONS

What else do you need to know about money matters? Banking? Just open a local Vacationland account and perhaps even get a free skillet or a bedside clock. The local banks are accustomed to winter accounts and offer all sorts of deals: free checking, free (no fee) traveler's checks, no minimum balances, reserve credit in the account, free checks, and free mailing envelopes, and they will print your name and address or that of your boat on the checks for nothing. If you want to save, there are innumerable savings-and-loan associations, all government supervised and insured to $40,000 per account; some offer certificates of deposit that pay up to 7½ percent. In general, your personal check is good anyplace in the South, with identification. Credit cards are widely accepted, especially at marinas and for fuel. In the Bahamas and Mexico, carry cash; credit cards and checks are not usable.

Part-time work? Why not? Lots of winter boaters do it. Work at anything you wish: your trade or skill, part-time teaching, Kelly girl, truckdriver. I know several men who, partly out of boredom, work part-time as dock-masters or marina night watchmen. One fills in on a charter boat, drift fishing each morning. One helps a marine surveyor; another is a part-time yacht broker. Several men offer their skills in boat painting; varnishing; top engine overhaul; tuning up; electronic, TV, and radio repair; compass adjusting . . . and all live aboard as originally planned.

Chartering out? Beware. There are pitfalls. Ask any yacht broker or dock-master. Do it only if you have full insurance. If your own services are required, you will need a limited license to carry passengers for hire (not more than six). By and large, though it is done often, especially for Bahamas cruises, try to avoid chartering your own boat. It seems never to work out well for anybody. Leave it to the professionals, who have learned the hard way.

TRANSPORTATION

And one more cost faced by many live-aboards: transportation. By far the best plan is to ship a bike or two, or a very small, light motorbike, and rent a car occasionally as needed. To move your own car down is expensive and ruinous of the vacation spirit of your sojourn south. It will cost about $300 to and from New England, for example, either by a delivery service or by flying up and down to "get the car." In some areas, there are parking fees of about $8 to $10 a month. If you stay more than three months, the local gendarmes will want you to buy a license at a cost of $40 to $60. Further, a car breaks up the cruise if, as many boaters do, the wife goes ahead with the car and meets the boat every evening at the next marina; or if, every few days, somebody buses back for the damn car. That isn't what you took to this life for! The cost runs much higher than the cost of renting a car.

A dodge in case of dire necessity is to buy a "clunker" near your winter port and leave it there when you cruise or return north. This can save a few dollars, but not many, and opens you to double insurance, operating, and maintenance costs that hardly seem worthwhile.

Either way, transportation involves costs that you must reckon with. By far the greatest number of people solve the problem by shipping take-apart bikes fitted with market baskets and a stout lock and chain.

Unfortunately, the welcome habit of marinas keeping a courtesy car for anyone to use (for shopping and local driving), or of eager store managers "sending a car for you," is rapidly disappearing. You definitely need transportation, and it is a legitimate component of your overall costs.

TABLE OF DOCKAGE RATES IN FLORIDA (1976)

(Per-month charge for a 40-foot boat, winter rates.)

Municipal marinas	1 month	5 months
Fernandina	$ 80	$ 65
St. Augustine	100	78
Daytona	110	100
New Smyrna	80	80
West Palm Beach	120	108
Fort Lauderdale (New River)	100	100
Miami (downtown)	150	130
(Dinner Key)	90	70
Key West	88	N.A.
Naples	60	60
Fort Myers	60	54
Sarasota	160	92
Bradenton	85	64
St. Petersburg	90	81
Clearwater	110	95

(Electricity and 4 percent sales tax are extra.)

Commercial marinas (by area)	1 month
North Florida to Eau Gallie	$100 to $150
Indian River to West Palm Beach	180 to 220
West Palm Beach to Lauderdale-by-the-Sea	300 to 400
Fort Lauderdale	600 to 850
Miami	400 to 700
Upper Keys	400 to 900
Naples Area	200 to 250
Fort Myers area	140 to 200
Sarasota-St. Petersburg	150 to 275

Private Docks

Area	1 month
Stuart	$ 50 to $125
Jupiter	100 to 150
Boynton Beach	100 to 200
Fort Lauderdale	125 to 250
Miami	125 to 250
Naples	75 to 125
Sarasota	85 to 150
St. Petersburg (beaches)	75 to 125

Usually includes utilities (except phone), parking, and trash collection; private owners seldom charge sales tax. Seasonal rates by negotiation, but about 20 percent lower.

Chapter 4
Waterway Navigation

Navigation, as an art, on the Intracoastal Waterway is quite different from, say, navigating at sea, well offshore. You do not need a compass or a foghorn, the charts are on a different scale, the aids to navigation are entirely different, there are some special techniques required, and you are never more than about 12 feet from land—straight down.

First, the small-craft charts. For some reason the chart makers produced them in the scale of statute miles (5,280 feet to the mile) instead of the usual and normal nautical mile scale (6,080 feet per sea mile). There's nothing too wrong with it, save that every other chart that covers or adjoins the same area is on the nautical mile scale and thus forces transposing (and possible error) when working two charts (as at an inlet or a crossing, half of which would be on a chart on the nautical mile scale). It is something to remember when laying down courses and estimating time and distance.

When using the logarithmic speed scale of the small-craft charts, the speed will be shown in knots, which is a measurement in nautical miles. You must therefore convert statute miles to nautical miles *before* making the calculation (by dividers), and reconvert to statute miles *after* obtaining the answer in order to use this information with the Waterway charts. If you use an automatic speed-time-distance calculator, be sure that it also has a scale for statute miles. The entire length of the Waterway is divided into units of five statute miles, making it somewhat easy to make a quick approximate estimate of distance run. For the first northern 200 miles or so, a five-mile marker is placed just *off* the channel. It is usually a black spar (pile) with a white, rectangular sign noting the appropriate mileage from Mile Zero (15, 20, 25, etc.). Be careful not to confuse these markers with the normal day marks.

You should have, handy by, a quick conversion table for converting nautical miles to statute miles, and vice versa (*see* page 88). All small-craft charts have this scale for use with dividers, but it is necessary to step off the distance to be converted. Quick tables may be found in Coast Pilot 4 (Cape Henry—Key West).

Particularly helpful on the small-craft charts are these special features: recommended compass courses on open bays and sounds (true courses); a magenta line indicating the continuous Waterway in the best water; large purple numbers and leaders indicating a public marine facility (marina, fuel, dockage, etc.) and keyed to a Table of Facilities, printed inside the jacket of the chart; local tide tables (of most use to deep commercial vessels); noted anchorage areas for yachts (marked N-1 in a circle); schedules of marine weather broadcasts; and a quick digest of navigation laws, chart symbols, and Rules of the Road. Most experienced skippers know most of these things well, but a review can do no harm and might do some good.

Navigation on the Ditch is essentially the seat-of-your-pants variety. When it fog mulls, you simply do not move, for it is impossible to predict the currents, depths, and course changes along the magenta line. There is no tolerance for error; indeed, it is impossible to lay down a course that fine. Thus, you do not need a compass; or RDF. Even the very few sounds of any distance (Pasquotank River, Albemarle Sound, Neuse River, St. Andrews Sound) are well marked by closely spaced day and lighted markers. Albemarle Sound even has huge steering targets across its width of 15 miles, and they are visible at all times during a crossing. By waiting no more than five minutes, one can pick up another boat and follow; it's that easy.

The banks of both sides are visible the entire length of the Ditch, and they are readily identifiable by features noted on the chart and by snap-bearings, proximity to bridges, day marks, junctions, and habitations. A sounder (using a foot scale, not fathoms) can be very helpful. An easier way to determine depth is to understand the character of your normal quarter waves. If they rise unduly, or begin to break a few feet inshore, or the boat becomes difficult to steer, or, by *herself*, she sheers *away* from the bank, you are getting into shallow water. Get in the middle . . . fast. Some of the banks in dug canals are layered sandstone and, further, they may have dangerous water-logged trash lurking there. Incidentally, most displacement boats will lose speed in shallow water, due to the accumulation of displaced water under the hull, which requires them to . . . mildly . . . steam uphill. This occurs at about the time there is only about four feet under the keel, and when the hull is being pushed beyond its hull speed. The cure is to reduce speed *to* hull speed and until the steering becomes easy again, the wake recedes, and there is no unusual vibration in the power train.

It is simple to forecast the course for some miles ahead, because almost always there are from two to 10 day markers visible ahead, defining a path through the waters. Often this path is miles from either shore; sometimes the day marks are on land. The channel is inboard of them by about 12 feet, for the cut is not steep-sided but sloped to a bottom width somewhat smaller

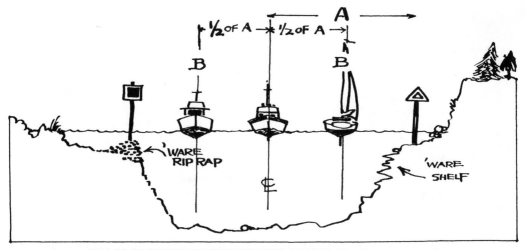

CROSS SECTION OF CUT OR DUG CANAL (depth exaggerated)

Normal transit is in about the middle of the cut, about midway between port and starboard markers. Pass or overtake, keeping about the relationship shown. Some markers have been rip-rapped with stone and should be avoided by at least 15 feet. Some shorelines extend varying depths under the surface and may be exposed rock strata. If in doubt, use the sounder.

Targets are used to indicate direct courses across an open sound or bay too exposed to hold day marks or buoys in place. They are colored with white opposing checks and are read the same as day marks and other ICW aids. While not lighted, some are painted with light-reflective coatings and are readily picked up by a searchlight. Albemarle Sound was thus first marked across its widest part.

than the top width. Markers are sometimes set in rip-rap and should never be left close aboard. Ranges should be observed, as they often define the only channel of depth, even in wide waters. Line up the fore-range (low one) with the far-range (high one, and usually a different shape than the lower one) and stay on that course until another mark (day mark, buoy, or another range) instructs a change. Guard against sagging off (as in a cross current or wind) and take particular pains when steaming *away* from a range. This requires watching your course from over the stern. A hand at the wheel, an autopilot, or a stern lookout helps here. Entering inlets or crossing creeks in flood are apt to move you sideways off course and into shallow waters. If possible, compensate *before* you feel their force.

The marking system of the Intracoastal is a special system, quite simple and obvious until you reach a junction with the standard coastal system. The key

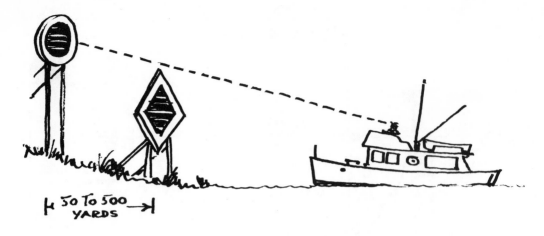

A typical range. The farthest and highest is usually circular; the nearest and lowest, a square or diamond. The color is read just as for a buoy or day mark and means the same thing when you arrive at the end of the range or its junction with another channel (itself often also marked). The most important ranges are lighted (white and the appropriate color, green or red).

is: *All* markers have a yellow band or border, identifying them as Waterway markers. From the *north*, those colored red (frequently orange, yellow-orange, and seldom a true crimson red) are left to starboard and mark the starboard side of the channel. Those colored black (or green) are left to port and mark the port side of the channel. Buoys and lighted markers having the distinctive yellow band (or sometimes a yellow triangle) mean the same. Starboard hand markers are numbered, consecutively, from a beginning number in that Coast Guard buoyage district, with *even* numbers. Port markers bear *odd* numbers.

At a junction, the usual system merges and, if the Waterway and harbor entrance coincide, the coastal marking system takes over temporarily. The illustration here helps define the combinations that may appear. It is often confusing. Best to slow down and sort it all out, aided by the chart, and pay attention only to aids with the yellow band, stripe, square, or triangle of the Intracoastal.

The Waterway marking system conforms to the coastal system in that north to south on the east coast is indicated by *red* to starboard. This carries around the Florida peninsula and *up* the coast (even though trending *north*), across the Gulf states, and again south to the border . . . *red to starboard all the way*. This system also prevails across the Okeechobee Waterway to the Gulf.

Nighttime navigation is no problem. All markers have appropriately colored reflectors on both sides (north and south). Red markers (starboard hand going south) have white or *red* lights, fixed or flashing. Black or green markers (port going south) have white or *green* lights, fixed or flashing. Special care must be taken to prevent sagging off the straight course between markers at night. Judicious use of your searchlight is recommended to confirm marker numbers

(continued on page 64)

INLAND WATERWAY MARKERS

A mileage marker, denoting miles to or from Mile Zero at Norfolk.

An older day mark, red to starboard going south and black or green to port. Being replaced, though still used at times between modern marks (below).

A starboard-side marker going south. Red, orange, or yellow-orange field with yellow frame and numbers.

A port-side marker going south. Black or green field with yellow frame and numbers

Either of the above two markers may be lighted. Usually sited on a concrete square pile. The addition of a letter (7 A, 16 B, etc.) only continues the sequence and in no way changes the meaning.

TYPES OF AIDS TO NAVIGATION
INTRACOASTAL WATERWAY

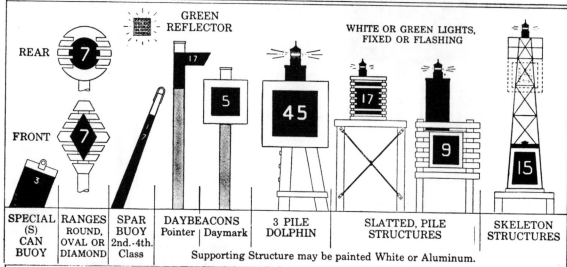

SPECIAL (S) CAN BUOY	RANGES ROUND, OVAL OR DIAMOND	SPAR BUOY 2nd.-4th. Class	DAYBEACONS Pointer | Daymark	3 PILE DOLPHIN	SLATTED, PILE STRUCTURES	SKELETON STRUCTURES

GREEN REFLECTOR

REAR FRONT

WHITE OR GREEN LIGHTS, FIXED OR FLASHING

Supporting Structure may be painted White or Aluminum.

PORT Side of channel (Black with Odd Numbers) entering from north and east and traversed to south and west respectively.

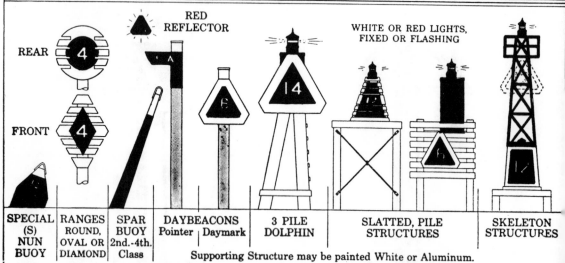

RED REFLECTOR

REAR FRONT

WHITE OR RED LIGHTS, FIXED OR FLASHING

SPECIAL (S) NUN BUOY	RANGES ROUND, OVAL OR DIAMOND	SPAR BUOY 2nd.-4th. Class	DAYBEACONS Pointer | Daymark	3 PILE DOLPHIN	SLATTED, PILE STRUCTURES	SKELETON STRUCTURES

Supporting Structure may be painted White or Aluminum.

STARBOARD Side of channel (Red with Even Numbers) entering from north and east and traversed to south and west respectively.

All borders are bright yellow. Yellow on any navigational aid indicates an ICW aid. Spar buoys have been largely replaced by standard buoys.

RED
BLACK
YELLOW

When the ICW and another system of channel marking join and use a common channel, ICW markings are temporarily abandoned and the common channel is marked by the "other" system, usually red to starboard and black to port entering from seaward. Aids used by the other system are marked as shown above; markings are the reverse of the ICW system, i.e., a yellow square indicates that buoy or marker is to be regarded as a nun (red). But the meaning is not always reversed: when steaming south on the ICW, and it joins another system also trending south (from seaward entrance), markings apply to both users. Since ICW markings have been omitted, the aids, even though correct for the ICW user in this situation, are marked with the square or triangle. Thus it is possible to find a red nun also marked with a yellow triangle, meaning that it is to be regarded as a nun (which it already is!).

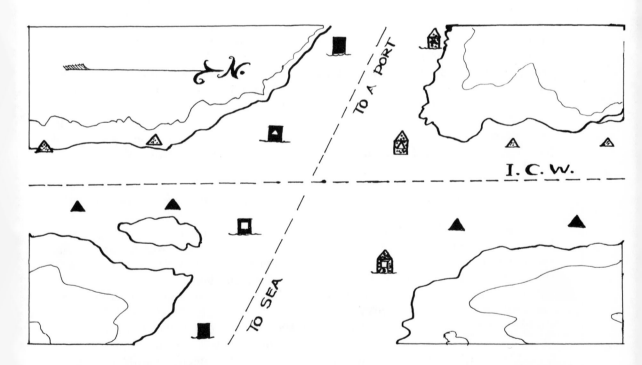

A junction of the Waterway and an entering channel. There are several such situations along the Ditch, notably in areas with a seaport west and upriver of the ICW. Note such areas as Norfolk, Cape Fear River, Georgetown-Winyah Bay, Charleston, Port Royal Sound, Brunswick, Savannah, Fernandina, Jacksonville, West Palm Beach, Fort Lauderdale, and Miami.

as picked up. It is a good practice always, but especially at night, to spread the chart out flat and keep track of your progress by buoy number and location, noting the buoy passed, or the buoy next ahead, by a pointer. (Pencil, folded dividers, a draftsman's "duck," or cute gadgets made for this purpose by those marine gift shop suppliers will serve.) The buoy number is *always* shown on the chart in quotation marks: "14"; not just 14, for that could be a nearby sounding.

There are no speed limits on the Waterway except in a very few places, usually to protect a submerged bank, and this is so marked in an official manner. However, there is a strict wake law, and it effectively controls speed. The wake law simply says that you are responsible for damage caused by your wake . . . and you had better slow down to *minimum* wake in areas likely to suffer damage. Marine patrols, sheriffs, and the U.S. Coast Guard all can determine the threat of your wake and cite you then for operation to endanger or reckless operation of a boat. In Florida it is illegal to display anything but an official sign or warning (usually state or county), and you need pay no serious attention to imploring signs in some populated areas begging: "No Wake," "5 MPH," "Slow Down," etc. Yet you are still under restraint not to do damage to anything or anybody with your wake. This means docks; boats; anchored or moving small boats; fishermen; work crews; bridge painters; buoy tenders; grounded boats; passing, overtaking, or over-taken boats; sea walls; navigation aids; sea cows (manatees); alligators; swimmers; scuba divers . . . you name it. And go slow! It is not a nuisance law; it was much needed and still ought to be enforced more often. A charge in court must show damage or well-witnessed reckless operation for con-viction, so local sheriffs, to whom all wakes appear large from their small patrol craft, can't just get "nasty." "Watch your wake" is an excellent watch-word.

Below are some very special Waterway situations quite apt to require solu-tion as you wend your way to the sun. . . .

Bridges. Fixed bridges have a controlling clearance of 52 feet, though some have more. And at least one has less, that at the railroad crossing on the St. Lucie Canal, just before entering Lake Okeechobee. It is 48 feet, because a few years ago they *raised* the controlling level of the lake.

Swing, bascule, and other opening bridges operate night and day. The standard signal is three blasts on the horn or foghorn. Some bureaucrat stumbled on the fact that this is also the backing-out signal of a departing liner, and that there might be confusion. There is, but not at the bridges. So now the Coast Guard is conducting experiments to specify a different signal and reeducate thousands of boatmen instead of a few liner masters. It appears that, though it is not official, we might find the signal become a combination of longs and shorts. At present, a bridge tender recognizes three blasts . . . or, if he is a nice family feller, a good loud holler. This may soon change.

If a bridge has two openings (left and right with the bridge pivot in the middle), use the normal one, to the right. If there is only one opening, the boat *with* the tide or current is the privileged vessel and may clear first. The boat heading upstream, being able to stem the current with an idling engine, must give way.

The bridge tender need not open until five minutes after his last closing. You must wait. Most tenders, seeing traffic coming, will hold the first boats and wait for the last ones, putting them through in a fleet. In general, bridge tenders are friendly to yachtsmen: the more boats, the more openings, and the better chance of the state's continuing the bridge and their jobs.

From West Palm Beach south, there are more bridges than in any other section of the Ditch. And more communities and more people. And there were more car traffic delays due to bridge openings . . . until the government denied the fundamental Marshall Decision of 1824—which stated that the waterways were the natural roads of the nation and all other roads must give way to their prior rights—and passed some new laws. The laws are sound and equable (heresy by a yachter!), but they do result in delays for the cruiser. These bridges are designated as "time bridges," meaning that they are closed during certain hours of the day, usually from 7:30 to 8:30 A.M. and 4:30 to 6:00 P.M. Some open on the even and half hours to allow waiting boats to pass. All open for a commercial vessel, tug, or government vessel, and wise yachtsmen sneak through with them. Obtain the times for these bridges from local marinas, from the table below, and from posted notices on the bridge abutments. There are isolated time bridges in other places, of course, notably at St. Augustine, Daytona Beach, the Titusville-Cocoa area (because of the Cape Canaveral traffic), West Palm Beach, and also the Fort Myers area.

In an emergency, any vessel can "open a bridge" by blowing four blasts. The bridge *must* open. The vessel opening it may have to prove an emergency in the event of a checkup by the Coast Guard. On the Gold Coast, watch the habits of the sportfishermen; they time their movements to bridge openings. Also watch (or follow) the "tour boats," which *can* open bridges, and slip through with them. If you have a retractable antenna, retract it if it will give you clearance; you can be fined for unnecessary opening of a bridge. (See chart on next page.)

Locks. Locks are no great bother on the Waterway. There is one at Great Bridge, Virginia (about a six-foot rise to the Ditch), two on the Dismal Swamp route, if you elect that, and five on the Okeechobee Waterway across the state. All are federally operated and free. The signal to open is two longs and two shorts, though tenders will open for three blasts, as for a bridge. The lock master is in charge. Enter when he shows a green light, lay to where he indicates, and do not leave until signaled to. These locks all provide the lines needed. Fenders are required only on large boats. In general, these lock tenders are gentle and not pressed for lockage, so they keep their pumps at a slow, nonturbulent pace. Passage is open all night at Great Bridge; others have closing hours, usually from 10 P.M. to 6 A.M., with openings during the "closed" period upon advance notice of four to 12 hours.

At times, when water is low, all but the Great Bridge lock (which is tidal) may institute operating hours or hold boats until a lock-full has accumulated.

FLORIDA–EAST COAST WATERWAY BRIDGE SCHEDULE

Miles From Norfolk	Bridge	Clearance Closed	Restricted Period	Regulated Hours
778	St. Augustine Bridge of Lions	25'	**Mon-Fri	7:00 am to 6:00 pm, opens on hour and half hour; but need not open at **8:00 am, 12:00 noon and 5:30 pm**
			Weekends and holidays	7:00 am to 6:00 pm, opens on hour and half hour
824	Ormond Beach	21'	**Mon-Sat	7:30 to 8:30 am; 4:30 to 5:30 pm; but opens at **8:00 am and 5:00 pm**
836	Port Orange	20'	**Mon-Sat	7:30 to 8:30 am; 4:30 to 5:30 pm; but opens at **8:00 am and 5:00 pm**
878	Titusville	9'	Mon-Fri	6:45 to 7:45 am; 4:15 to 5:45 pm
885	Addison Point	27'	Mon-Fri	6:45 to 8:00 am; 4:15 to 5:45 pm
914	Eau Gallie	9'	Daily	8:15 am to 4:15 pm, opens quarter of and quarter past the hour
			**Mon-Fri	6:45 to 8:15 am; 4:15 to 5:45 pm
918	Melbourne	6'	Daily	8:30 am to 4:00 pm, opens on hour and half hour
			**Mon-Fri	6:45 to 8:15 am; 4:15 to 5:45 pm; 8:15 to 8:30 am; 4:00 to 4:15 pm; opens on signal
952	Vero Beach	22'	**Mon-Fri	7:45 to 9:00 am; 12:00 noon to 1:15 pm; 4:00 to 5:15 pm; but opens at **8:30 am, 12:30 and 4:30 pm**
1018	Riviera Beach	14'	Daily	8:00 am to 6:00 pm, opens on hour and half hour
1022	West Palm Beach: Flagler Memorial	17'	Dec 1-Apr 30 Daily	7:30 am to 6:00 pm, opens on hour and half hour
1023	Royal Park	14'	Dec 1-Apr 30 Daily	7:30 am to 6:00 pm, opens quarter of and quarter past the hour
1025	Southern Blvd.	14'	**Mon-Fri	7:30 to 9:00 am, 4:30 to 6:30 pm; but opens at **8:15 am and 5:30 pm**
1055	Pompano Beach: NE 14th St.	15'	Daily	7:00 am to 6:00 pm, opens quarter of and quarter past the hour
1056	Atlantic Blvd.	15'	Daily	7:00 am to 6:00 pm, opens on hour and half hour
1059	Ft Lauderdale: Commercial Blvd.	15'	Nov 1-May 15 Mon-Sat	12:00 noon to 6:00 pm, opens every quarter hour
			Sun	9:00 am to 6:00 pm, opens every quarter hour
1062	Sunrise Blvd.	16'	Nov 15-May 15 Daily	7:15 am to 6:15 pm, opens quarter of and quarter past the hour
1066	17th St. Causeway	25'	Daily	7:00 am to 7:00 pm, opens 15 minutes after last closing
1072	Hollywood Blvd.	10'	Nov 16-May 15 Daily	10:00 am to 6:00 pm, opens on hour and half hour
1074	Hallandale	22'	*Nov 15-May 15	10:15 am to 6:15 pm, opens quarter of and quarter past the hour
1078	Sunny Isles	19'	Mon-Fri	7:00 am to 6:00 pm, opens quarter of and quarter past the hour
			Weekends and holidays	10:00 am to 6:00 pm, opens quarter of and quarter past the hour
1082	Miami: Broad Causeway	16'	Nov 1-Apr 30 Daily	8:00 am to 6:00 pm, opens on hour and half hour
1088	Venetian Causeway, West Span	8'	**Nov 1-Apr 30 Mon-Fri	7:00 to 9:00 am and 4:30 to 6:30 pm, opens on hour and half hour
1088	MacArthur Causeway	35'	Nov 1-Apr 30 Daily	7:00 to 9:00 am and 4:30 to 6:30 pm, opens on hour and half hour
1089	Dodge Island Rwy. & Hwy.	22'	*Mon-Sat	7:30 to 9:00 am; 11:30 am to 1:30 pm; 4:30 to 6:00 pm; opens quarter of and quarter past the hour
1092	Rickenbacker Causeway	23'	Mon-Fri	7:30 to 9:00 am and 4:30 to 6:00 pm, opens on hour and half hour
			Weekends and holidays	11:00 am to 6:00 pm, opens on hour and half hour

All hours closed except where openings are noted in bold face.
*Regulations given are existing; changes have been proposed and may be in effect by the time this is read.
**Except holidays.

(Chart courtesy *Waterway Guide*)

Such controlled openings will be posted and shown in the *Notice to Mariners.* Many locks have convenient tie-ups for waiting boats. Some, like the Franklin Lock on the Caloosahatchee River, have elaborate picnic areas and anchorage basins. (See the next chapter, on anchoring out.)

Look for turbulence only when, by chance, you are locked through with a commercial tow or large, heavy vessel. In such situations, put out fenders and double lines and get all hands on deck to fend off; the turbulence can be severe when twin eight-foot wheels turn in confined waters.

Passing Tows and Large Vessels. As mentioned in Chapter 2, the Ditch has a great deal of commercial traffic. When a large flattie appears, headed against you, in a narrow canal, its beam just about the width of the bottom of the cut, it behooves you to be exceptionally patient and understanding. He can't do a thing about the situation, because he needs all the water visible just to float. Be assured that the skipper is a skilled pilot, that he knows the bottom and the sides better than you do, and that the last thing he wants is even a slight rub with a yacht. His record is almost perfect and he deserves your respect. First, when such a flotilla appears, you have no rights save that of survival. The tow will signal what he expects you to do—pass left or right, or stop—and you should do it, promptly and even with exaggeration, so that he

Florida's St. Lucie locks. (Florida Department of Commerce)

can see and understand the situation. Usually, unless in confined waters or on a sweep or sharp bend, he will edge over to your port bank and reduce speed, giving you the proper passing signal (one long). Slow down to steerageway and hold steady course between his port side and the channel as defined by an *imaginary line between markers*. Proceed when clear of propeller wash.

If he seems to be having difficulty, by full astern signals, or a call for his mate (by whistle), or sheering off a bank, stop and get out of the way. He cannot stop, or even turn. He's got a much better chance of solving his problem and keeping the channel clear if he doesn't have to worry about you too. Don't challenge him on turns, pass when the waters open, and, by chart examination, you know there is sufficient water for both boats. And do signal him. If he doesn't answer, it's because he doesn't agree with the proposal your signal makes. He *is* the boss here!

The phenomenon of "attraction" may apply in some situations of passing and overtaking, with the smaller vessel (you) taking the beating if not understood. When some vessels proceed in narrow and shallow waters, they can drag along certain areas of water that may affect the navigation of passing or overtaking smaller vessels. It is seldom dangerous when passing, though collision *is* possible (sideswiping is a good term here). But when overtaking, because the situation prevails for some minutes, there is often marked suction, described as follows: as the overlap commences, the overhauling vessel may expect her bow to be attracted slightly toward the vessel overtaken. The stern will simultaneously be repulsed. As the vessel hauls abreast, the attraction forward increases and the stern repulsion slowly turns to attraction. Then the bow attraction changes rapidly to repulsion and the stern attraction becomes stronger, diminishing only after a brief repulsion when entirely clear of the overtaken vessel.

The attraction may be so great as to cause the smaller vessel (especially if of considerable lateral plane, as in a keel sailboat) to yaw wildly, hit the bank, or hit the overtaken vessel. The force of attraction decreases at slow speeds and in deep water—difficult factors to achieve in the shallow Waterway and

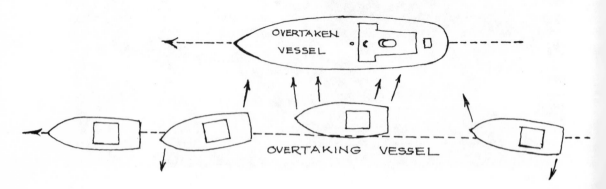

The effects of attraction when passing.

with big, unwieldy tows that must have speed to maneuver and maintain control. This can occur in very narrow channels, with 20 feet or less between barge side and the bank, and can "set" a small boat high in the mud, after a husky bump on the beam. The tow can do almost nothing about it. It's up to you, and your sole, sane defense is to wait your chance and pass *only* when the Ditch widens, or the water deepens, or both. Then open 'er up and pass rapidly on a compromise course between the tow and the bank, swing smartly into the course of the tow (mid-channel), and proceed.

Beware, when following a tow close aboard, as is sometimes necessary, to keep out of the turbulence. Not only is it difficult to steer, but tows, sliding along on the bottom, almost, often throw up logs and wreckage that can foul you up fast.

Passing a Working Dredge. Slow down and study the situation. If the cutter-head is out and working, the dredge will fly a black ball. Its head (underwater) is usually surrounded by temporary buoys, often oil drums. Keep clear. Avoid the suction pipe, which is usually supported by steel pontoons and leads off into an adjacent marsh. The way will "open up," possibly assisted by a waved arm. If in doubt, signal the dredge (four blasts), and he will respond with one blast (pass to starboard) or two blasts (pass to port). Some barges work with tugs, or linkages to anchors, which enable them to move the entire rig from the channel when a boat approaches. If the channel seems blocked, wait a moment and listen for the all-clear signal (passing signals). And slow down; they can do without your wake.

To Pass and Be Passed. Passing is a gentle art that is understood by all slow boats and disregarded by far too many fast boats. Nothing makes *both* slow and fast boats madder than wild passing. There have been lawsuits about it and fist fights and garbage thrown and shots fired. But as long as we have selfish, thoughtless idiots with us (probably fewer than two percent of the fast-boat skippers), this will go on, and all fast boats will forever be the mortal enemies of slow boats.

The cure for the situation is a cooperative effort . . . and consideration and decency . . . by both skippers involved. The passing boat has a right to pass, and to pass he *must* go faster than the passed boat. Therefore the passed boat has an obligation to slow down so that the difference in the speeds while passing will be so little as to also require slow speed by the passing boat—and, hence, no wake.

This is the way to do it:

Passor, coming up on the passee, gives usual overtaking signals (which are the same as the passing signals, i.e., one blast to pass on the starboard side or two blasts to pass on the port side). When answered (and not before!), he moves up, as far away from the passee as the channel will permit. Meanwhile, the passee has slowed down to, say, three knots, or stopped and drifted, and then only gives acknowledgment to the passing signal. The passor now carefully, with minimum wake, passes, maintaining course and speed while the passee, once clear of the stern quarters, swings sharply into the wake, so as to cross obliquely the quarter wave of the passor; then he straightens out *in the*

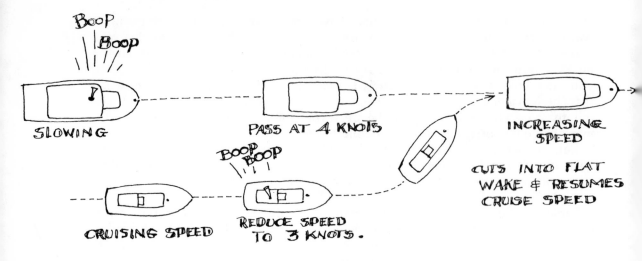

How to pass—and be passed.

wake of the passor. The passor, say, 100 feet ahead, resumes speed, slowly, and ditto the passee.

No sweat, no smashed dishes, no broken legs, no lawsuits, no buckshot into the transom—gentlemanliness, decency, and sanity have prevailed. A dream to strive for, indeed!

By and large, with the education from our boating periodicals, public boating courses, seamanship manuals, and the example of prudent seamen, the ancient passing horrors are disappearing. Much is due to the professional skippers (but not the sportfishermen), who move the big stuff up and down each season. They know how to pass; indeed, they are under orders not to cause wake damage of any kind. It's better than it was, but there is still room for improvement. I used to get "shook" by every boat faster than I was; now it's only every third boat.

If a passing results in real damage, more than ruffled feelings, report the matter to the next local sheriff, or the marine police, and have the boat stopped. Bridge tenders do this with glee. Then bring charges. Even if you do not collect . . . though you usually do, and out of court . . . you can spoil the speed hog's schedule and cause him delightful delay and inconvenience. Be sure to obtain witnesses, on your own boat or others. I was once canvassed in Charleston after a day's run by an irate owner who wanted witnesses against a certain hog who had scandalized the moving fleet. He found 44 skippers who would testify! A certain speeder on the Waccamaw River upset a johnboat, drowning one man. He was apprehended about 50 miles north, his boat was impounded, everybody aboard was jailed, and the owner/skipper was sent to prison. It does pay to squawk!

Tides. In general, the tides flow in and out of closely spaced inlets, and nothing can be gained by trying to "use the tides." Just proceed, and the day's run will average out, no matter what the tide. It is possible for the purist to get a slight free ride on favorable tides if he is willing to run day and night, to lay over and wait for favorable tides, and to be a big bore to his guests. The tide tables on the small-craft chart covers are for commercial boats and are of little practical interest to yachtsmen unless with a very deep draft (like eight or 10 feet, keel boat). They might be helpful in estimating when and if you are going to float off a bar, if you have that kind of bad luck.

In many places, such as inland sounds (Albemarle, Currituck, Indian River, etc.), there is no tide. There is only water level variance caused by wind. Other areas (Brunswick and Savannah, Georgia; Fernandina, Florida) have tides like Maine: nine feet normal. The west coast of Florida, subject to Gulf tides of 18 inches or less, often carries tides three or four times this when the winds blow for extended periods on the Gulf of Mexico. The Gulf, itself shallow, either backs up into the rivers and harbors or draws the water from them. On some of these rivers, the tide can be used: notably, the St. Johns, Cape Fear, Caloosahatchee, Manatee, and the harbor entrances (from the sea) of Tampa, Miami, and Jacksonville.

The level of Lake Okeechobee is subject to slight variation, hardly bothersome to the cruiser remaining in the regular channels. It might be of concern to the skipper needing to get under the Port Myakka railroad bridge (a lift bridge), or the boat going north to the bass fishing grounds. The lake level is posted at all locks. A call to a lock master will get you the information. The lake, too, is subject to wind "tides," usually only after heavy winds of several days' duration. Six to seven feet can be taken across readily.

Inside the canals, between locks, there is no change in level save in extreme dry summer spells.

Chapter 5
Anchoring Out
(with complete directory of all anchorages)

Until very recently, perhaps only one in 20 boats traversing the Waterway anchored out. It was inexpensive—and sometimes fun—to tie up at a marina or boatyard, explore the town, have a sundowner with friends, and be off, tanks filled, in the morning. As we have seen, those days are gone for many of us, and we now anchor out *most* of the time . . . and love it, for an anchorage is quite apt now to have friends in it and give us a pleasant, quiet night and save not only hard cash but almost certain frustration. Many a gleaming gold-plater that had never before launched one of her white-enameled anchors has discovered this new way of life afloat. The anchorages are by no means filled with boats that "can't afford marinas." They are filled with boats whose owners have discovered a new and satisfying value in this Ditch life; many of them are members of the younger generation who seem to be able to get down to basics and fundamentals so much better than their fathers.

The art of finding an anchorage is simple. The small-craft charts are very detailed and show or note every factor required to discover the anchorage to suit your boat and the weather.

Know these aids in selecting the exact spot to anchor.

1. The depth of water is indicated by the soundings, in feet, at mean (average) low tide. On the inside flap of every small-craft chart jacket, there appears a tide table for that area, calibrated for every day and hour of the year the chart was issued.

The predicted times of high and low water are also noted, so you can, by a direct sounding, forecast the stage of the tide at the moment of anchoring.

Since the chart soundings are at mean *low* water, you are not interested (save for reassurance) in the plus readings, which indicate the predicted tidal stage *above* the chart soundings. But do follow the column down for the *minus* readings. These predict the tidal stage *below* the chart readings and could very much interest you if the predicted subnormal tidal stage is on the day you anchor. Always check the data against the date. Remember, too, that the tidal stage can be significantly affected by the wind, especially wind of long duration (as in a nor'easter). Onshore winds tend to raise tidal levels, offshore winds to lower them. Select an anchorage that gives you at least two feet more than your draft under the probable conditions of your stay. Remember that the wakes of fast-moving boats are not all wave crests. Between them are troughs, with their lowest levels below the mean water level; you can be set on the bottom by a series of steep "wakes." Barges and tows, while seldom creating much wake, nevertheless drive huge volumes of water ahead of their bluff bows and draw depressions off their quarters.

More tidal information is contained in the *Tide Tables*, East Coast, North & South America ($2 in 1976), from the National Ocean Survey or most chart outlets.

2. Search for anchorages in the white areas of the chart. The blue areas indicate low-tide depths of less than seven feet. Often there are suitable six-foot spots along the joint border of the two colors.

3. Check the character of the bottom. An abbreviation will be printed in the general area as follows:

S	sand	Co	coral
M	mud	Sh	shells
Cl	clay	Oys	oysters
G	gravel	Grs	grass
Rky	rocky		

Moreover, the character of the bottom will be further described by the following:

sft	soft
hrd	hard
stk	sticky

With this information, it is possible to predetermine the type and weight of the anchor required, the scope, and whether (as in coral) a chain warp might be best. A look at the anchorage itself on the chart will suggest one or two anchors for bow-stern or a Bahama mooring. Thus, some time *before* arrival at the anchorage, the necessary gear can be readied and laid out for immediate use.

An anchorage in a creek or inlet on the *east* side of the Waterway is apt to lead directly to the sea and, because of current, apt to be scoured and have a hard bottom (hrd). An anchorage of any kind on the *west* side of the Waterway is apt to be "dead" water, having less or no current, and is apt to be mud (M) and probably slick (sft, stk). Coral is no threat until you reach the Bahamas or the lower Keys. Clay, shell, and gravel hold best, mud and grass the least. Always know exactly where your anchor is, using a marker buoy if necessary. You or another boat, in these shallow water conditions, could easily hit or settle upon an arm or a fluke and get into serious trouble.

4. A lee, such as a high bank, or a "berm," should be sought out in a breeze of wind, anchoring on the leeward side. In some parts of the Waterway, natural woodlands (especially jack pine, cypress, and coastal cedars) afford excellent lees. Conversely, in still, hot weather, they hold swarms of mosquitoes and other bugs and should be avoided—or at least kept downwind. Insects, save no-see-ums or midges, do not wander far offshore, a good point to remember when anchoring.

5. Those inviting "loops"—created by straightening the original winding creeks by dredging—are not often accessible, attractive as they may appear. In order to keep the current moving and the channel from silting, the dredgers have usually filled the entrances. Some have opened, of course, and might be tried. There is usually creek-deep water (to 10 or 12 feet) inside, even though it is shown in blue on the chart (in this case meaning not navigable). Those open are listed among the anchorages given at the end of this chapter. Beware of the ones you can negotiate at high tide; low tide might bottle you in.

6. Avoid anchorages in or near a fairway. Not only yachts during daylight, but shrimpers and netters at night (all night!) can keep you rolling constantly. Try to get a spit of land between yourself and the Waterway. Major creeks, such as Teakettle Creek and those marked "rivers," usually have fishing ports at their headwaters, and fishermen move as the tide allows, night or day. Notoriously scornful of yachts and yachters, they seldom slow down or change course. The worst "roller" is the anchorage off St. Augustine, Florida. For 3 hours every dawn (4 to 7 A.M.), the entire shrimper fleet passes, one at a time, scornful of the wake law and rather gleefully rolling the yachters out of their bunks.

7. Security at anchor is no cause for concern if you stay near the Waterway or habitation and avoid the remote creek heads in the marshes of South Carolina and Georgia. There have been almost no "incidents" reported. However, deep in the marshes there are some tiny settlements where poverty reigns. They are inhabited usually by fishermen or oystermen, who must resent the parade of wealth and success that passes them by and tempts them. The best defense is to stay away from these areas, however charming or primitive. The local watermen of the Southland are often uneducated and somewhat crude, but they are not criminal; they live the way they do because they want to live that way. They get drunk occasionally, they may appear unfriendly or uncooperative, but they are not an active threat to safety on the Ditch.

If you have the control and the necessary sense to carry weapons, do so. There is no law against it. Probably most yachts have a handgun on board. Many carry Mace or an inexpensive tear-gas gun. It would be wise not to show or use any. A situation heated up by confrontation is bound to end to your sorrow and perhaps be costly. If a situation develops, call in the sheriff or the state troopers (CB or VHF-FM, using Channel 16 to call and Channel 22 to talk). Genuine, professional sneak-thief activity is, thus far, confined to the land.

The best general-purpose anchor for the Waterway is the CQR or plow anchor, with a few fathoms of chain lead; then marked nylon rode—25 pounds for boats to 30 feet, 35 pounds to 45 feet, and 45 pounds to 55 or 60 feet is about right for powerboats. Move up one grade for keel sailboats, trawlers, and motorsailers. Holding is no great problem *if* you can get the anchor not only down but *in*. The CQR seems to do this best. The Danforth type is quite suitable, as is the Herreshoff (old fashioned), but they are apt to foul with the changing currents that are present throughout the coastal sections of the Ditch. In certain areas with black ooze-mud bottoms, all but the Danforth or Northill types will slide or drag, and these types may have to be set. Or a different bottom will have to be found.

Rules for cable scope do not necessarily apply, especially on hard, scoured bottoms. Give it the usual five times depth; then throw another few fathoms after it and tend the anchor until it is set and holding; test it even against power. Be very sure that the swinging circle does not include shallower water, the bank, or other boats. If possible, set an after sail (mizzen) to prevent wandering.

Many anchorages are not large or have small, safe areas within the general anchorage area, and special techniques may be required in these.

1. Use the Bahama mooring (see sketch). Set two anchors, either one of which is able to hold the vessel, and take a short lead from the middle of

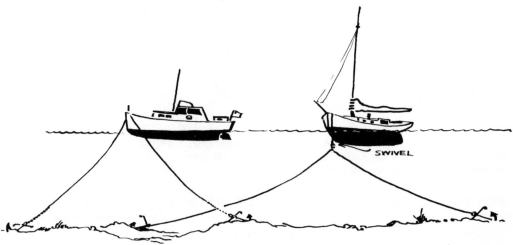

THE BAHAMA MOORING

The power cruiser lies to an "overnight" or temporary mooring with a line in each bow chock. The sailing vessel lies to a more permanent mooring, with a swivel so that she can swing through tide and wind changes.

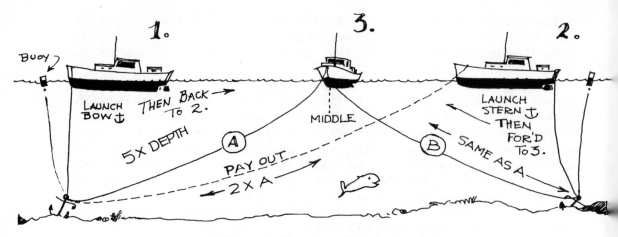

Setting a double anchor (Bahama mooring).

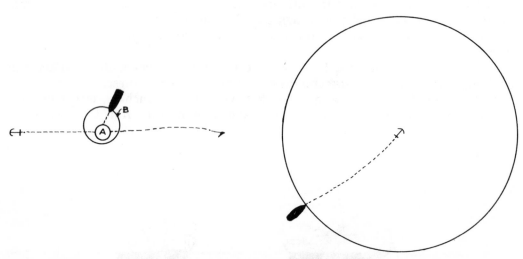

The swinging area required in an anchorage, conventional mooring versus Bahama mooring. Both boats lie to the same scope of cable. Circle (A) is inherent slack in the lines. Circle (B) is the swinging area required by the moored vessel.

their cables to your bitts, via a swivel. This will keep your boat within an area with a diameter of about three times your boat length. Set the anchors along the axis of the wind (present or predicted), not across the wind.

2. Moor "bow and stern" (see sketch). Set the anchors as above and with the same warnings, but bring the warp from the windward anchor to your bow bitts and the other warp to your quarter bitts; then middle the boat between. The boat will not move at all, save for a side-sag in a wind shift.

To set the anchors for either of these situations: set the first from the bow *against* the wind or current, having available and ready to pay out *twice* the length of warp needed. Dig it in with a burst of power after a length of five times the depth has been reached, snubbing the warp to the bitts temporarily. Then cast off and drift or back down to the chosen location of the second (leeward) anchor. Launch the second anchor from the stern, run *against* the wind or current, toward the first anchor (watching the warp in the wake), while a hand takes in the warp of the first anchor (at the bow). Dig the stern anchor in with a burst of power. Then, by hand or power, middle the boat between the anchors and belay the cables tautly, the bow anchor to the bow and the stern anchor to the stern. Or, in the case of the Bahama rig, bring both cables to the bow and belay, introducing a swivel if desired (not necessary for an overnight anchorage, but good seamanship if for several tides or wind changes).

So enjoy a really great style of life on the lovely Waterway. Keep your radio low, don't run your generator after 8 P.M., don't pitch your trash overboard, have a kind thought for the poor skippers tied up at a marina—and you will discover a new and most happy facet of life on the Great Ditch.

ANCHORAGES ON THE INTRACOASTAL WATERWAY

The following pages contain a complete listing of all the reasonable, safe, and practical small-boat anchorages on the Waterway, Norfolk to Key West, the Okeechobee Waterway, and the popular cruising areas of the west coast of Florida. All the anchorages listed are depicted on the chart as having at least one fathom depth at normal low-water stage. Approaches are not delineated; work this out from the chart. However, some seemingly good anchorages have been skipped because the approach is unsafe or impractical; use these if you feel that you can negotiate the entrances.

It should be stated here that anchorages in certain sections of the Waterway have been omitted because of local conditions. These are in areas where there is objectionable commercial traffic (such as shrimpers arriving from sea all night long), where there are objectionable odors (as from paper or fertilizer mills), or where local inhabitants object to visiting boats.

The tables are keyed according to the following pattern:

Mile   Refers to the nearest mileage notation on the small-craft charts.
Marker   Refers to a marker near the mileage notation, always an Intra-coastal marker, and by charted marker number.
Bearing   Refers to a bearing *from* the marker to about the center of the anchorage.
Distance   Refers to distance, in yards or miles, from the marker to the anchorage *in a straight line*. Suggest use of dividers here, setting the points to the scaled distance on the chart scale, then, with one point exactly on the marker, swing in the noted direction (bearing) to the obvious anchorage area.
Notes   Special instructions, cautions, suggestions to consider, and names of anchorages (if any).

WORKING THE TABLES

In this hypothetical situation, an anchorage can be found at or near Mile 430, with the nearest marker being number 17. With this located, the divider is set to the distance given (in this example, 90 yards). Distance is taken from the scale on each chart. The bearing is given as approximately SE, so southeast along this arc there should be an anchorage. Under Notes, this anchorage is described as being in 9 to 11 feet of water and protected from east wind but open to northwest wind. Thus:

Mile	Marker	Bearing	Distance	Notes
430	17	SE	90 yds.	In 9 to 11 ft. Good in easterlies. Open to northwesters.

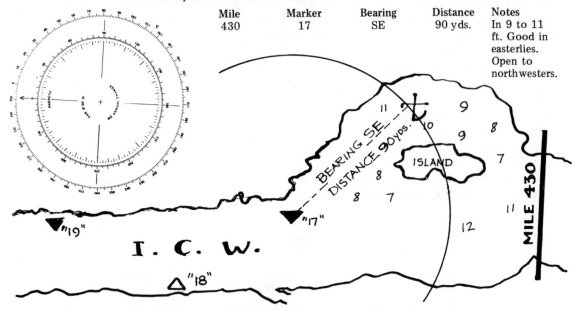

Norfolk to Alligator River Entrance
via
Albemarle-Chesapeake Canal

Mile	Marker	Bearing	Distance	Notes
10	76	SE	250 yds.	Industrial area; emergency anchorage.
27	34	SW	100 yds.	'Ware wrecks on creek banks.
28	41	SW	100 yds.	'Ware wrecks on creek banks.
29	42	SW	60 yds.	Open roadstead.
56	149	S	150 yds.	Good in southerly breeze; Buck I.
58	157	NE	175 yds.	Good in N and NE breezes; Buck I.
60	161	NE	1100 yds.	Mouth of Lutz Cr.
61	164	W	2 mi.	In Broad Cr., mouth or inside 50 yds.

Norfolk to Alligator River Entrance
via
Dismal Swamp Canal

Mile	Marker	Bearing	Distance	Notes
8	-	-	-	Emergency anchorage just off channel in Deep Creek.
40	-	-	-	Just off channel near Possum Quarter Landing; yacht traffic only until South Mills lock closing about 6 P.M.
44	11	W	1.7 mi.	Close under S bank of Goat I.
47	-	-	-	300 yds. S of RR bridge, in 9-ft. creek. There are no anchorages between the locks in the canal itself. Boats may tie up (free) at lock bulkheads.

Alligator River Entrance to
Southport, North Carolina

Mile	Marker	Bearing	Distance	Notes
82	8	W	1.8 mi.	In Little Alligator R., W of Sandy Pt.
88	18	E	2.5 mi.	In Milltail Cr. 'Ware stumps at entrance. Watch branches.
94	26	NW	2 mi.	Behind Catfish Pt. Enter over 6-ft. shoal.
103	43	N	200 yds.	Off Deep Pt. 'Ware stumps close to shore.
105	52	W	900 yds.	W side of Tuckahoe Pt. 'Ware stumps.
114	-	-	-	Feeder creek N of Fairfield Bridge, about 100 yds. in (old dock).
127	23	W	1500 yds.	Behind Marshy Pt.
132	15	NW	1 mi.	Mouth of Upper Dowry Cr. 'Ware stumps.
137	10	W	3 mi.	In Pungo Creek fairway, buoyed.
140	4	NE	2 mi.	In Slade Cr. Go in on bush stakes.
147	PR	SE	4 mi.	Follow buoyed channel to S of Dick Pt.
154	7	SE	1100 yds.	Mouth of Eastham Cr. Shell and oyster bottom.
158	11A	E	300 yds.	Just E of Waterway. Some light local traffic.
172	4	NE	3 mi.	Follow day marks in to Burton Cr. feeder.
187	9	E	300 yds.	In Cedar Cr.
205	6	E	100 yds.	Public anchorage in 9½ ft. Light traffic.
209	7	N	250 yds.	Near mouth, Peletier Cr., or near boatyard.
229	47	N	150 yds.	Off Swansboro docks, to highway bridge.
244	66	N	100 yds.	In 10 ft. inside unused Marine Corps basin. Follow marked entrance, turn N.
263	86	SW	1.5 mi.	Leave Waterway via buoyed channel into Topsail Sound. Anchor W of small island near Marker 13.
287	132	E	150 yds.	In creek, 7-9 ft. Scoured bottom.
309	-	-	-	State marina. Enter, turn W (left) and anchor in 7-8 ft.

Southport, North Carolina, to Charleston, South Carolina

Mile	Marker	Bearing	Distance	Notes
330	75	N	800 yds.	Off docks in Shallotte R.
342	2	N/S	-	In Little R., under W bank.
342.5	6	N	150 yds.	In bight of river, in 7-8 ft. 'Ware current.
348	20	SW	1.3 mi.	In dredged basin, near mouth.
365	-	-	-	In loading basin, W side of channel.
371	-	-	-	In turning basin, W side of channel.
375	25	NE	200 yds.	In Enterprise Cr.
375	1	-	-	Anyplace in Waccamaw R. to Peachtree Landing. Only small-boat traffic.
377	35	W	125 yds.	Enter S of island, in Old R.
380.5	-	-	-	In Prince Cr. Anyplace.
381	-	-	-	In Bull Cr. and its N branch. Anyplace.
384	57	W	100 yds.	In 7-11 ft., Cow House Cr.
389	73	W	-	In the Pee Dee R. and various creeks. This is old rice-paddy country.

Mile	Marker	Bearing	Distance	Notes
395	83	NW	-	In Jericho Cr.
395.5	84	SW	550 yds.	W of Butler I. in 25 ft.
401	94	NE	-	Up Pee Dee R. Fixed bridge with 20-ft. clearance 1.2 mi. up; then clear for miles.
411	2	SE	.5 mi.	On W bank of Cat I. Little traffic.
415	4	W	150 yds.	In 13-21 ft., in Minim Cr.
417	-	-	-	Up or down the North or the South Santee R. 'Ware current. Shrimpers likely in season.
425.5	29	S	-	In Casino Cr., behind island at entrance.
435.5	48	S	900 yds.	In 13 ft. in Awendaw Cr.
448	84	SE	400 yds.	In Price Cr.
452	96	NW	800 yds.	In Whiteside Cr.
455	109	W	-	In Dewees Cr. or Long Cr.
461	119	S	-	In Inlet Cr., either side of Waterway.
470	5	N	-	At dolphins, S side or 250 yds. SE of them. Also near bridge on E side of channel.

Charleston, South Carolina, to Fernandina, Florida

Mile	Marker	Bearing	Distance	Notes
471	6	SW	300 yds.	E end of bight, behind island.
475.5	19	N	250 yds.	In 8 ft., near range marker "A".
480	39	N	200 yds.	In bight (Note: W entrance is blocked).
487	77	SE	-	In Wadmalaw Sd. E of New Cut Landing.
491	93	S	100 yds.	Behind island in 33 ft.
497	110	S	1.1 mi.	Leave Waterway, to marker "2" in N Edisto R.; then up Steamboat Cr.
501	128	S	300 yds.	In Dawho R., behind island, in 10-16 ft.
504	145	W	.7 mi.	On N bank in 20 ft.
510	161	SE	3.2 mi.	S Edisto R. Some local traffic, oystermen. Down river into St. Pierre Cr.
514	167	-	-	Up Ashepoo R. ½ mi.
515	172	-	-	Down Rock Cr. 1 mile.
518	186	S	1.5 mi.	Behind Marsh I. spit.
522	-	-	-	Up Bull R. to island or into Parrot Cr., then into Bass Cr. or up Morgan R.
530.5	-	SE	300 yds.	Bight off Brickyard Cr. behind island.
536.5	1	SE	17 mi.	In Factory Cr., east of shrimp docks, off W bank.
536.5	-	-	-	Off city park at marina, W of bridge.
543	34	-	-	Up Chowan Cr., some local traffic.
562	-	-	-	NW of March I. Enter close aboard Barataria I. from N.
564	1	-	-	Up (N) Broad Cr. to E of Possum Pt.
566	-	-	-	Up Bull Cr. beyond first bend in 13 ft.
573	-	-	-	Up Cooper R. or down New R. or up or down Wright R. Strong currents.
584	35	W	150 yds.	In general (public) anchorage. See chart.
590	-	-	-	In general (public) anchorage. See chart.
592	60	E	100 yds.	Behind island, enter from N.
595	-	-	-	Up Moon R. 3/8 mile in 9 ft.
612	-	-	-	Up Buckhead Cr. or up Kilkenny Cr.
618	114	SW	2.2 mi.	In Walburg Cr. Also (from S) enter at Marker 124.
630	135	NW	1 mi.	In Wahoo R. in 16 ft.

Mile	Marker	Bearing	Distance	Notes
633	11	SW	1.1 mi.	SW on creek to Blackbeard Landing. Moor to piles if free.
645	-	-	-	Up Crescent R. or in New Teakettle Cr., at mouth, or up South R., or up Doboy Sd. to Folly R., or in Duplin R., N of plantation wharf.
650	-	-	-	Up Beacon Cr., or up North R., or up Darien R. (traffic), or up Rockdedundy R.
656	202	SW	1000 yds.	Behind marshy island, in 28 ft.; enter from W.
660	211	W	850 yds.	Behind largest island; enter at Marker 211 from E.
666	229	-	-	In Frederica R., off Fort Frederica, or in any bend with 10 ft.
666	231	NW	1000 yds.	In Walleys Leg, W of island, in 14 ft.
674	242	SW	.8 mi.	In Mackay R. near bridge (9-ft. tides).
687	-	-	-	Umbrella Cr. or down from alternate (storm) route at Umbrella Cut.
693	37	SE	150 yds.	Emergency anchorage, in 9 ft. E of marker.
697	40	-	-	Up Mud Cr., to 20-ft. depth or up Brickhill R. to W of 3-ft. shoal.
704	121	W	.7 mi.	Up Crooked R. in 9 ft.
710	19	NE	1 mi.	Off Dungeness shore in 25 ft.

Fernandina, Florida, to Stuart, Florida

Mile	Marker	Bearing	Distance	Notes
725	37	N	800 yds.	Junction of Alligator Cr. and Amelia R.
729	66	SW	-	In bight of old creek, in 7-9 ft.
730	48	E	-	In Sawpit Cr. to bridge, or to W of Bird I. under 15-ft. fixed bridge.
735	72	E	-	In bight, N side, 250 yds. E of marker, or in 14 ft., Ft. George R., S bank.
736	75	W	300 yds.	In Horseshoe Cr. Enter from S.
738	82	E	200 yds.	Lay to dolphins in 7-12 ft. (industrial).
765	25	NE	400 yds.	In creek around Pine I. Average 10 ft.
777	-	-	-	Off fairway, N or S of Bridge of Lions, off Castillo de San Marcos or municipal marina.
802	-	-	-	At Palm Coast development, in mouth of unused canals (2).
807	3	N	100 yds.	In old cut, 75 yds. in, after 6-ft. bar.
831	44	SW	750 yds.	Open roadstead in 13 ft.
840	1	E	800 yds.	In 12-ft. creek near Inlet Harbor.
869	-	-	-	Dredged basin (abandoned) W of lift bridge in Haulover Canal (9 ft. in 1975).
877	-	-	-	In lee of RR bridge, near spoil island.
885	-	-	-	In lee of causeways, E or W.
894	-	-	-	In lee of W causeway.
898	-	-	-	In lee of causeways, E or W.
909	-	-	-	In lee of causeways, E or W.
914	-	-	-	Follow markers into Banana R. Anchor in 10-14 ft. S of swing bridge.
915	2	W	1 mi.	Take buoyed channel into Eau Gallie Hbr. Anchor off fairway, to S, in 6-8 ft.

Mile	Marker	Bearing	Distance	Notes
918	-	-	-	In lee of E causeway.
925	-	-	-	In lee of numerous spoil islands, in 7-8 ft.
958	137	E	-	In creek under E side of island. Good.
965	185	W	300 yds.	In basin under N shore, in 27 ft.
981	220	NW	750 yds.	S of W causeway, in 7 ft.
988	-	-	-	In Manatee Pocket, clear of midstream traffic, in 6-9 ft. Anywhere.

Stuart, Florida, to Miami, Florida (Dinner Key)

Mile	Marker	Bearing	Distance	Notes
992	19	E	250 yds.	In pocket dredged out of Peck Lake, in 7-8 ft. Compass course 66 true.
998	40	W	300 yds.	Under high bank, W shore, in 8 ft.
1000	46	NW	500 yds.	Off fairway, W in 9 ft.
1001	49	W	150 yds.	Under bank, W shore, in 9-10 ft.

From this point to south Miami, there are very few anchorages that anybody would want to remain in . . . or, for that matter, that anybody would want *you* to remain in. This is the Gold Coast, densely populated, studded with huge high-rise apartment buildings and interlaced with a network of residential canals—hardly a place to anchor unless in an emergency. If you must, search the chart for that tiny patch of white that may clue you in. Wherever it is, there will be heavy day and night traffic, much noise, highway traffic, lights, smells. The only time my wife ever became seasick was at anchor off a Fort Lauderdale bridge.

These are the only places where you might, with extreme luck, get a decent night's rest on the hook:

At Lantana, on Lake Worth, on the lee side of the west bridge causeway, near the bulkheaded shore.

At Fort Lauderdale, on the south side of the west approach of the Las Olas Boulevard Bridge. The basin is a city anchorage, and you *must* pick up a mooring, at a daily fee ($2 in 1976).

At Dinner Key, *outside* of the dredged yacht basin, either northeast or southwest of lighted marker #15. Usually crowded, open to easterlies. Free . . . as a few score of hippies have found out.

Hurricane Harbor on Key Biscayne.

No-Name Harbor, at Cape Florida on Key Biscayne, just off the Cape Florida Channel. Delightful, palm- and pine-shaded lagoon, with usually only a few boats (say, up to eight), some daytime picnickers; free. This is a favorite of experienced cruising people.

THE FLORIDA KEYS

The anchorages in the Florida Keys are not many, and there are almost none on the outside (Hawk Channel) route. Many are "fair weather" anchorages, as at Elliott Key, where a sizable fleet from the Miami area gathers every "good" weekend and anchors near Sands Key or off the western shore of Elliott Key. I have seen the entire fleet haul anchor and leave at 3 A.M., when a night norther appeared. But I have also laid there a full week and never moved.

The Sands Key anchorage is at the mouth or inside (if you can find space) the tiny basin shown on chart 848 (11465). It will accommodate six feet maximum. Along the west shore of Elliott Key is a county park and marina, and many boats anchor off it, partly because there is a footpath across the key to the ocean side.

Another anchorage . . . tricky, but passable for boats with up to five-foot draft . . . is that around Adams Key. The approach is from the northwest, over a five-foot bottom; then follow the stakes into the current basin west and south of the island. With care, it is possible to creep behind Rubicon Keys and lay to bow and stern hooks.

There are several creeks entering Angelfish Creek that afford good, colorful, and remote anchorages for boats drawing up to seven feet. Beware of strong currents here (excellent fishing). In the lee of Pumpkin Island, off Snapper Point, many yachts find pleasant anchoring. A careful approach to Steamboat Creek, west of Jew Point, will produce a lovely, remote wilderness anchorage . . . and the same on a southern approach. The creek carries about eight feet, but not past the new highway culvert, which has recently stopped through-passage of this ancient waterway.

In Barnes Sound, there is fair anchorage under the southwestern shore of the Barnes Point peninsula in anything but a heavy southwester.

Tarpon Basin, the next body of water when steaming south, is a popular mooring. Anchor in the bight of eight-foot water, just north of marker 48 A; or southeast into eight-foot depths off the shore.

An interesting, if tenuous, anchorage is in the cut through the Cowpens, anchoring just off the fairway, bow and stern. The interest is in the flocks of roseate spoonbills, often nesting, in the surrounding mangroves. It is well protected, and traffic usually slows down in the cut. Nearby, Snake Creek will accommodate boats of five-foot draft. Enter carefully from the northwest, following the bush stakes. Similarly, a course into the bight southwest of Wilson Key may be negotiated.

Lignumvitae Key affords a lee from all but easterlies, in eight feet, just offshore. Matecumbe Harbor, small but secure, lies inside the lighted marker (#2) and is limited in size. Good in a norther.

A popular anchorage at Marathon, on Vaca Key, is Boot Key Harbor. It is necessary to go under the Key West Highway (U.S. Route 1) via Knight Key Channel or via the Moser Channel, south of Pigeon Key. It is usual for southbound yachts to exit from the inland route via Moser Channel (though vessels under 20 feet high may exit at the Bahia Honda Channel). There are no anchorages, save one, for the stranger from here to Key West. A marked channel leads around the southern tip of Newfound Harbor Keys (Marker #2) and into a deep bay with two arms. The easterly one is the best, with anchorage off an abandoned marina (the site for the filming of the movie *PT 109* in the 1950s), or in the marina basin. The southwesterly harbor, Newfound Harbor itself, is best in a norther. This is coral (rocky) area and chain cables should be rigged.

At Key West, the only anchorages for small craft are in Key West Bight (off the docks and strand) or in Garrison Bight, with eight feet. The former is nearest the "old" and scenic Key West. Key West is an important commercial and naval harbor, and small craft should not attempt to anchor in the turning basin, the submarine pens, or areas noted as "restricted" on the harbor charts.

The lack of harbors in this last leg of the Waterway is made up by the fact that not many yachts cruise or winter in these waters. You are apt to find the anchorages unoccupied, save in Key West itself. They are, rather, transient harbors for boats "on the way." Yet some, such as Newfound Harbor, are beautiful and remote, ideal for loafing, fishing, and sunning, and some Ditch crawlers spend months in their crystal-clear waters and steady, tropical weather patterns. All . . . truly all . . . are free.

The Okeechobee Waterway
to the
West Coast Intracoastal Waterway

(Chart 855-SC (11428). Scale is in statute miles)

Mile	Marker	Bearing	Distance	Notes
12	37	SE	-	Anyplace in original St. Lucie R., with exit at Marker 39, 10-16 ft.
15	49	W	50 yds.	In basin, under spillway, close to N bank (avoid during runoffs).
39	2A	-	-	In basin, W of gate fender.

Okeechobee Waterway Route 2 (or Rim Route)

Mile	Marker	Bearing	Distance	Notes
60	-	-	-	In bight, W of channel, N of swing bridge.
68	92	-	-	Leave Waterway, turning north to small
70	94	-	-	anchorages behind wooded spoil islands.
71	96	-	-	Limited. Very scenic.

Rejoining Route 1

Mile	Marker	Bearing	Distance	Notes
71	-	-	-	At Liberty Pt., E into old canal, ½ mi.
77	-	-	-	Off lock entrance canal or in abandoned canal to N.
78	-	-	-	Off fairway, E of town dock (little traffic).
83	-	-	-	Enter Lake Hicpochee, 2nd opening going W. Anchor just inside in 7-8 ft. 'Ware water snakes on hyacinth flotillas.

(There are many loops off the main channel, now straightened, which are the old winding river, from Mile 100 to Franklin Lock at Mile 122. Some may be entered with care for bow and stern anchoring. Few will accommodate more than two boats. Depth is usually six feet. Possibility of dense tropical vegetation and overhanging branches. Test entrance; some have been closed. West entrances are apt to be deepest.)

Mile	Marker	Bearing	Distance	Notes
122	-	-	-	Anchorage and picnic grounds (federal) E side of lock, on N bank, in old river.
125	5	NW	500 yds.	In Owl Cr. or its western branch. 8 ft.
135	46	NW	-	To NW of Loftus I. in 7 ft. Note old piles shown on chart.
150	"H"	SE	200 yds.	In 5-6 ft. bight, E of channel and of range light "H".

THE WEST COAST OF FLORIDA

The west coast of Florida is quite unlike the east coast and presents few of the anchorage problems of the Atlantic Waterway. This is chiefly due to the fact that it is far more open—meaning many fewer miles of canal or canalized creeks—and natural anchorages have been preserved and are readily discovered by chart examination. This does not mean that there is an abundance of anchorages, for, alas, the west coast is quite shallow in most of its parts, and many beckoning coves or "lees" are inaccessible to all but boats of very shallow draft; or to centerboard sailing craft.

Starting at its southern reaches, the Everglades are by far the most productive of anchorages. There are literally hundreds of deepwater anchorages in the Shark River area available to boats drawing up to seven feet. Access is from the Gulf, at the light at the entrance to the Little Shark, just south of Ponce de Leon Bay. From the river, deepwater channels lead to the Shark and to Whitewater Bay and its many arms. All have excellent wilderness anchorages. Access for vessels no higher than 10 feet 3 inches (to clear a fixed bridge) is available from Flamingo, the headquarters of the Everglades National Park service. (Check the water level and bridge clearance; they may

Clumps of trees on "hammocks" pepper the sawgrass in the Everglades.

be changed after heavy rains.) This area offers all the very tops in fishing ... snapper, snook, trout, redfish, and panfish. The only supply center is at Flamingo, where there is a store, fuel dock, ice and bait station. It is best reached by dinghy if anchored north of the bridge.

There is a small-boat passage, well marked since 1972, from the Shark River area to the Chokoloskee-Everglades City area. Large boats must go north outside, reentering at the Baron River. Here, where there is anchorage off the Rod and Gun Club, northwest of the island in a feeder creek (shown on chart), is another supply base. Several natural bights off the river afford anchorage.

The course from here (north) is offshore, with a possible duck-in at Naples (where there is anchorage off the yacht club or the city marina), past the mouth of the Caloosahatchee River, and into Pine Island Sound, where there are some major anchorages. These are: in the St. James City area; on the southeast side of Chino Island; on the east shore of Upper Captiva Island; in Roosevelt Channel on Captiva Island; in the area of Cabbage Key and of Useppa Island; and into Pelican Bay, via Pelican Pass. In general, this, like most of this coast, is shallow water and, off the marked channels, care must be exercised. There is no coral (mostly mud or sand bottom), but there are submerged oyster bars that can tear up a bottom.

Charlotte Harbor has a few good anchorages, notably near entering rivers (the Peace and Myakka rivers), and so has the Englewood region, on the Palm Island side. At Sarasota the resort communities take over and continue, with one interruption, to above Clearwater. The "interruption" is at Egemont and Mullet keys, off the Tampa ship channel, both of which are popular cruiser's anchorages in suitable weather. The Clearwater anchorage is at Clearwater

Fort Myers, Fla., is the terminus for many northerners who annually migrate southward. (Florida Department of Commerce)

Beach, off the beach and marina area. Above here, the water is extremely shallow and the channel well offshore, and the only anchorages are up the few rivers or creeks, which are entered by locally marked channels and usually produce most limited anchoring areas. Major rivers north of here (the Homosassa and the Crystal) have anchoring areas, but they are entered from channels *miles* offshore and with controlling depths of five to eight feet only. Check the charts and cruising guides for navigating these waters.

The annual migration from the North ceases in the Fort Myers area . . . fully covered for anchorages herein. A far smaller number of boats migrate from the Mississippi system, and all of these cross the Gulf from Carrabelle to Cedar keys; then coast to Clearwater, St. Petersburg, Tampa, Fort Myers, and Naples; or to the east coast's Gold Coast. They do not require anchorages, save, possibly, when cruising locally during their stays. The Waterway, as such, ends for the northerners at Fort Myers and for the midwesterners at Carrabelle, when they leave the Ditch for the open Gulf of Mexico and their terminal ports.

I suggest that you mark your chart with the standard symbol for anchorage as you plan your day's run (see sketch), and particularly "case" the entrance to it. Just remember that the small-craft charts are scaled to statute miles and that adjoining charts may be scaled to nautical miles. (Use standard conversion tables, found in the *Coast Pilot* and presented following—see box.) Get a weather forecast, or make your own by observation; then select an anchorage or two near where you predict the end of the day's run to be. Check the character of the bottom in the best lay considering the forecast weather. Well beforehand, prepare the anchor and cable. Run your generator *before* you anchor (if needed) and happy anchoring, an ever-more-popular way to cruise.

It is wise to mark your chart with the anchorage symbol as you plan a day's run.

CONVERSION TABLE FOR NAUTICAL AND STATUTE MILES
1 nautical mile = 6,080 feet;   1 statute mile = 5,280 feet

Nautical miles to statute miles

Nautical miles	Statute miles	Nautical miles	Statute miles
1	1.151	51	58.690
2	2.302	52	59.840
3	3.452	53	60.991
4	4.603	54	62.142
5	5.754	55	63.293
6	6.905	56	64.444
7	8.055	57	65.594
8	9.206	58	66.745
9	10.357	59	67.896
10	11.508	60	69.047
11	12.659	61	70.197
12	13.809	62	71.348
13	14.960	63	72.499
14	16.111	64	73.650
15	17.262	65	74.801
16	18.412	66	75.951
17	19.563	67	77.102
18	20.714	68	78.253
19	21.865	69	79.404
20	23.016	70	80.554
21	24.166	71	81.705
22	25.317	72	82.856
23	26.468	73	84.007
24	27.619	74	85.158
25	28.769	75	86.308
26	29.920	76	87.459
27	31.071	77	88.610
28	32.222	78	89.761
29	33.373	79	90.911
30	34.523	80	92.062
31	35.674	81	93.213
32	36.825	82	94.364
33	37.976	83	95.515
34	39.126	84	96.665
35	40.277	85	97.816
36	41.428	86	98.967
37	42.579	87	100.118
38	43.730	88	101.268
39	44.880	89	102.419
40	46.031	90	103.570
41	47.182	91	104.721
42	48.333	92	105.871
43	49.483	93	107.022
44	50.634	94	108.173
45	51.785	95	109.324
46	52.936	96	110.475
47	54.087	97	111.625
48	55.237	98	112.776
49	56.388	99	113.927
50	57.539	100	115.078

Statute miles to nautical miles

Statute miles	Nautical miles	Statute miles	Nautical miles
1	0.869	51	44.318
2	1.738	52	45.187
3	2.607	53	46.056
4	3.476	54	46.925
5	4.345	55	47.794
6	5.214	56	48.663
7	6.083	57	49.532
8	6.952	58	50.401
9	7.821	59	51.270
10	8.690	60	52.139
11	9.559	61	53.008
12	10.428	62	53.877
13	11.297	63	54.746
14	12.166	64	55.615
15	13.035	65	56.484
16	13.904	66	57.353
17	14.773	67	58.222
18	15.642	68	59.091
19	16.511	69	59.959
20	17.380	70	60.828
21	18.249	71	61.697
22	19.118	72	62.566
23	19.986	73	63.435
24	20.855	74	64.304
25	21.724	75	65.173
26	22.593	76	66.042
27	23.462	77	66.911
28	24.331	78	67.780
29	25.200	79	68.649
30	26.069	80	69.518
31	26.938	81	70.387
32	27.807	82	71.256
33	28.676	83	72.125
34	29.545	84	72.994
35	30.414	85	73.863
36	31.283	86	74.732
37	32.152	87	75.601
38	33.021	88	76.470
39	33.890	89	77.339
40	34.759	90	78.208
41	35.628	91	79.077
42	36.497	92	79.946
43	37.366	93	80.815
44	38.235	94	81.684
45	39.104	95	82.553
46	39.973	96	83.422
47	40.842	97	84.291
48	41.711	98	85.160
49	42.580	99	86.029
50	43.449	100	86.898

CAMPING ALONG THE WATERWAY

While hardly the problem of most cruisers, there is a notable number of hardy souls who annually travel the Great Ditch in canoes, kayaks, Foldboats, sailing dinghies, and (true) . . . rowing dories. These chaps depend upon camping at night, and they have their problems more often than not.

In general, not *all* the Waterway can turn up suitable sites for an overnight tent. Some of it is wild, swampy land, often studded with cypress trees that grow *in* the water, often thick, matted, and overgrown—and too much of it is populated and privately owned land. The bugs and no-see-ums, the greenheads and the mosquitoes must be a problem; possibly the alligators, raccoons, and snakes also. Nevertheless, the trip is often made by these small-boat enthusiasts.

It is said that jack pines (the tall, straight evergreens that cover much of the terrain from Mile Zero to the true tropics at about Mile 950, Vero Beach) will grow only in dry soil of at least six feet above sea (Waterway) level. They, of all the varied vegetation of the Southland, seem to afford a dry and reasonably sane camping ground. The mangroves stand in water. The palms are buggy and snaky. The Virginia and Carolina vine growths are impenetrable.

Along much of the Waterway, the dredgers have left long stretches of "spoil islands," small islets of one to three acres of pure sand, now well grown in Australian and jack pine, sometimes sabal palm. These are unowned, though claimed by the state; they are very clean, fairly high, and seldom more than 200 yards off the yacht channel. I have seen many a paddler camped on one of these lovely little islands—seemingly without challenge. These spoil islands occur, some stretching for 20 or more miles, at: Bogue Sound, south of Spooner's Creek; various areas to Fernandina, Florida, usually and especially in the wide sounds near ocean inlets; on either side of passages to the sea; in Mosquito Lagoon, south of the Indian mounds below New Smyrna; almost the entire length of the Indian River and in a few local areas near Fort Pierce, Jupiter, and Lake Worth.

In the marshlands of South Carolina and Georgia, there are frequent unmarked private landing docks, obviously for small-boat parties of surveyors, game wardens, and wildlife patrols. Most lead to high ground and often to "berms," usually treed and protected. The Caloosahatchee River, in its easterly reaches, cuts through high prairie land, with good camping spots on both shores. At the locks, there is always a parklike area (some have tables, fireplaces, and rest rooms) open to the camping public who come in both boats and travel-camper vehicles. (Best is at Franklin Lock, near Alva.) On the lower river there is camping in Owl Creek, near the mouth on the west side; on Loftus Island, off Fort Myers; and, of course, on the endless islands and keys of Everglades National Park, starting at Naples. The offshore keys of Pine Island Sound also offer good camping, a popular spot being a county park (free) on the north end of Cayo Costa. The Peace, Myakka, and Manatee rivers are popular canoeing rivers, with state-established camping grounds along them.

It is beyond the scope of this guidebook to list all the parks that border the Waterway; a road map or a camper's guidebook will do this. There are many, and from the deck of a passing yacht, most look very well run, clean, and much used by smallcrafters.

Believe me, they are most welcome on the Ditch, for they are one with the original users, when the now-connected links of the Waterway were the paths of the pre-Columbian Indians as they, too, followed the sun southward.

Chapter 6
The Leisurely Life

Truly learning the art of loafing is an accomplishment vouchsafed to few. It often leads to boredom and is usually much too abrupt a change from the hectic lives most of us spent to acquire the monetary means to be able to loaf. And boredom can lead to other evils... vegetation, regression, dependence upon alcohol, drugs, lack of interest in anything or anybody. It flourishes especially in the confines of a small craft, in the general atmosphere of relaxation and retirement rife in boating centers, and with the withdrawal from the local civic responsibilities we left behind.

The successful live-aboards have in one way or another solved the problem of boredom. They probably have much reduced their involvement in large and public affairs, yet they "keep busy" in many ways that are often of no importance to anyone save themselves. There is, at last, time to do what you have always wanted to do; to be yourself and enjoy being just that.

There are endless activities and interests possible for the live-aboard, suddenly complete master of his own time and inclination... and there need be no sacrifice of relaxation. It is a matter of just taking it easy, just recognizing that whatever the diversion, there is no time deadline for its completion. You can often recognize the crew that has achieved true loafing, or relaxation, status by the boat they own. It is very apt to be a slow, eight-knot boat, or a cruising sailer with a little-used powerplant. The owners have learned that enjoyment is measured in terms of time and not distance or speed, and that undue regard for distance and speed simply steals away from the hours of enjoyment. You are "there" sooner, but you didn't have as much

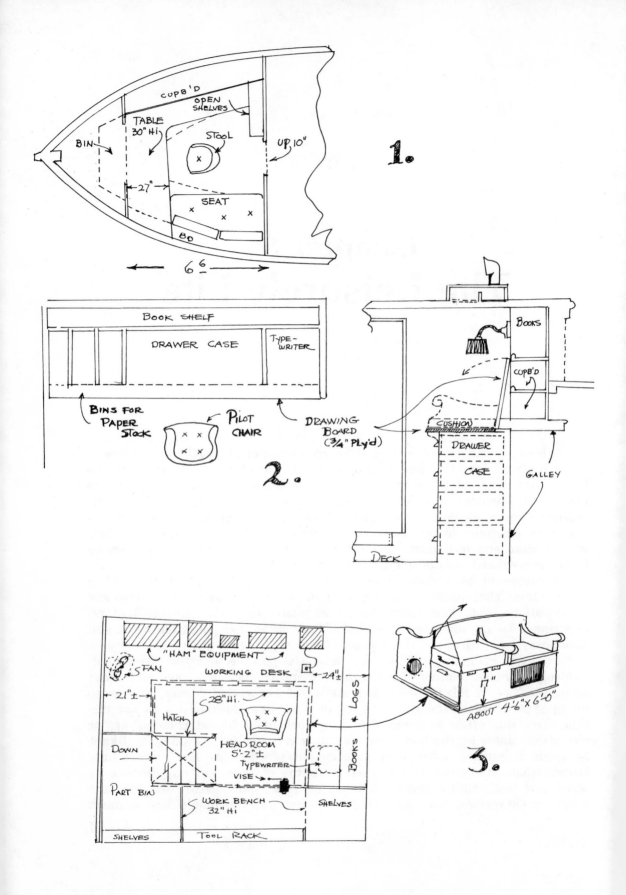

1.

CUPB'D
OPEN SHELVES
TABLE 30" Hi
STOOL
BIN
UP 10"
27"
SEAT
BD
6'6"

2.

BOOK SHELF
DRAWER CASE
TYPE-WRITER
BINS FOR PAPER STOCK
PILOT CHAIR
DRAWING BOARD (¾" PLY'D)

BOOKS
CUPB'D
CUSHION
DRAWER CASE
GALLEY
DECK

3.

"HAM" EQUIPMENT
FAN
WORKING DESK
24"±
21"±
28" Hi.
HATCH
HEAD ROOM 5'-2"±
LOGS
DOWN
TYPEWRITER
VISE
PART BIN
BOOKS
WORK BENCH 32" Hi
SHELVES
SHELVES
TOOL RACK

ABOUT 4'-6" X 6'-0"

Left: REDESIGN OF SPACE TO SERVE DUAL PURPOSES

The live-aboard family takes along hobbies and leisure-time diversions and activities, so these pursuits deserve some permanent location on the boat. Indeed, in the case of working live-aboards, it may be essential to survival.

(1) Conversion of the unused "crew's quarters" on a 46-footer into a utilitarian and attractive "hobby shop," where the owner and his wife make jewelry and shell novelties. Such a space needs a large skylight hatch and, possibly, a fan as well. This area also serves as the "ship's office."

(2) Author's conversion of the observation seat in the wheelhouse into a large drawing board and worktable. The back folds down (after removing 3-inch foam cushion) and forms drawing board. Beneath are bins for storage of drawing papers, 8 drawers for gear, and a slide-in bin for the typewriter (with a "trash basket" under). Dead ahead (or aft in this case) is a row of necessary books and shelves for working tools. I use the pilot stool, since the table is about 50 inches high, like the drawing board in a studio.

(3) Unique "ham station" on Hank Budlong's Ilyna. *In the center of the large, open cockpit, he constructed a combination scuttle and seat, as shown. Under it, with only 62 inches of headroom (because his is a "sitting" hobby), he operates a world-girdling ham station, complete with library and workshop. Many older-type boats can accommodate such a fitment.*

fun getting there! Once "there," you must, in time, turn to interests and activities that will keep you alive, awake, and happy. These are many indeed.

Before blindly settling down in some port by accident, you should certainly look into it via the local Chamber of Commerce, or by talking to other experienced live-aboards. Are there chapters of your northern service clubs? Are there churches of your choice? Are there courses in whatever you might want courses in? Can you play golf, bowl, dine out well, join a hobby group, play bridge, attend sports events, take scenic rides by car or bicycle, go swimming, fly out (for travel)?

Most large yachting centers on both Florida coasts can offer a dizzying variety of diversions and activities. Probably one of the best ways to find and join some of these activities is via a church affiliation; or join a national service or fraternal club (Lions, Rotary, Masons, Odd Fellows, etc.). Just appear . . . and display interest in what is there; you will soon be on a committee and become involved. More passively, join one of their groups: the choir, the Men's Club, the Ladies' Good Cheer Society, the vestry, whatever interests you. Both the U.S. Power Squadron and the U.S. Coast Guard Auxiliary are very active in most Florida cities, and you are welcome to join the local unit as a fully qualified member, either by transfer or by attending the next course. If you are an officer, take a class and become an instructor, a role offering much pleasure and personal satisfaction. This is a natural for a boatman.

Close to this is sail racing. Many live-aboard groups have organized local dinghy sailing clubs and entered these into regional groups for competitive sailing in local waters. Scuba diving clubs are to be found in many areas, particularly on the east coast and in the Keys, and some specialize in searching for sunken Spanish treasure ships. (I know of a skipper who thus shared in a found treasure off the Marquesas to the extent of $118,000!) Sportfishing or drift fishing (in chartered boats) is the interest of not a few retired skippers.

Gentler diversions include attending art or craft classes, available universally in Vacationland. Sometimes these are offered by universities (as at Coral Gables and Fort Myers), which give academic credit. Most are informal groups, under an interested instructor, and these turn out some of the best "art" of the hundreds of annual art exhibits. Most any large city will offer classes in jewelry-making, pottery and ceramics, macramé, knitting, shell art, etching, portrait painting, photography, and cinematography. Weekend editions of Florida papers often carry "activity round-ups," which list what's going on, and where . . . and some names and addresses.

In the Keys and on the west coast (in the Sanibel Island region), great numbers of people collect seashells, mount and display them, and compete for prizes and blue ribbons at the many local shell shows. Sanibel Island, once the mecca for this hobby, has become so crowded that the beaches are picked clean before the sun is up every morning. Find the more remote beaches—from Marco Island to Clearwater—and search for shells on them. There are few shells on the east coast (though sometimes, after an easterly storm, Scotch Bonnets will come in in great numbers). The Keys, the Bahama islands, and the Dry Tortugas all have good shelling. By all means, acquire one of the many shell guides to help in finding and recognizing the worthwhile species.

The cleaning, classification, preparation for exhibition, and the making of the mounts, cases, or "tables" extend this popular hobby far beyond the mere searching. Craftsmen create many interesting objects (lamps, paperweights, jewelry boxes) using shell decoration. It is a natural Florida hobby.

Along with shell collecting is the hobby of fossil collecting. Fossils are found on many Gulf beaches, centered around the Boca Grande-Siesta Key region on the west coast of Florida. In ancient times, when the seas receded and left large saltwater lakes, animal life gathered round and there eventually died. The sea returned, filling these basins choked with animal bones, and they are now . . . after storms . . . again opening, and their grisly deposits, now hardened into fossil rock, drift onto the beaches. Thus it is no trick at all to find, in the sand or in the swash channel off the beach, huge quantities of sharks' teeth, the anvils of shell-cracking fish, the barbs of stingrays, the carapaces of turtles, deer and cat and bird bones, sometimes the huge leg bones of mastodons, camels, and three-toed horses . . . all millions of years old. The collection, identifying, and mounting of these fossils make for a fascinating hobby.

The Southland, in a way, provides its own local pastimes. Fishing is ever-popular . . . and helps the larder as well. Free saltwater fishing is available all along the Florida coasts and up the rivers, usually to the first bridge or dam (beyond which is fresh water, under state control). There is no license required in federal waters.

Sportfishing on charter boats (these are out of Fort Lauderdale) is a favorite activity in Florida waters. (Florida Department of Commerce)

Tackle stores abound . . . with abundant advice available in each. The east coast, bounded close inshore by the Gulf Stream, is where the sportfishing goes on . . . marlin and sailfish and dolphin and wahoo in record-breaking sizes. There, also, are bluefish, trout, grouper, flounder, snook (a protected game fish, sometimes called robalo), and many varieties of pan fish. The west coast provides less flashy species: kingfish, mackerel, bluefish, cobia, sheepshead, redfish (channel bass), snook in great quantities, pompano, trout, flounder, and the big-game king, silver tarpon. Many varieties are also found in the Keys, both offshore and in the shallows of the inside waters. It is here that the gamiest of all, the bonefish, is taken. All this fishing is available even to small craft. It is nothing to see 100 outboard boats trolling for kings 20 miles offshore. We seldom sail these coasts without picking up a dolphin or a Spanish mackerel for dinner. (Silver spoon on 150 feet of monofilament at three to four knots is just right.)

Here also are to be found oysters by the bushel for the picking. Most are the small, sweet 'coon oysters, the kind that raccoons search out at night. They are found at low tide, in bars, in many places. Knock them off in clusters with a hammer, or hand pick them, wash them, and store them in a gunnysack hung overside; they'll stay alive for weeks. Along shores of mud, overlaid by sand, clams are readily found; all quahogs (hard) and the cherry-stones (small, for half-shell serving) are at half-tide marks; the big "hen" clams (for chowder, fritters) are *below* the low-tide mark, *in water.* These are readily located by searching for a hole in the sand that looks like a keyhole. Mr. Clam is beneath. Six will make a chowder for four.

The fine arts of fishing include scalloping, shrimping, live-bait catching, and specimen gathering (tropical fish, seahorses, and exotic types) . . . any one a worthwhile hobby. Open to anybody on the beach is the gathering of a bucket of coquina. These tiny, twin-winged clams are found in shoals, just at the low-tide line of most sand beaches. Note the sandpipers . . . they feed on coquina. Dig out a bunch, sand and all, and capsize them into a "strainer" (a wooden frame about 15 inches by 20 inches with one face covered with ¼-inch mesh hardware cloth). Wash out the sand. The coquina will remain—alive, of course. A bucketful, brought to a boil but *not* boiled, will yield a delicate nectar fit for a god. Serve it hot or chilled. Coquina broth, a gourmet's broth: base for a chowder, liquid for making fritters or patties. One chap at Coconut Grove uses it in a martini!

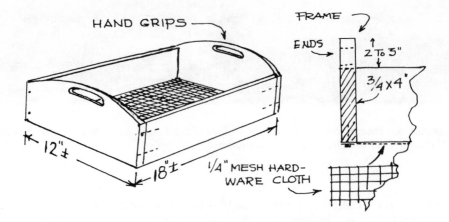

A coquina "strainer" is easy to construct.

A warning: even in federal waters, where no state fishing license is required, there are still some game fish laws, usually referring to season or legal size. Tarpon, snook, and trout are thus protected. Be sure to check at your fishing tackle store for the current game regulations. The manatee (sea cow) and the alligator, both of which are frequently seen in southern waters, are protected by law. Neither should be fed or encouraged to live in yacht basins or marinas.

Bird lovers find the South a bonanza of song and color, for the birds, too, winter here along with northern yachtsmen. Exotics—parrots, roseate spoonbills, the tall flamingos—are often seen in the wild, especially near the Everglades, where they have been protected since egret feather hats went out in 1900. Hunters, too, find game in northern Florida: deer, bear, wild hog, turkey, and small game are plentiful. A license is required, of course. Also, wear snake boots (which are lengths of iron stovepipe slipped over the shoes and extending from ankle to knee), for the South does have its reptiles (rattler, moccasin, and coral snakes are the dangerous ones), and no true southerner would even go to his own backhouse without snake boots or snake sticks.

Gardening is not a strange pastime for boaters at all. Many communities have garden clubs. Some have small patches that may be reserved in a county park. Fort Myers has a beautiful 10-acre garden along the yacht channel. It is reserved for and beautified exclusively by men! Lovely, happy, potted varieties may be grown on board, of course . . . and they are a joy to watch. (P.S. Just keep them out of my wheelhouse!)

Florida is geared to vacation-oriented attractions by the hundreds, since 20 million people annually visit the state. It is liberally equipped with theatres, concert halls, exhibition halls, art galleries, movie houses. Some of the best talents in the fields of music, entertainment, and the theatre arts appear "on tour" in even the smaller cities. There is no end to what is offered in the daily press and the Chamber of Commerce monthlies. You have only to choose. We have always felt that we see more theatre in Florida than we ever possibly could in our small Maine community. There are endless festivals and pageants throughout the state. Most of them are fun for all, free, and have good weather pretty much guaranteed. The Orange Bowl Parade starts it off in Miami, Fort Myers picks it up with the Edison Pageant of Light in early February, Sarasota brings on the opening of the circus season. Even the little town of Moore Haven, in the Seminole Indian country, stages the Chula Nitka, honoring the bass of Lake Okeechobee.

Sports attractions are in abundance: horse racing, greyhound racing, boxing, wrestling, basketball . . . and most of the national baseball teams come to Florida for spring practice and are happy to have an audience. Some major yacht racing takes place here (like the St. Petersburg-Fort Lauderdale race and the lesser ocean races). Even the swamp-buggy races (Naples area) draw huge crowds, many of them winter visitors.

Florida is liberally sprinkled with public parks, many of them on or near the waterways of both coasts. Disney World is the best known park (though hardly public) and may be reached from Sanford at the end of the St. Johns Waterway or from the Daytona-Orlando area by local bus. Everglades National Park is ever-popular and accessible by boat (drawing up to five feet) at Flamingo or at Everglades City. In northern Florida are many state and county parks, which include the colorful "springs" country, some with real, live mermaids. Of special interest to winter boaters are at least the following:

Elliott Key	National park on Elliott Key; docks; natural.
Crandon Park	Park on the sea, with world-famous zoo. Miami.
Matheson Hammock	18 miles south of Miami, on Biscayne Bay. Pleasant day's boat ride.
Cape Florida	Tip of Key Biscayne. Old lighthouse.
Virginia Key	Miami. Seaquarium, marine stadium.
Jonathan Dickinson State Park	Wild, huge, accessible by car or by dinghy via the Loxahatchee River. Chart 845-SC (11472).
Haulover Beach Park	At Bakers Haulover, Mile 1079. Ocean beach, picnics, docks.
Hugh Taylor Birch State Park	Fort Lauderdale, on beach and Waterway. Antique railroad, picnics.
John Pennekamp Coral Reef State Park	Underwater park, diving reefs. Key Largo.
Sebastian Inlet State Park	Treasure museum, ocean beach, trails, picnics.
Caladesi Island	Off Dunedin. Wild, natural island. Wildlife, canoe trails, picnics.

Miami's Crandon Park Zoo, a tranquil oasis. (Florida Department of Commerce)

A.L. Anderson County Park	Near Tarpon Springs. Lovely gardens, lakes, birds; picnics.
Ding Darling National Wildlife Refuge	On Sanibel Island. Natural bird refuge, off Pine Island Sound
Carl Johnson County Park	On Black Island, south of Fort Myers Beach. Ocean beach, picnics.

The local Chamber of Commerce will provide a complete list of *all* parks and their facilities. Most are free, though charges may be made for their "attractions," rides, admissions to special features, etc.

There is no end to golf courses in Florida. Almost all are open to the public, and many are free of greens fees. Because of the climate, it is usual to take a cart, preferably one with a sun shade, because many southern courses lack natural (tree) shade. Championship courses are at Hilton Head Island, South Carolina, and at Ocean Reefs Club, on Key Largo, south of Miami. The mild game of shuffleboard is played all over Florida, and many marinas have 'board decks. The usual "visitor centers" in public parks often have banks (up to 36 courts) of decks, always free to the public. Competitions go forward all winter long, with state playoffs in late March. Along with the growing interest in tennis, many communities have provided courts in their parks. Most are free; a few charge token fees. The retiree would do well to do his tennis playing during the weekdays (rather than on weekends, when local folks want to use their courts) and quit by 5 P.M.

Cape Florida Lighthouse, near Miami, is open to the public, as are its attractive surrounding beaches. (Miami-Metro Department of Publicity and Tourism)

For those who like to move, there are many marked "bike trails," usually utilizing routes off main traffic arteries and traversing the more rural areas. From any city in the Southland, package bus "tours" can take you to every possible resort or attraction in the state . . . Disney World, the Florida "springs" country, the many animal "safari" farms (like Busch Gardens in Tampa and Lion Country on the east coast), the Everglades, Cape Canaveral and its rockets, and Key West with its turtle crawls and goombay dancers. Tours from Florida also go to Las Vegas, the New Orleans Mardi Gras, the Orange, Cotton, and Rose Bowl events . . . even the Canyon de Cobra bit to Puerto Vallarta, Mazatlan, and Mexico City. From Port Everglades, which is an enormously busy seaport at Fort Lauderdale, world-girdling cruise ships stop to pick up passengers. Many cruises, particularly to the Bahamas and the lower Caribbean islands, originate here; some of the all-inclusive short package cruises cost as little as $40 per person per day, and a long weekend in Nassau may be had for the bargain price of $99.50 each. Facilities for air travel are equal to those in any area of the country. There are international airports, with direct flights to anywhere in the world, at Jacksonville, Tampa, Fort Lauderdale, and Miami.

No, there is no reason to become bored with life aboard a small boat in this winter wonderland. There is plenty to do, and often, especially if you maintain your boat yourself, not enough time to do it. If you do not wish to conform, to join the throngs who amuse themselves in the resort areas, how about digging in ancient Indian mounds, scuba diving a quarter-mile beneath the surface in limestone springs, canoeing 770 miles on a state park canoe trail? You can do them all in Florida.

Chapter 7
Going Foreign

Most winter dwellers in Florida break up the winter with one or more major cruises during the season. Locally, they include the lovely St. Johns River cruise, about 500 miles of sweetwater cruising in northern Florida, well off the beaten tourist track and in the midst of scenic splendor, great freshwater fishing, and a Florida not known to many. Then, too, there is the popular "great-circle" cruise, embracing a one-way track from any point and return on this "circle"; Miami, to Stuart, across the state via the St. Lucie, Lake Okeechobee, and the Caloosahatchee River, down the Gulf Coast to Naples, Everglades City, and Flamingo; then across Florida Bay to the mid-Keys (Vaca Key, usually) and north through the sounds to Biscayne Bay and Miami. Another is the Key West round trip and still another the Dry Tortugas cruise, which is an excellent "trainer" for a genuine foreign cruise.

The obvious foreign countries are the Bahamas and Mexico. While this book can hardly become a guide to these foreign lands, we will happily undertake to get the reader started on his way to still another beckoning live-aboard adventure.

THE BAHAMAS

Warning: The Bahamas is no longer the British West Indies (BWI). Do not refer to these islands, or to a Bahamian, as such, or refer to money as "Beewee dollars" or in any way suggest that this island nation is anything but Bahamian.

The islands lie just 48 to 55 miles, port to port, from the United States, an easy daylight run from Fort Pierce, West Palm Beach, Fort Lauderdale, or Miami. The run involves crossing the Gulf Stream, which has a northerly current of up to five knots at all times and can, and often *does* kick up a huge fuss. Unless you have a truly large, seakindly craft, it behooves you to realistically "watch the weather." Anything from the north to east can make for a rough passage—like 24-foot waves and strained gear and seasickness even for old hands. However, even during the winter season, there are days of utter calm, periods of gentle offshore winds when the Gulf Stream is docile as a creek. You must wait for such a period. The roughest crossing I ever had was in June; the smoothest, in mid-January.

Once over, once "on the banks," almost all problems cease. Normal weather here is calm to light southerly, warm, sunny, with short runs between ports and gay adventure at the end of the run. A norther, especially in one of the canyon-deep arms from the sea, can still bother, but the lack of the Gulf Stream current prevents seas of anything but ordinary and expected size. It may still be more comfortable to stay on the hook until it blows out, but who cares? You are over here for fun and games, and time is not to be considered.

The islands are charming, truly foreign in flavor, friendly (especially if you came to spend money, for tourism is almost the sole source of national income), and ready to show you whatever you define as a "good time." There are lonely islets and remote backwaters where you won't see a "tourist" boat for weeks. There are lively, sophisticated ports with nightlife, gambling, casinos quite as wild as Las Vegas or Reno . . . and quiet lovely "clubs" on sunny islands where the Tahiti dream can come true within two martinis. You can, literally, pick the kind of vacation you want. Even the island groups differ from each other in subtle ways. The Abacos, still very English and "white," are quiet and relaxing, just a bit cooler in winter than their neighbors. Nassau, in the New Providence group, is alive and vibrant, usually jumping with fun-bound tourists (from many calling cruise ships). The Exumas and Eleuthera, very lovely and recognizably "civilized." The Out Islands (meaning "out" from Nassau, the seat of government) are almost undiscovered. Great, huge Andros Island is primitive, beautiful, all native, the nearest of the "unspoiled" islands. Any and all are worth inclusion in a long cruise. Most are the type that easily induces relaxation and laziness as you swing to a hook in crystal-clear waters teeming with fish and turtles and shells and the sun a-warming from behind the tremendous, billowing banks of Gulf Stream clouds. It is the nearest that we in the States can come to the idyllic dream of the South Sea islands, and still get back to the good old U.S. in five or six hours.

The best possible guide obtainable is *Yachtsman's Guide to the Bahamas*. It includes all information necessary to a successful cruise and has detailed local chart extracts of considerable help in an area where navigational aids are scarce. The 1977 edition is available for $4.95 most anyplace in the South that sells charts, or it may be purchased by mail (include $1 for postage and handling) from: Tropic Isle Publishers, Inc., P.O. Box 340866, Coral Gables, Florida 33134. This firm also publishes a series of charts with sketch views of the harbor entrances, light structures, etc., which are most useful. Standard charts (National Ocean Survey) are:

NOS#1002 (11013)
N.O.#11161
N.O.#26240
N.O.#26260
N.O.#26280
N.O.#26300
N.O.#26320
N.O.#27040

Helpful also is a publication of the U.S. Naval Oceanographic Office entitled *Sailing Directions, the West Indies*, volume 1, publication #21.

Good background reading is:

Bahama Islands, J. Linton Rigg; revised by Harry Kline. Charles Scribner's Sons (New York), 4th ed., 1973.

History of the Bahamas, Michael Craton, Collins (London), 1968.

The *National Geographic* and many boating journals have published many feature articles on the islands, some by cruising men of the stature of Carleton Mitchell, Dick Bertram, etc.

The following sources provide excellent free introductory material on the islands:

Bahamas Tourist Office, 200 SE First St., Miami, Florida 33131

Cape Eleuthera Resort and Yacht Club, 7880 Biscayne Blvd., Miami, Florida 33138

Walker's Cay Club, P.O. Box 22493, Fort Lauderdale, Florida 33315

Xanadu Princess Yacht and Tennis Club, Freeport, Grand Bahama

A Few Helpful Notes on The Bahamas

Dockage is usually at a "club," often quite fancy. It runs from a minimum of 25 cents per foot per day to 50 cents. Both 110 AC and 220 AC dockside power are included, often on the unreliable side and subject to much voltage fluctuation. Water is usually limited, so boat washdowns and excessive tank filling are sometimes frowned upon, especially in the more remote Out Islands. Most marinas have restaurants and swimming pools; some have tennis courts or nine-hole golf courses, skeet shooting, and sportfishing. The islands of Bimini, Gun Cay, Nassau (Paradise Island, formerly Hog Island), Chub Cay, Walker's Cay ... the sportfishing hang-outs ... are apt to be quite expensive. Reservations are definitely needed in season.

Fuel is available in all populated ports. In 1976 gasoline and diesel were both close to a dollar a gallon ... a U.S. gallon, not an imperial gallon. Water in quantity averages about five cents a gallon. In the remote islands, where roof water is the sole source, it may run as high as 10 cents a gallon. On the other hand, I once asked for water at Marsh Harbour, in the Abacos, and the marina operator cheerfully told me: "Sure, boss, an' it's five cents de gallon. But was I you, I'd sail me down to de gov'ment dock an' buy him fo' only a dollar fo' one t'ousand gallons." Which I did, there and at several other "gov'ment docks."

Engine parts (flown in), possibly needed to keep going, carry a 33 1/3 percent tax at the point of entry. So do boats and their equipment *and freight* (meaning personal items aboard, such as cameras, radios, TV, sporting equipment, books) if you plan to be in the islands more than 180 days. Imported groceries, liquor other than rum, and other "native" products are subject to this 33 1/3 percent tax also, *plus* shipping costs. All in all, there is about a 50 to 60 percent markup of costs over U.S. prices.

You may bring in unlimited (but not wholesale) quantities for personal consumption but can take back to the U.S. only one quart per adult. There is no limitation on beers or wines. Don't try to "sneak" liquor in; you may be the tenth boat that is searched, and detection means the automatic seizure of the vessel, plus personal charges punishable by fines or jail or both.

Don't try to bring firearms in, especially hand guns or automatic weapons. The Bahamians are still afraid of revolution, Cuban takeover, and dark plots by American "gangsters," and they propose to control it by strictly forbidding guns to everyone. If you want a gun for hunting, you should obtain official permission well beforehand; you may have to post a bond. The greatest fear is the automatic weapon. I have entered with a .22 hand gun, not hidden and not searched for . . . just luck that time. Another time, I entered with the same .22, plus an "over-under," and had them both taken from me and held against my departure. There have been stories of guns not returned after such seizure, or of high bribe money being necessary to regain possession. The best course is to leave *all* guns on the mainland. They are not needed in the islands, save, possibly, against American criminals, for the Bahamian government has been extremely successful in holding down petty crime and robbery. It is recognized that their true national wealth stems from the tourist trade, and the tourist must be made to feel safe in the islands. Nevertheless, most boats carry tear-gas or Mace or both and do not invite strangers aboard, and certainly not below decks.

There have been quite a number of unexplained disappearances of both boats and their crews, many of them pleasure yachts. The Coast Guard warns that drug interests needing a onetime boat to run a load in from the 12-mile limit will pirate a boat; kill and toss the crew overside; load from another ship; and be in, unloaded, and gone within six hours. A frequent device is to appear to be in trouble, by signaling, or flying a capsized U.S. ensign, far offshore but on a popular crossing track; then take over the rescue boat. It is prudent advice to *not* go to the aid of any boat, not to take anybody aboard at sea. If help is needed, radio in for the Coast Guard or BASRA (the Bahamian counterpart of the Coast Guard, meaning Bahamas Air-Sea Rescue

Association). Be very sure that you personally know all your passengers and crew members. Do not pick up dockside hands, sea cooks, unknown pilots or guides. They could be working with a drug runner offshore. Of the 250 disappearances at sea in good weather, only three have been positively linked to this sort of hijacking operation. It is truly a *spürlos versenkt* bit of piracy, sunk without a trace.

On a happier note: Pets may be taken into the Bahama Islands under the following conditions:

(1) You must obtain a Pet Import Permit from the Director of Agriculture and Fisheries, P.O. Box N28, Nassau, New Providence Island, Bahamas. (It is wise to apply 60 days or more in advance.)

(2) You must have on board a valid rabies vaccination certificate *and* a U.S. Veterinary Health Certificate dated within 24 hours of leaving the U.S.

These conditions apply to any and all pets—birds, cats, goldfish, dogs, monkeys, mice, elephants, and dinosaurs—one set of papers for each animal.

You may *not* take into the Bahamas any plants, cuttings, cut flowers, oranges, trees, or bushes. Boarding officers will check this out at the port of entry.

Be sure to have at least the following radiotelephone crystals:

U.S. Coast Guard	2182 kHz
	or Channel 16, VHF
Miami marine operator	2118 kHz
	or Channel 25, VHF
Nassau marine operator	2198 kHz or 2522 kHz

When in the islands, using the dial telephone (land phone), precede the full phone number with the numeral 809, thus: 809 plus seven-digit number. When dialing overseas (or to an overseas operator), add the numeral 32, thus: 809 32 plus area code plus seven-digit number.

Traveler's checks are good in Nassau, West End, Lucaya, etc., but not good in the Out Islands. Personal checks sometimes are accepted if you are known or have Bahamian banking connections. Credit cards are not accepted. U.S. cash is acceptable anyplace; also British pounds, although Bahamian currency is no longer tied to them.

Cruisers going over the first time, or preferring to travel in a group, can get in touch with the local U.S. Power Squadron or Coast Guard Auxiliary, who arrange group crossings as often as needed. The Bahamian Ministry of Tourism provides pilots for such groups as they organize and request guidance. Crossings are advertised in local papers. Dockmasters, yacht brokers, and marine chandleries usually know of such groups. It is highly recommended that novices, outboards, houseboats, and small sailers travel in groups. In season it is seldom necessary to wait more than 10 days for a group of your destination and speed to leave. There is no charge.

Fishing regulations in the Bahamas are strictly enforced in an effort to control their national source of food. Check with local authorities before taking lobsters, turtles, conch, whelk, and certain species of fish. The best fishing is *off* the banks, at just about the demarcation between the green (shallow) water and the deep blue (deep) water, producing all the usual Gulf Stream "sport" fish.

While we cannot go into navigation here, understand that it is in no way much different from any ocean navigation. The chief problem is that of allowing the correct compensation for the drift of the Gulf Stream as you cross, usually at nearly 90-degree angles. The drift (or set) is all northerly and varies between three and six knots, depending upon the wind and tide. A rule-of-thumb allowance for the set is 2.5 to 3.0 knots, which is multiplied by the estimated hours needed to cross (edge to edge, not shore to shore). Your compass course is adjusted *against* the set by the result. Example: If the current during the time of crossing will set you 15 nautical miles to the north of your objective, adjust the compass course by 15 miles *south* of your objective. Maintain course and speed, and you should make an accurate landfall if your ETA has been figured correctly. It is quite possible, of course, to cross entirely on RDF bearings by steering an *approximate* course to about the middle of the Stream, then homing in on the beacon.

When "going foreign," an American yacht does not need to clear an American port. Just depart . . . being very sure to carry identification and the boat's papers; also any permits for pets or for weapons. Upon reaching a Bahamian port, the vessel must officially enter. This is a simple procedure, but it must be accompanied by the display of the U.S. ensign (not the yacht ensign) in the usual place (taffrail staff or from a gaff on the aftermost mast) *and* the Bahamian flag in the starboard rigging (as from a spreader or shroud). The Bahamian flags are shown in the sketch. They may be purchased stateside at all southern marinas. The Bahamian "yacht ensign" is acceptable. The usual yellow quarantine flag must be flown as well, signifying request for medical clearance.

Proceed to the customs dock (see list of ports below) and do not . . . repeat DO NOT . . . permit any passengers ashore, or baggage of any kind, until

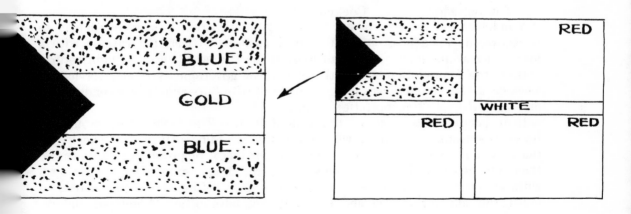

The Bahamian flag (left) and the Bahamian yacht ensign (right).

cleared. Only the master (skipper, owner, or adult member of the crew) may go ashore and to the office, usually dockside. After identification and a few questions relating to citizenship of all hands, the cargo, purpose of the voyage, etc., a transire is issued. This is a permit to cruise to any part of the islands and is returnable within 180 days (or, at times, less). You then break with a longtime custom and pay an entry fee now, rather than a departure fee, as formerly. This costs (in 1976) $2 each, and another $2 might be added if the inspecting officer has to use "transportation" to reach the dock. (He usually does.) You are then *in* and free to cruise. Your "cargo" has been checked as to guns, cameras, optical gear, appliances, electronics, etc., and listed on your transire, and these items must appear when departing. If not, you are presumed to have sold them, and duty is applied. Henceforth, no one will bother you. Be sure to keep your Bahamian courtesy flag flying night and day and be sure to dip your own U.S. colors to any official vessel, patrol, fort, etc., for the Bahamians are a very young and very proud nation and quick to demand official courtesies.

Ports of entry are:

The Abacos	Walker's Cay, Grand Cay, Green Turtle Cay, Sandy Point, and Marsh Harbour
Andros Island	Nicoll's Town, San Andros, Fresh Creek, Mangrove Cay, Congo Town
Berry Islands	Great Harbour Cay, Chub Cay
Bimini	Alice Town (also nearby Gun Cay)
Eleuthera	Rock Sound, Hatchet Bay, Georgetown, Harbour Island, Governor's Island
Exuma	George Town
Grand Bahama	West End, Freeport, Lucaya
Inagua	Matthew Town
Mayaguana	Abraham's Bay
New Providence	Nassau (any marina or yacht basin)
Ragged Island	Duncan Town
San Salvador	Cockburn Town

You have three options for surrendering your transire to be sure your departure is registered: (1) deposit it with a local customs officer; (2) leave it with a local marina operator; or (3) mail it from the United States after your return.

Both the United States and the Bahamian governments render service on weekdays. Overtime charges may be made in off-hours and on weekends. Both may also make a "transportation" charge.

It is necessary to "enter" the United States. The yellow flag should be flown (requesting pratique), whereupon the boarding officer will check out the crew and cargo, check for aliens and for illegal or prohibited cargo (more than one quart of liquor per person aboard, drugs, some pets, certain agricultural species, etc.). There is no charge save as before noted. You may then lower the quarantine flag and proceed; you have officially entered and rejoined your homeland.

U.S. Customs offices are at the following ports:

Miami	In Government Cut, Miami Beach (near sea entrance, north side) or at Miamarina.
Fort Lauderdale-Miami	Bakers Haulover Cut, at marina, inside entrance, north side of channel.
Fort Lauderdale	Pier 66 Marina; or other nearby marinas.
West Palm Beach	Anchor off in turning basin or call 844-4393 from any marina or dock.
Fort Pierce	Stop at any marina, or the Coast Guard wharf, and call Customs. An officer will arrive dockside.

Very helpful in the matter of customs, as well as many other matters, is the Florida Marine Patrol, readily reached by radio or shore phone along the entire Gold Coast (Miami to Jensen Beach).

Entering procedures are gradually changing so that it soon will not be possible to find and report in at an official dock or marine station. Rather, the vessel may proceed to any local marina and tie up, and the skipper calls the immigration office. An officer will shortly appear, via automobile, and check and issue immediate entry permission if all is well. Miami already has its Miamarina, a facility at the inshore end of Government Cut, where any yacht may tie up, briefly and at no charge, for the purpose of entering.

If in doubt, or in trouble, radiophone the nearest office (the same ones called to request a clearing officer) as follows:

Miami	350-4334
Fort Lauderdale	525-7575
West Palm Beach	844-4393
Fort Pierce	461-1200
Key West	296-5411

(*Note:* the nearer you are to a Customs office, as listed before, the faster an officer will arrive. Check locations against chart and your immediate plans.)

If you plan to seek out docks for your stay in the islands, here is a current list (1976). Be warned, however: a great many yachtsmen have displayed displeasure at the high dockage rates charged by many of these marinas and clubs. In fact, they have avoided them in such numbers, by anchoring out, that not a few have had to shut down operations. Do not be surprised to see some abandoned and closed down. (Those already closed are not included in this list.)

ABACO CAYS

Walkers Cay
Green Turtle Cay, White Sound
Treasure Cay
Man of War Cay
Hopetown, Elbow Cay
White Sound, Elbow Cay
Cooperstown, Great Abaco
Marsh Harbour, Great Abaco

ANDROS

Nicholls Town
Fresh Creek
Mangrove Cay
Mastic Point
Lisbon Creek

BERRY ISLANDS

Great Harbour Cay
Chub Cay

THE BIMINIS

North Bimini
South Bimini

CAT CAY

CAT ISLAND

Bennetts Harbour
Smiths Bay
The Bight
Hawks Nest Creek

ELEUTHERA

The Current
Hatchet Bay
Rock Sound
Cape Eleuthera
Davis Harbour

HARBOUR ISLAND

SPANISH WELLS

EXUMA CAYS

Highborne Cay
Normans Cay
Sampson Cay
Staniel Cay
George Town, Great Exuma

GRAND BAHAMA

West End
Freeport/Lucaya Area
Deep Water Cay

LONG ISLAND

Stella Maris
Salt Pond ·
Clarence Town

NASSAU, NEW PROVIDENCE

RUM CAY

SAN SALVADOR

Cockburn Town

THE DRY TORTUGAS

While not "foreign," an excellent training cruise for the Bahamas or other open-water cruising is a mini-cruise to the Dry Tortugas, technically part of Florida. The passage is much the same as to the Bahamas, the ocean clear and blue and very tropical. The seven islands of the group are much like those of the Bahamas. There is top fishing, excellent snorkeling, and bird-watching. On the largest island (Garden Key) stands ancient Fort Jefferson, now a national park. There is a large dock, a good anchorage, and a welcome from the park rangers. This is a favorite anchorage for shrimpers out of Gulf ports. It is only about 70 miles out of Naples, Florida, and a little less from Key West, via the Marquesas Channel. It may prove wise indeed to test out both boat gear and the crew with a short cruise to these lovely islands. Chart 585 (11438) is the correct one for this venture.

MEXICO

Our only other handy-by foreign cruise is to Mexico. However, it's a long, rather dreary trek around the Gulf Coast and into Mexican waters (well over 1,200 miles). Across the Gulf, it's about 400 miles, but there's a smart chance

Fort Jefferson, a National Park in the Dry Tortugas, Fla. (Florida Department of Commerce)

of foul weather or utter calm . . . bad sailing for a sailer and almost too far for a powerboat. By and large, there is almost no American yacht travel to Mexico's east coast, and few local residents own pleasure boats. As a result, the region is not yet ready for the boat-borne tourist. The nearest Mexican area, via the Ditch route around the Gulf Coast, is highly industrialized (Tampico, Vera Cruz) and boasts scarcely a single resort port. Moreover, it is flat and sandy, has few natural anchorages and no marinas, and the so-called Mexican waterway is shallow and largely unimproved. As in the rest of Mexico, the fuel is foul, of frighteningly low octane, and quite expensive. Diesel is not considered "good" unless it smokes! Further, there are few if any waterside fueling stations. In some fishing ports, diesel may be found, but there is almost no gasoline. It is necessary to arrange (sometimes by sign language) for a truck to service the boat and, understandably, the local people are not overjoyed at the prospect of selling 35 gallons of their scarce gasoline in this way.

Hardy souls do cruise in Mexican waters, usually offshore, with self-supported stops in a few colorful areas, mostly in the south and the Yucatan. But there is just no cruising of the type that is accepted as natural and enjoyable in Florida and the Bahamas.

Chapter 8
The Boat

It would be utter folly for me to specify the exact boat for *you*—even if you would follow the advice—for a boat is a different critter to every individual. And this is as it should be. Further, few people buy a boat for the waterway life; they either own one designed for other types of nautical life or pick up a used one that is, basically, somebody else's idea of a boat and may never have been intended for extended life aboard. I have never heard of an architect's being commissioned to design a craft for live-aboard uses to the exclusion of all other uses; nor does it require an architect, for the ideal live-aboard boat already exists in great numbers, readily available to all; namely, the common garden variety of houseboat.

For creature comforts, use of space, cost, there is no better type. For dual use—that is, to cruise offshore, make long passages to and from a northern home base, ride out a hurricane—there is no worse type. To be sure, houseboats do these things, and in safety and comfort, just as salty deep-sea vessels remain dock-bound for months with winter live-aboards. But then all vessel design is a compromise among the many factors that go into "design." I venture to say that there can be no such animal as a 100 percent ideal live-aboard boat. The specifications change with personalities, budgets, location, weather changes, cruising needs, draft, future and present plans, and health, among other things. Thus the ideal boat to live aboard may well be a dog at sea, or incapable of creature comforts in port, or too deep or too slow.

The selection of the ideal boat starts not with the boat itself but with a carefully thought-out set of creature demands that the proposed boat must

110

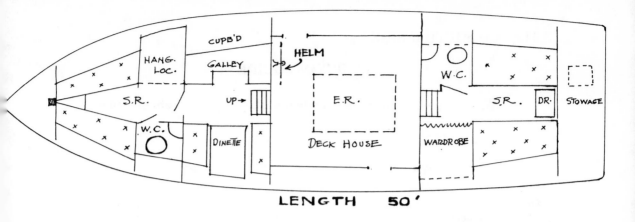

LENGTH 50'

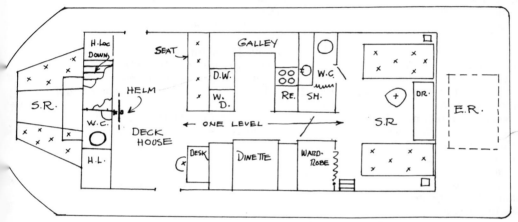

LENGTH 42'

Both these craft—a conventional displacement cruiser 50 feet long and a typical houseboat only 42 feet long—have the same accommodations. The houseboat is on one level save a guest stateroom in the bows. The cruiser has three levels, and two of them are deep in the hull. The deckhouses (living areas) are the same in both designs. The houseboat has a spacious galley with dishwasher, washer-dryer, and 12-foot refrigerator-freezer. Note engine room locations: one in living area, the other aft and away from living areas. There is unlimited outdoor lounge and sunning space on the houseboat, almost none on the cruiser. If new, the cruiser would, in diesel, cost three to 3½ times as much as the houseboat.

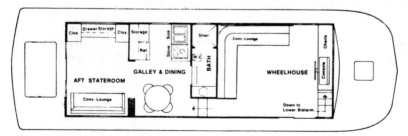

A typical houseboat accommodation, in the Burnscraft fiberglass 43-footer. She sleeps six in separate spaces, has shower, separate galley area, walkaround decks, and lots of main deck outdoor living space. She also has large sundeck and optional flying bridge. A variety of power options and sizes are available.

BUYING GUIDE

What to seek, what to avoid when looking for a live-aboard boat

VITAL

Full headroom (6 ft. 6 in. min.)
Walk-around decks
Berths at least:
   single, 33″ x 78″
   double, 54″ x 78″
Shower
Heat (winter)
Air conditioning (summer)
110 AC & 12 DC electrical circuits
Combination refrigeration: 110 AC, 12 DC,
   LP gas (any two)
Overhead insulation (main deck)
Shatterproof for'd glass areas
Ventilation system
Galley exhaust system
Hot water system
Insect protection
Sunning and lounge areas
Adequate stowage space

AVOID

Conversions
Experimental designs, layouts
Antiques and classics
Amateur ferrocement hulls
Underpower (a "dog")
Overpower (a "splasher")
Wooden decks (except teak)
Canvas sails, awnings, etc.
Extreme draft (5 ft.+)
The boat you can't afford
Uninsurable boats

IMPORTANT

TV-hifi center
Large refrigerator (10 ft.+)
Oven
Vacuum cleaner
Curtains
Dining table for entire crew
Seating space for entire crew
Lounging space for entire crew
Shoreside electrical and water hook-up
   systems
Protection for valuables
Security systems (locks, etc.)

NICE TO HAVE

Flying bridge
Fireplace
Swim platform
Auxiliary fuel tankage
Auxiliary water tankage
Dinghy (and davits)
Deck awning(s)
Double sink
Radio (CB and/or VHF)
Two or more heads
Electric heads
Generator
Diesel power
Glass or aluminum construction
Phone connection (dockside)

fulfill or be a failure, no matter how well built, how fast, or how good a bargain. Below are the minimal factors that should be the subject of honest research and pre-action conference:

1. The boat *must* be able, in terms of sea-ability, to negotiate safely *all* the waters in which you propose to sail her, whether these be waters you must traverse in the to-and-from passages or waters in which you propose to cruise during your "stay."

2. The boat must be able to sleep, in solid comfort, every member of the ship's company and guests, and have adequate wardrobes and stowage space for all hands.

3. The boat must be able to accommodate every member at the dining table and in living and lounging areas, and also have sufficient numbers of heads and showers for all hands.

4. The boat must have sufficient small boats (dinghy, liferaft, inflatable boat, in any combination).

5. She must have the ability to be space-heated in winter and possibly air-conditioned in summer.

6. She must have adequate means of preparing and storing food.

There are many other things that the ideal boat should have, but unless the above six requirements are satisfied, the boat will be a disappointment and unfit for the purpose of the purchase.

Some of the borderline items much to be desired—and possibly spelling the difference between success and failure as a live-aboard boat—are the following: reliable, safe power, including diesel and twin screws. Communication (VHF, CB, and SSB, with ship-to-shore facilities). Space for everybody, and space for luggage, scuba gear, folk guitar, clothing, kite, books—for of these things is living made. Full headroom for the tallest, together with a berth long enough for him. Opportunity to live outdoors, in shade, and possibly with insect protection. Means to combat emergencies (fire, fume removal, deck leaks). Privacy—a place on board that is invasion-proof. A basic plan, an organization of talent and brawn, geared to the greatest good for the greatest number, with work watches specified and scheduled; plus an acknowledged leader (not necessarily the owner of the boat). Utterly compatible ship's company, preferably pretested.

It is now evident that considerations anything but physical deeply determine vessel design. Perhaps this helps to explain why, in the ever-changing accents as the ship's uses are changed (i.e., from dockside living to waterway cruising, to ocean racing to ocean passagemaking, etc., etc.), there is no such thing as an ideal boat. It brings us back to the houseboat. Houseboats are available as stock boats, in endless combinations of accommodations, speeds, power options, as the ideal boat to live on *tied to a dock.* They are perfectly capable of local cruises, in fair weather; or up and down the Ditch. They may *not* be safe at sea, or in northern waters out of season; or even wanted for use, say, in Nova Scotia in September.

It is all a matter of this delicate balance of all the factors both required and desired in an ideal live-aboard boat.

Possibly the best we can achieve in stock designs are the so-called trawler types, though a trawlerman would vomit if he had to go to sea in some of them! These are followed by the splashers, those big glass boats that plane at high, noisy speeds and look like anything but a proper boat. But they do indeed have very roomy and rather wonderful living accommodations.

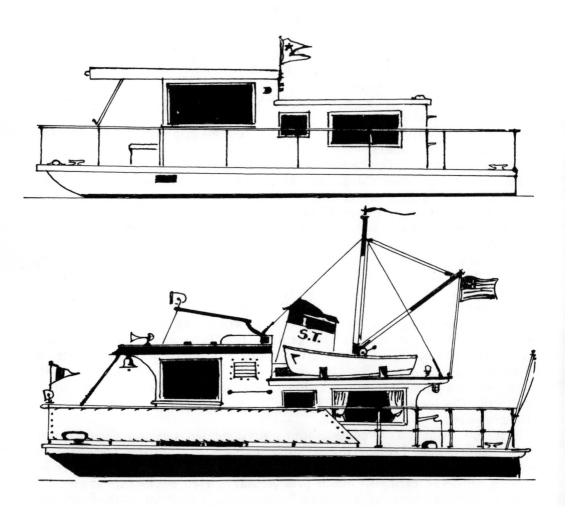

AN ANSWER TO THE TRADITIONALIST

The stock houseboat does not have to be plain and ugly. A little imagination, some talent, and $1,000 will improve even a little 32-footer. This houseboat has the accommodations of a 42-foot trawler yet costs one-fourth as much, has superior live-aboard features, and cruises nearly as well on inland waters. Army Engineers and the Coast Guard operate vessels of this character and flavor. In a 45- or 50-foot size, such an apology to nautical design can result in a superb character vessel with unbeatable accommodations.

Thus, if you are in the market for either a new or a used boat, you should look for a solution, or a partial solution, to your demands of houseboats, trawlers, or wide, roomy "family" stock boats. If the basics are there (items 1, 2, and 3 previously listed), the others might be added.

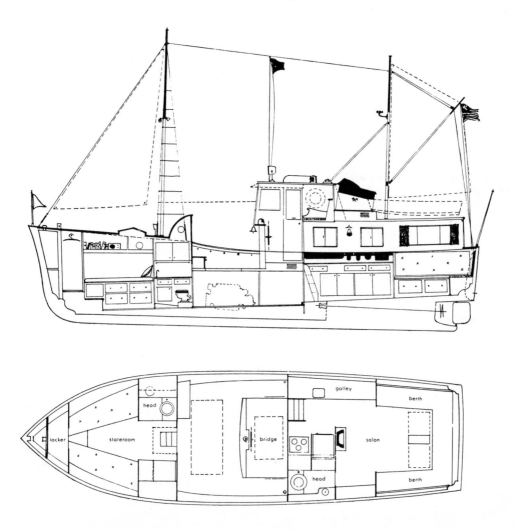

This is a fine "character" trawler affording private owner's stateroom and space for four guests if after berths are installed as uppers and lowers. She is designed for long winter vacations for two, with space for individual privacy. Note two heads, separate shower stall, generous hanging wardrobes, entertainment center in after lounge, fireplace (Franklin stove), and he-man's wheelhouse and bridge. She has walkaround decks, a midship well-deck (à la trawler) with reefing awning rigged over it, and can fly enough canvas to sail downwind. She is a single-screw diesel-powered boat, with 600-gallon fuel capacity, and cruises at 10 knots at 5.5 GPH. While only 42 feet long, her generous 13'6" beam provides exceptionally spacious quarters. She has a large hold under the wheelhouse for luggage and all the gear needed for long-term onboard living.

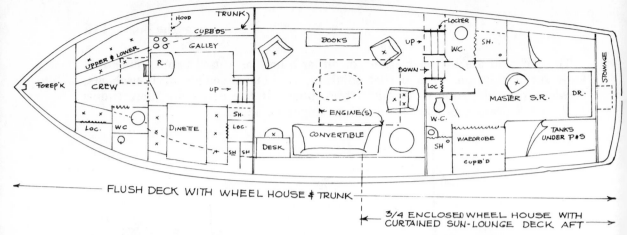

FLUSH DECK WITH WHEEL HOUSE & TRUNK

3/4 ENCLOSED WHEEL HOUSE WITH CURTAINED SUN-LOUNGE DECK AFT

This common stock layout in 45- to 50-footers meets most requirements of a live-aboard couple. Guests are accommodated in crew quarters or in the main saloon, using a convertible and "guest" bath. There are generous living areas; a fixed dining area with fixed table and benches; a fine galley; space to entertain in the saloon or in the large outdoor lounge; and a completely private master stateroom and bath—all vital. In slightly larger lengths, some stock boats offer, just forward of the master stateroom, a small guest cabin and head. By judicious "stealing," this is managed with a length increase of only about six feet and no power change.

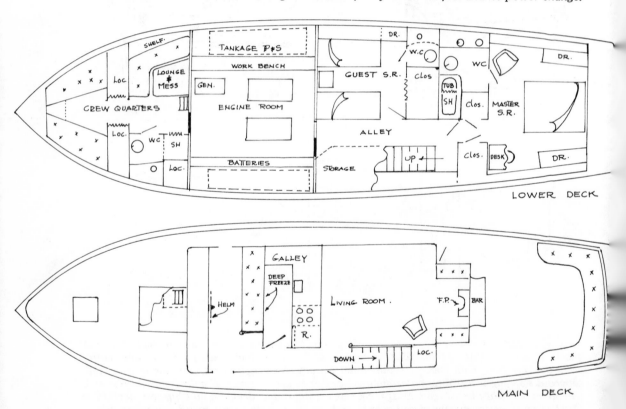

LOWER DECK

MAIN DECK

A typical accommodation plan for a two-decker, one of the best live-aboard types in the 60-to-80-feet, $300,000+ category. Some have two guest staterooms below and a convertible in the deckhouse. A crew is almost a necessity just to keep up with daily ship's chores, for these deluxe yachts are garnished with much varnish work, chrome, plate glass, and large teak deck expanses.

For the person who wants to sail, there is a wide choice of quite roomy, able boats...but very few of them in ordinary sizes have civilized accommodations for more than four people; and few can accommodate children on a long-term basis. Probably the most spacious is the Chinese junk, but there are few worse sailers, or investments. The really big wind boats have difficulty finding deep-water dockage and anchorage. The medium-sized sailers, utilizing a centerboard (quaintly called a swing keel in the South), sacrifice the very space they need for shallow draft to a trunk...and come out about even.

Actually, there is little opportunity to sail the Waterway in anything much above 40 feet on deck and a normal six foot draft; both spar height and draft usually will dictate an offshore passage. A 40-foot sailing boat has the accommodations of a 30-foot powerboat—not very spacious or comfortable, save for a couple who never have guests; or who only have the kids down for Christmas. Yet the sailboat people seem a very experienced group, many quite Spartan, and they are willing to trade some creature comforts for values they consider important.

Increasing in popularity is the so-called motorsailer, a fat cruiser type with accommodations equal to a straight powerboat (and a hull that is neither fish nor fowl) and a moderate sail rig that might satisfy the sailor if he doesn't seek speed or racing ability. These, in the double-cabin or center-cockpit editions (often with below-decks communicating alleyways between cabins), make quite passable live-aboard boats, their chief lack being sun and weather protection above decks. They do, however, disappoint the man who appreciates a well-balanced, lively sailboat, and they are quite sluggish to windward because of the excessive beam and depth necessary for living accommodations.

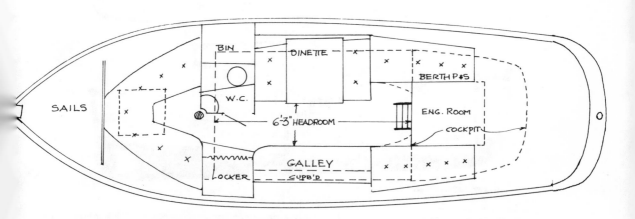

This 43-foot cruising sloop demonstrates how little live-aboard space exists on sailing vessels. She has a pitiful 26 square feet of cabin floor in which one can stand upright! Both sleeping compartments lack headroom and must almost be crawled into. She is by no means an extreme example; few sailing craft under 60 feet can produce much better, save the so-called motorsailers, and very few of these can sail the way a true wind sailor wants them to.

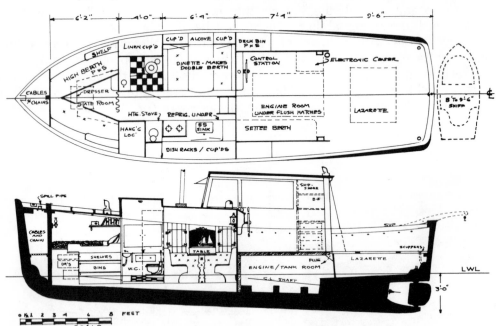

This 36-footer is about the smallest-size boat practical for four persons to live aboard—and two should be temporary guests! She is powered by a single 135-hp 6-cylinder diesel and uses 3.9 GPH at cruising speed of 9.2 knots. She has full headroom throughout, a fine wheelhouse with full weather protection (via a draw curtain aft), and generous "outdoor" living space and fishing cockpit. While the sparring is mainly for "flavor," a steadying sail can be carried as when on an ocean passage. Note heating stove, generous main hatch, ample stowage spaces, and many small bows to comfortable long-term living. Small as she is, there are several of this model annually making the long cruise from New England to the Southland.

Living space on all boats is composed of length, beam, and depth, forming volume. Length is the only component of the volume formula that costs money, since dockage, hauling, and taxes are reckoned in terms of length. Therefore it may be of importance to some to search out the ideal boat on the basis of length, for an extra length charge per month and per year can run up costs considerably. Here, again, the houseboat comes nearest to solving the problem.

The notion that living space may be gained in the multihulls (catamarans, trimarans) without an increase in length is not very sound. There are also other and rather serious objections to these types for live-aboard craft. First, the gained spaces are small, not one of them large enough to accommodate *all* the people the boat will sleep. Nor is there a table large enough to permit the full crew to dine at the same time. This may be acceptable for a weekend cruise, but not for an entire winter afloat. Other objections are: Difficulty in arranging above-deck living spaces, or providing insect protection. Difficulty in heating (or cooling) two or three separated "cabins." The need for constant climbing up and down, in and out, in getting about the complete ship. Dockmasters often refuse to take in multihulls; they just take up too much space. Or else they may require double dockage (at double prices, of course). Further, they seldom need much, if any, fuel, so there is little opportunity for dockmasters to "make a buck." Better to save the dock for a straight powerboat that might buy 300 gallons of fuel! This is no indictment of the multihull boat, merely the suggestion that it is far, far from a satisfactory live-aboard craft.

Now, if sailing is the accent: if fast, thrilling, riding the wind is the all-essential factor, then you should settle for a cat or a tri by all means. The novice probably should stay away from the type. It takes considerable know-how and experience to skipper a multihull successfully, especially at sea. (Actually, and as a note, I have the feeling that the popularity of the type has diminished a great deal since it was first introduced some 15 years ago. Multihulls remain with us as small, sporty afternoon sailers—Hobie cats, for example. Many cruising types have disappeared from the stock-boat market, and they are difficult to sell as used boats—all due to what I consider inherent clumsiness in accommodations and to a long history of structural failure at sea.)

I am sure that all these comments have left you confused and a bit confounded, for they have offered little of concrete value that will help you to select the ideal boat. They have, rather, suggested what you should *not* buy. More than many things in life, a boat is a compromise all the way. Boatbuilders, naval architects, and the used-boat markets can provide us with suitable boats that meet *most* of our needs afloat. We can, within reason, make alterations or additions to the physical plant. If we need to sleep four, there is no great problem. However, just *how* we sleep them can become a major problem and ruin an entire winter. The sleepers must be carefully analyzed and their habits and preferences considered and given weight in

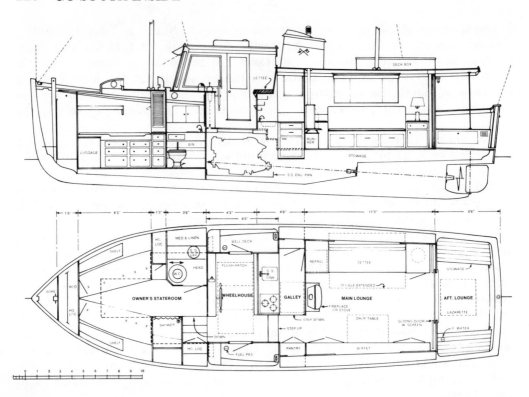

This 40-foot "character" cruiser has been the author's home in the Southland for nine years and leaves nothing to be desired . . . for TWO people. There are generous accommodations for temporary guests or family members via a convertible in the deck lounge. The "head" is available to both sleeping areas, since there is a louvered door between the forward stateroom and the stair landing area. Most-appreciated features include the settee in the wheelhouse, the wheelhouse itself (a genuine ship-style navigation center uncluttered by other cruise or living features, such as galley, berths, etc.), the fine after living lounge and adjoining "back porch," large enough to entertain in, fish from, or loaf in. The stack conceals three LP gas bottles. There are generous deck boxes for stowage. The mizzen carries a small steadying sail for ocean cruising and crossing the Gulf Stream. She has walkaround decks, carries her 9-foot glass dinghy over stern horn davits, and handles anchors with an electric winch and short anchor sprit. She draws only 38 inches at the heel, has a completely protected wheel and rudder, and has a full-molded hull of traditional Maine model for a steaming speed of 10 knots. Were she to be built today, the author would install a small generator (since anchoring out is now the way to go), build the hull of strip-planking covered with grass (her deck and houses are glass), place the refrigerator outboard of the galley space and use recovered space in the main cabin for TV and hi-fi. He would also increase tankage from 240 gallons to about 500 for buying fuel at quantity discounts and avoiding high fuel costs of the U.S. Gold Coast and the Bahamas.

reaching as near the ideal as possible. I can sleep in a narrow quarter berth, without a reading light, in a sleeping bag sans linen, my clothing bundled into a wad on the deck beside me—but damned if I'm going to sleep like that all winter! I'm sure that I'd become a nasty old man, make life miserable for all hands, and jump that ship fast. Yet all I want is six inches more berth width, a little bulkhead lamp to read by (because I *always* read in bed before corking off), a sheet or two and a clean blanket, and, handy-by, a hanging closet or wardrobe. Is that asking too much? I'm sure that such a boat could have been found had my preference been taken seriously and not discounted as I grabbed at some other feature—such as a "bargain" price, or speed, or a nice color on the topsides. Too late, I realized that I had not placed all the factors in realistic perspective; I had failed to recognize that I wasn't going on a weekend club race-cruise but was going to live for months and months on this boat, my only home.

This is all-important, this careful weighing of personalities and individual habits and preferences . . . quite as important as the powerplant, the boat's age and condition, and the cost. Of course, these too will be subject to compromise, but they cannot be completely brushed under the rug. You can live aboard a boat with painted decks just as well as on one with teak decks, but you can't live aboard at all if your bunk is six feet long and you are six feet six inches tall! Or if there is no room for Susan's high chair. Or if your wife has no oven, no hot water, only a two-burner stove, and limited fresh water. All these trivia, in terms of people and personalities and life habits, must be considered, or the life afloat may be doomed before you put any blue water under your keel.

Of course, you are not going to find the ideal boat. You are not even going to have it if you design it from scratch. All you will find is somebody else's

The author's live-aboard vessel, a 40-foot "one man" boat with a single diesel for 10-knot cruising speed at 4.8 GPH fuel consumption.

Above and below: *After living cabin of the author's vessel. Floor measurement is 9 by 13 and provides comfortable living for two to four. Convertible sofa makes guest double. Opposite is folding table for four with chair stowage outboard of it. The stove burns briquettes, stowed in bunker beneath. Note writing desk and screened wide doorway to after lounge deck.*

notion of an ideal boat . . . for them! You will have to compromise, and the plea in these paragraphs is that you place correct and realistic values on your needs and demands *as people*, and compromise the least with these. You can re-engine, or repaint, or alter and fuss on the boat, but you cannot change people without unhappiness, opposition, and defeat. Eventually you will see and understand what is wrong with your boat in terms of you (wife, family, guests). Why not make the effort to reduce the risk, even obviate it, by careful, sane selection of the boat now?

Boatbuilders, like car manufacturers, will swamp you with "literature." They will show you sister ships, give you demonstration rides, arrange financing, take trades, sell you insurance. It is not at all difficult to buy a boat.

Naval architects will design you a boat, presumably the ideal boat for you and your needs. This will cost a great deal more than the "stock" boat; and it will take a great deal more time to be built than everybody assured you it would take.

Used-boat markets are maintained by all dealers in stock boats (their trade-ins, of course)—not only their own brand, but others as well. In addition, there are huge used-boat markets in numerous areas of the country; these are accessible through direct contact with owners via the classified columns or in yachting journals, and also via yacht brokers, as selling agents for the owners.

You can also build a boat, preferably from the designs of an *experienced* naval designer (as distinguished from those nice chaps with facile pencils who seldom see their "designs" actually built), or from a kit, or from a completed hull that "you finish up."

New boats carry a "floor" price. You usually pay for delivery from the plant, sometimes a "dealer's prep" charge, in most states a sales tax. You can usually count on another 10 percent for "extras," which include electronics, air conditioning, compass, dinghy, fenders, second anchors and their tackle, cradle—plus furniture, deck chairs, possibly drapes and carpets, engine spares and tools, TV and hi-fi, etc. If you have no trade-in, it is often possible to coax the dealer into furnishing much of this "extra" gear. He works on about a 25 percent markup, and on a high-tag model he can well afford to meet you on price. He usually does this of his own volition; indeed, he would be staggered if you failed to "deal." Fear not; he's ready for it and you.

Naval architects work on a flat 10 percent fee (of the contract price) for the drawings and specifications of a new boat concept. If it is a "file" design (one that he has built before) and requires no deep original engineering, he will adjust the fee downward. If *no* changes are required, he may well ask a very nominal fee. If the architect is required to inspect the work as it progresses, to guide the builder, to prepare supplementary drawings, he will make additional charges, including traveling time and costs. The trick in such an arrangement is to achieve and maintain absolute control over the situation; naval architects and boatbuilders are old associates and intend to keep it that way. Not many boats today are so built, and those that are, are in the quarter-million-dollar-and-up class.

Used boats make up the bulk of the market; there are thousands available. Most of them are quality boats, possibly weak in the cosmetics, but quite worth salvaging. You can save up to 75 percent over new boat prices. Unless you are a genuine professional, best leave the evaluation to others, especially in southern waters, which inflict their own local damages on boats.

Go see a broker, never forgetting that he knows little more about the boat offered than you do but will go out on a limb (but not in writing) to extol its glories. He will charge 10 percent of the selling price, payable by the seller, and a little less if the price reaches the $50,000-and-up bracket. You may look at the boat, talk to the owner, investigate and dig all you wish. You will not get a demonstration until you have posted a deposit, usually about 10 percent. At that time, a sales agreement is drawn up providing that you will pay the agreed-upon price (after offers and counter-offers, of course) if the boat meets her sea trials (performance, speed claimed, etc.) and passes her survey. If she fails these tests, or any portion of them, you may withdraw your offer and request return of the deposit. Brokers (who are controlled by state law in Florida at least) have placed your deposit in an approved escrow account (in no way accessible to the owner). Many are further regulated by membership in one of the many broker's associations, which discipline or expel shady members.

A survey is most emphatically recommended. This means calling in the professional, who goes over your proposed boat in every last detail . . . right down to a complete hull check and an engine and machinery survey; indeed, *everything* except an actual test run (which may also be arranged for with him). He submits a complete and detailed report, with recommendations. His charge is about one percent of the selling price, depending upon the number of engines, size, age, etc. It is then usual to consult with the broker and owner in an effort to have any deficiencies brought up to recommended standards at the seller's expense—or at least to that point of "as represented." Example: if a boat is represented as having "no rot" by broker or seller or the listing, there should be no rot. If there is, you can reasonably reject her or request that the seller remove the rot and bring the boat up to standard. About this time, the broker will suggest that you hold sea trials before the seller commits himself to the repair. Again, the surveyor can help here. The boat should be up to the speed claimed, the engine should turn the rated rpms, show the proper oil and other pressures, and completely satisfy you as to handling, maneuverability, seakeeping, etc. If you don't like the way she handles, don't take her . . . it's that simple. If you do take her, the seller must complete the work required by the survey, pay the bill, and you then complete the transaction and take over ownership.

Pay particular attention to claims of a free and clear title (check in the local courthouse) and promises to provide parts or services *after* closing the deal. Sign nothing until you have the check (less commission and with a sales tax receipt) in hand (and bank approval).

It is usual to attach to the bill of sale a full list of all the parts sold with the boat. Insist upon this, and check it against the inventory (small boats, sails, spars, tools, furniture, electronics, radio, TV, dishes, galley gear, heaters, spares, etc.). Sometimes the surveyor will do this as part of his job . . . and also evaluate the small parts.

This book can be of little use to those hardy souls who build their own boats from scratch or via a partially completed kit. If you are a skilled technician—an all-around one—go ahead. I suspect these chaps have quite as much fun building the boat as using her. By and large, home-built boats seem to look home-built. They lack the slight detail, the professional swing of a line, the seamanly treatment of the professionally designed and built craft. They never sell readily. Some are uninsurable, some unsafe. And they all cost—when eventually sold—as much as and more than a "real" boat. If this book discourages home-building of boats in the live-aboard size . . . great. Those who can build don't need this book; those who can't, shouldn't start.

No matter how you acquire the boat, she will present some basic problems. Wise evaluation of them, in the light of southern, winter, live-aboard use, with limited cruising, is the subject of the next sections.

DISPLACEMENT VS. PLANING HULLS

A displacement hull is one designed to be pushed through the water. It has refined, efficient lines, can be made an excellent and safe seaboat, and usually is available in realistic sizes quite able to accommodate spacious interior compartmentation for living areas. It has a terminal speed, usually in the seven- to 11-knot range, beyond which it can be driven only slightly, and with enormous additional power and fuel costs. Cruising sailboats of all rigs are displacement boats, quite able to use efficiently all the *wind* power presented but seldom able to move at more than terminal speeds. Retention of certain hull lines is essential to smart sailing and safety, and thus a sailer cannot be modified effectively to achieve more speed—save in very minor considerations reserved for the racing enthusiasts, and possibly by the addition of special sail rigs.

The powerboat can be improved upon by changing certain lines, usually at the entrance (bows) and the run (after sections), so that the boat partially lifts, or planes, as she is driven forward. This converts some of the forward pushing power into a lifting power and, since it is far easier to push a boat forward in air than in water, the boat, now lifted partially into the air, gains considerable speed. We now have a semi-planing boat. Basic lines have been changed to achieve and hold speed with power applied, and this change somewhat reduces seakeeping ability—within reason hardly dangerous, possibly slightly uncomfortable at times, but, nevertheless, a universal practice and not at all to be frowned upon.

Opposed to this concept is the full-planing type. This hull is very flat, with most of her seakindliness sacrificed to speed, and urged up (into the air) by enormous initial power, moves forward mostly in air and with a minimum of

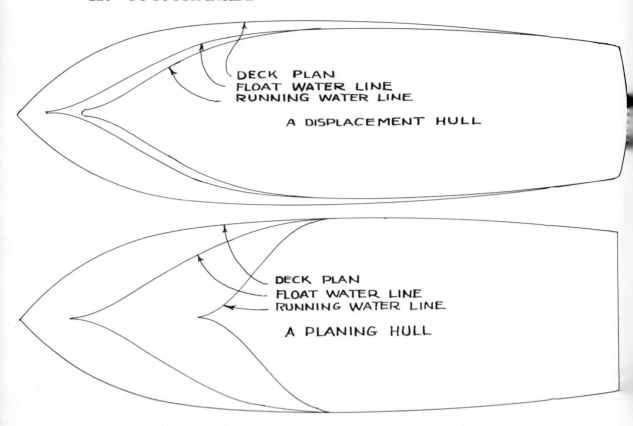

DECK PLAN
FLOAT WATER LINE
RUNNING WATER LINE

A DISPLACEMENT HULL

DECK PLAN
FLOAT WATER LINE
RUNNING WATER LINE

A PLANING HULL

The displacement hull (top) is a conventional cruiser form, level riding and a good round-bottom seaboat. It is economical of fuel, seakindly at any attitude, and can be driven only slightly beyond its theoretical "hull speed," usually 10 to 12 knots maximum. The planing hull is a chine type, using much of its power to reach a planing, lessened-immersion running attitude. It is not an ideal seaboat, though hardly dangerous. Because of much-reduced skin friction, it can be driven at high speeds by the application of appropriate and high power with consequent high fuel consumption. Twin engines usually are required. Note that the displacement hull while running retains a proper 1:3.5 length-beam ratio, while the planing type violates it rather drastically, reducing it to a 1:2 ratio.

water pushing, and then, even with power reduced, proceeds at dizzying speeds. The extremes of the type are the racing hydroplanes (110 mph) and the genuinely fast "commuter" cruisers (to 35 knots).

A great many modern stock cruisers are of this planing type for some sound reasons: i.e., ease of construction using sheet materials such as plywood, metal panels. Because of the flat bottoms, chine bilges, and excessively wide beam inherent in the type, it is easy to install preformed and prefitted accommodation units, achieving cost savings and economy of build. Further, a *fast boat* is the kind of boat most Americans, brought up in fast cars, want . . . and devil take the fuss-duddies who argue for safety at sea. (They contend that they

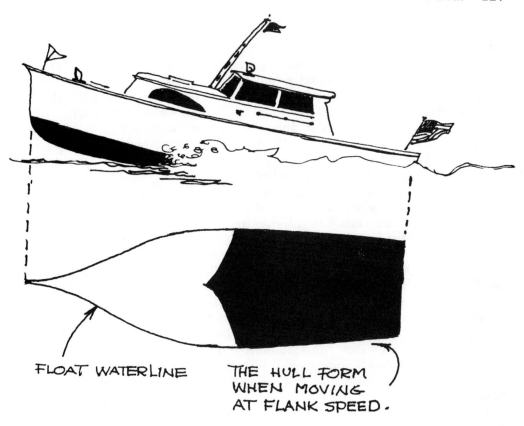

FLOAT WATERLINE   THE HULL FORM
                       WHEN MOVING
                       AT FLANK SPEED.

The importance of cruising attitude. This boat has a normal, if not ideal, hull form, and while meant to plane, fails utterly. The hull form under "squatting" conditions takes the form of the black area with a beam-length ratio of about 1.5:1. The ideal is 5:1; 3.5:1 is acceptable.

have the speed to beat dirty weather into port; the opposition contends that they haven't the wits or experience even to recognize dirty weather in time.) Meanwhile, not many boats are lost at sea.

There are some slight variations in hull types available (such as the Chesapeake cross-planked chine boats, tunnel-stern boats to achieve truly shallow drafts, the British "plank-on-edge" cutters, etc.), but all will fall into one of three basic categories. Which one will suit you is up to you entirely. You cannot help but be impressed by the spacious accommodations, wide decks, and unique layouts of the full-planing boats, and, if you do not plan to or need to navigate in extended open waters, there's nothing wrong with putting the emphasis on superior live-aboard features. The type will burn much more fuel, require much more engine maintenance work, shame you if you are a classic buff—but it certainly provides a beautiful platform for dockside living in comfort and style. Probably *most* cruisers afloat today conform to this style, and, therefore, investing your money in one isn't quite as risky as with some other types, particularly the multihull boats, junks, paddle-wheelers, and the like.

The sailboats for the most part represent the true displacement type; they *must* retain the ancient seakindly hull forms or risk poor or no performance. Planing sailboats there are, of course, but never in cruising sizes; there just isn't that much available power in a wind that would still permit safe sea conditions. The powerboats in this class are the semi-planers: sound, roomy boats able to run at 10 to 12 knots, at economical fuel-consumption rates . . . and at a lot less consumption at true displacement speeds in the eight- to nine-knot range. Motorsailers, the so-called trawlers (defined in the public's eye today as anything that isn't a Chris-Craft), and the old-time classics (Elco, Matthews, early Richardsons, and most custom boats before the 1950s) are all in this class. They, too, provide quite roomy accommodations but are apt to require much hand work to install the fitments (usually created right on board and in no way "stock") at considerable labor costs. Platforms and soles (cockpit decks and lower cabin floors, respectively) are apt to be smaller and narrower and not always have square corners.

No type should be selected for appearance, speed, or cost alone. The principal aim, obviously, is to live aboard in comfort, safety, and style. If, for example, selecting a planing boat because she has superior living possibilities in no way introduces other considerations (safety, economy, fuel consumption, investment) of relative importance, buy her. If you must annually cross the Bay of Fundy in October and May to reach the Southland, don't buy a planing type.

By observation, I conclude that most snow birds who have acquired a used boat for the specific purpose of living aboard in the South have chosen the displacement type. The full-planing types are boats already bought, for another location and another purpose, and pressed into winter service or multi-purpose boats (i.e., for sportfishing, corporate entertaining, status, or a true need for fast passagemaking). These displacement boats render maximum fuel efficiency at hull speed, and very modest at that (for example, 5 GPH diesel for a 40-footer at 8.5 knots; that's only $1.65 an hour or 20 cents a nautical mile). They give creature comforts equal to other types; and better than some. They fit the mood of the 1970s, with their high fuel costs, shortage scares, and general mistrust of the economy. They are definitely a safe investment as boats go. Like the compact car of the age, the displacement boats, the trawlers and motorsailers, are arriving fast.

Fuel-consumption tables will vary, of course, but they will work out something like this:

For a 40-foot cruiser, approx. weight 16,000 lbs.

Single Diesel	Displacement	Semi-displacement	Planing
Speed	8	10	14
GPH	4.5	6.2	11-12
Twin-Screw Diesel			
Speed	9	12	18-20
GPH	6	7.3	16+

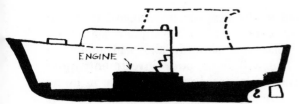 

Relative interior areas with six feet of headroom in two boats of exactly the same length, one power, one sail. Both boats are 45-footers, with 13 feet inside beam. The powerboat has 2,660 cubic feet of interior living space, all with at least six feet of headroom PLUS a generous weather-shielded deckhouse lounge. The sailboat has only 988 cubic feet of interior living space with the same headroom, plus a cuddy forward suitable for crawling into (for sleeping, storage), plus, of course, a small cockpit sans weather protection of any kind.

Gasoline would require higher gallonage as well as a higher cost per gallon. While it is true that the faster boat will cover more miles, the fact still remains that the *per mile* cost will exceed that of the slower boat by better than 50 percent. Further, fun and relaxation on the sea is measured in terms of time and not mileage. Why should you spend *more* money to get from it *less* time on the water? You have no need to rush, no need to pay a premium to arrive early.

In fairness to the subject, this needs to be added to the foregoing: *all* of these boats are misdesigned, and none satisfies the engineering formula for maximum speed, efficiency, and seakindliness. To achieve this, the hull must have a length-beam ratio of about 1:5 or 1:5.5, i.e., a waterline beam of about one-fifth of the waterline length. Thus, the ideal beam for a 50-footer would be 10 feet, and for a 40-footer only eight feet. Obviously, only quite crude accommodations can be worked into such narrow beams. If one adds, in these days, a strong insistence upon walk-around decks, requiring about five feet of beam amidships, one ends up with a house only an impractical three or four feet wide: utterly too narrow to accept wide berths, twin engines, dinettes, alcove arrangements for galleys, heads, and dressing rooms. The compromise with the length-beam formula seemingly is justified if there is an increase in pleasant, usable interior spaces; certainly it is far more livable than a layout somehow jammed into a long, narrow formula hull—an arrangement like the old railroad flats, in which no room had privacy and all spaces were, in fact, halls and communication alleys.

Yet there is a modern tendency to carry the compromise entirely too far by increasing beam still further for a relatively short length, by trying to increase midship accommodations by moving all engines and tanks into the stern and using V-drive units or outboard units, and by fattening up the entrance still more. The result is one of those horrible abominations that violate the basic rules of vessel aspect (or her appearance when running): one of those ships that stick the bow high in the air, dig the stern deep into the wake, send off dangerously high (and very expensive!) quarter waves (wake), and often require correction in the form of "trim tabs," literally wing flaps, which are supposed to raise the stern, depress the bow, and make the boat perform as she would if properly designed in the first place. I suggest that you not become tempted by one of these (discovered only by complete sea trials). She will cost, fuelwise, far beyond what she should; she will make an enormous fuss but not really go fast; she will be a poor investment; quite probably, she will open you up to considerable derision and ridicule in home waters . . . and someday she will throw you and all your deck gear right off the stern and into the drink.

Unhappily, there are producers deliberately specializing in this type of boat, winning novice sailors with admittedly generous accommodation plans and most irresponsibly saddling them with other deep, dangerous, and fatal characteristics that only experienced seamen could possibly know about. Any naval architect or conscientious yacht broker can advise . . . if he is willing to be that honest and brave. As a novice, then, beware of the boats that do not ride on a substantially level keel; the ones that sport antisquatting devices, themselves costly and thieves of much forward power; the ones that seem to throw unduly huge wakes (viewed from off the boat!); the ones that have engines in the stern; and those that have a length-beam ratio of less than 3:1. We go back to the common garden variety of houseboat . . . still the best balanced design if seakeeping is not the dominant requirement.

DIESEL VS. GASOLINE POWER

The day of the gasoline engine in large boats has passed. No one can afford it and no one can buy a gasoline engine of sufficient power to move today's cruisers, even slowly. Twin engines do *not* double the power. They move it upward somewhat, each taking the strain from the other—say, 30 percent as an average—and they produce a feeling of safety in case of one engine failure. And they drive up the fuel cost by at least 75 percent. Maneuverability is increased and quite possibly could be an advantage in certain situations, but not many. A single engine and a spring line will still do quite as well as double screws for true boatmen.

There are not many true marine gas engines available today. Small ones, up to 50 HP or so, are available for auxiliary sailboat power. All others are automobile blocks (with thin walls and automotive accessories), to which has been added a power clutch, reduction gear, thrust bearing, and water-cooled exhaust risers. Stock boatbuilders use these engines to keep down offering costs, and the builders usually specify inadequate power for the same reason. Unlike the automobiles for which they were designed, these engines pound out full, continuous horsepower every second on the run; they have no respite on downgrades or when coasting or slowing. Pound, pound, pound with the throttle in the corner, tight as she'll go all the time; that's marine use. No wonder they give up after a few hundred hours of use. And no wonder stock boatbuilders try desperately to switch the buyer up to either twin-screw gas power or diesel power. They know from sad experience that auto engines won't take it.

To be sure, small boats using inboard-outboard rigs still use gasoline power, and so do a few million outboard boats, but these are not fully found 40- and 50-foot cruisers, lugging a complete home for four or eight around the globe.

The trend toward diesel power is no longer caused by a desire to save fuel costs, though there still is a saving. But it takes a good many sea miles to make up the considerable difference in cost between gas and diesel plants. Few pleasure boats can ever make it up. However, in the diesel the modern yachtsman finds the really hefty, rugged plant that can serve him reliably for years; he buys it truly because there is no other suitable power for his modern needs. He is not disappointed; diesel *is* power.

In the diesel he has, first of all, a heavy, tested *industrial* power unit designed to move trucks and drill wells and dig trenches and pump liquids—not a lightweight auto engine designed for intermittent duty. He has tried-and-true auxiliaries, batteries, power trains, pumps, coolers, and injection systems. Incidentally, he gets away from the risk of explosion. Practically, he gets more ergs of power from a gallon of fuel that is somewhat cheaper than gasoline; he gets better "mileage." His overhauls are far less frequent. He has few running adjustments. Most diesel engines can be rebuilt in fairly simple processes, without undue cost or time wasted, and they seldom require deep overhaul under 10,000 hours. Above all, the yachtsman has reliable power, perfectly capable of delivering almost top output hour after hour and in no way requiring a "twin" engine to assist in attaining normal cruising speeds.

These are the reasons that the modern cruising man has gone not only to diesel power, but to a single engine again. It is becoming increasingly difficult to sell "gas" boats in the larger sizes; almost the entire pleasure fleet has been dieselized. These are excellent reasons why you, too, should go to single diesel.

The entire seaboard offers superior diesel service, due, of course, to the pioneering commercial users. Parts, dealers, and service are found in every port that supports a tugboat or two. If not, the tractor people are equipped to bring a complete machine shop to your boatside with service on your *exact* engine and model. This is not usually true of the gasoline engine service people; you are apt to wind up in a back-lot garage with your engine problems.

By all means, insist upon diesel power. It will almost guarantee a winter free of engine troubles.

SINGLE SCREW VS. TWIN SCREW

The gas-powered boat almost *requires* the relief of a second engine to share the enormous strain of continuous full-performance operation. Further, the single engine is utterly vulnerable to abrupt failure under the usual loads demanded, and a second engine could be a life-saver. Few twin-screw (TS) boats handle well under a single engine because of tiny rudders and off-center power application, but they can, *in extremis*, be brought to safety by one engine. Costs will multiply rapidly with a second engine, due partly to the necessity of carrying the additional weight of engine number 2, its batteries, tanks and fuel, power train, shaft, wheel, etc. Much of the extra power is used to carry the extra power! This is true, of course, whether the engine is gas or diesel.

The diesel plant, properly selected for the job to be done, can handle the load on a single engine; that's the kind of work the engine has been built for. There is no need, from a performance standpoint, to add a second engine. To obtain maneuverability, or as a safety precaution, a second engine may be justified in some cases. Not too many large cruisers have twin-screw plants; the really large ones (90 feet and up) have two and sometimes three engines for sound engineering reasons, and this in no way affects them as efficient cruisers. Presumably, this is not the province of this book.

There is no doubt that a TS boat can be maneuvered in tight situations, singlehandedly, better than a single-screw (SS) boat. The SS boat will tend to turn one way better than the other, which limits maneuvering in small quarters (as at docks or basin corners). This can be readily and swiftly controlled by "working" two props; indeed, a TS boat, handled by an experienced hand, using wind and tide, can literally *do anything.* This, conceivably, might be a sound reason to opt for a twin-screw boat. Believe me, however for straight steaming with reliability, economy, and freedom from worry, the single diesel is the correct answer.

A further consideration of the problem—that of vulnerability—is not to be dismissed lightly. Twin screws do not huddle safely behind a solid four- or six-inch deadwood and above a long, strong keel. They stick out into the quarters, like fans, exactly the same as the propellors of a "prop" plane. Shallow water is their enemy. So are coral heads, found in the Keys and the Bahamas. And so is driftwood. Those huge piles of trees, roots, snags, and timber encountered so frequently along the dug canal stretches of the Ditch are driftwood gathered and grounded by the several U.S. Army "snag" boats that operate year-round on the Waterway. Miles and miles of the Southland yield wood for the manufacture of paper pulp—cut on the spot into four- and eight-foot-long logs. These are piled to overflowing on the pulp barges, common from mid-North Carolina to Florida, and X-number on every voyage manage to fall into the water—to be sloshed back and forth until recaptured by the snag boat. Meanwhile, they lurk in wait for yachts. Oh, single-screw boats tick them occasionally, but twin-screw boats don't just tick; they gulp in the entire log, jam it between hull, strut, the wheel, and bottom, and something, obviously, must give. It is never the log.

A common reason given for the high cost of marine insurance is that of losses due to twin-screw damage, which is usually deep and involves the shaft and hull as well. I know of boats that "bang up" four sets of wheels and shafts every passage up or down—usually operated by those heavy-footed chaps who insist upon open sea speed even in the narrow Ditch. So this, in addition to other factors, is sound reason to compare sensibly the alleged advantages of "twin screws."

HULL MATERIAL

Alas, the traditional wooden boat has joined the dodo bird. It's even difficult to buy a new one today! For the cruiser thinking in terms of Florida and the tropics this is not bad news, for there is no hull more vulnerable to the nasty eatin' worms of the South than a wooden one. So let us shed a tear ... lovely, beautiful hulls they were, like beloved antique furniture, with the patina of age and the loving marks of hand tools, the hulls of Farragut and John Paul Jones, and ... shucks; *fiberglass is better,* so there.

There is glass and there is glass. Laid up; thick; well-braced; bulkheads and gussets bonded in; plenty of roving; a true, heavy "gel" coat outside; and expensive (even more than wood!) ... it's fine. Thin; shoddy; obviously slapped together; applied color (meaning painted on); no gel; little roving; see-through capability; large surfaces easily depressed; parts like deck, houses, and hatch frames pressed together over a compression bead ... uh, uh; think twice. Most laymen know little about glass, and even less about how to judge it. Let the surveyor (not the salesman or the seller) evaluate it. Be in no doubt; this is the ideal hull material for the Southland. To be sure, it requires protection against flora and barnacles and for cosmetics, but no teredo can ever invade it, and that removes in a single stroke the greatest enemy of the hull in warm waters. You must still protect the bottom with antifouling paints, however, for tropical waters support great varieties of growth unknown in cold waters. The barnacle and the oyster are still enemies, but fortunately nonboring ones. It is usual to paint the bottom twice annually—once in the mid-spring and again five months later; then not for seven months, counting on cooler winter waters and less use to keep the paint effective during the slightly stretched period.

Many experienced boatmen of the South paint with a hard paint in the spring and a soft coat in the winter, thus obtaining the advantages of a hard coat during the season of most use. This is necessary because of the general shallowness of the waters (seldom much more than a fathom below the keel) and the constant operation in a situation akin to sand scouring. The hard paint will resist this somewhat. On the other hand, it soon builds up to the point that a hull sanding will be required. The soft paint will "wash" off to some extent and slow the paint build-up. Thus we strike a happy medium and delay an expensive hull blasting for five or more years.

Every boatman has his favorite bottom paint. I recommend that you use the paint the local fishermen and commercial boats use. They have long since discovered the best paint for that particular area. It is seldom the highest priced paint; indeed, there is little practical need, save for racing, for excessively costly paints. A soft paint can be purchased for about $25 a gallon; a good hard paint costs about $45 a gallon. Any paint should be put on with a brush and worked into seams and depressions with care. Rollers do not do it; sprayers cannot properly handle thick bottom paint.

The wooden boat in the South needs at least the recommended protection and might well be examined by scuba *before* the estimated repaint date. When hauled, the boat must be searched diligently for teredos. These tiny worms, about the diameter of a pin, enter the wood via a tiny hole of about that diameter . . . and then proceed to grow fat and saucy on your planking, until they sometimes reach the diameter of a pencil. They never eat *through* the planking, but, rather, they honeycomb the wood until there is no strength left and its separation from the sea is only paper thick.

Teredos must be hunted out, after the boat has dried for a day, and then killed. The teredo keeps the after end of his body near the hole entrance in order to obtain water in which to live. When the hole is found, probe it with a fine, long needle; then hit the spot with a blowtorch until the wood chars. Along with this, search for a tropical villain, the putty bug. He is a mite, a bit smaller than a ladybug, that invades the puttied seams of a wooden hull. He actually eats the putty and can, in time, strip the seam bare. Look for his tracks in a puttied seam; then dig him out and squish him. Reputty the seam; he may have eaten to the cotton.

With glass, you have none of these problems . . . nothing that can't be cleaned off with a broom and high-pressure hose . . . and your precious hull is in no danger.

Now there is nothing wrong with metal hulls, either steel or aluminum. They, too, resist the worms. They do raise other problems, however: electrolysis and corrosion. Built by a builder of experience, working under an architect of experience, the metal hull can be successful and is often used for boats of larger size, say, the 75-foot and up class. The steel hull requires very special treatment during its building and a neutralizing system (of which there are several, all electrical) to protect it from consumption by the ravages of electrolysis, which is simply the "battery" effect of unlike metals in salt water. Such systems must be in constant operation while afloat, and they require various and heavy current drains; hence they are best used on a large vessel. There are several rather small cruisers available with metal hulls, and sometimes the builders do not trouble to provide hull protection. Unless it *has* hull protection, beware, because there will be thin platings for sure, even after only a few years. If it does have hull protection, ask yourself if you really want to bother with it: the risk of breakdown, of replacement, of constant watching (even when you are absent). The metal hull, it seems to me, takes the boat out of the class of pleasure boat; this is for the crewed boat, the corporation, the genuinely large ocean cruiser.

Until recently, the aluminum boat's great weakness was in the plate riveting: the rivets soon gave up due to electrolysis. Now there is sound aluminum construction, using aluminum welding, recently developed by the air-frame industry. While not common in small cruisers, there are several stock aluminum hulls in the 55-foot and up class that are properly welded. There is no particular reason for a live-aboard cruiser to seek out a metal-hulled boat. On the other hand, if he is offered one in the used-boat market and it appeals, it should be considered only with the expert advice of a competent surveyor with metal hull experience.

There is little difference in the performance of a metal hull over a wooden or glass one, weight being about the same. There *is* a difference in maintenance costs and in the constant need to uncover the rust and corrosion that goes on *under* the paint of a metal hull. Repairs are apt to be expensive and take you to yards that do not do or do not want yacht work. And, last of all, metal boats seem hard to resell; people do not seem to want the added headaches.

The last hull type to consider is the ferrocement vessel. It's new; it's impressive. Some very lovely boats have been so produced. And some horrors have also been produced . . . and usually abandoned. The art is just too young to reach any conclusions. Nobody has come up with a *better* boat because of ferrocement construction. The experts seem to agree that there is little money savings. Obviously, the result will be an extremely heavy, cold hull that nobody yet knows for certain can resist years of saltwater use, or continuous engine vibration, or the stresses of spars and sail rigs—nor for how long it will remain limber and seakindly, or cosmetically clean and worthy of the name *yacht*. There seems to be no practical reason to build with this material in small yacht sizes; it seems, rather, to be the material of barges and carriers and workboats that need in no way meet the standards of construction or performance that a yacht must meet. A lot of amateurs have engaged in ferrocement boatbuilding, encouraged by sellers of plans and materials, but I have never seen a successful one yet, so there must be many bugs in the deal. I have seen a very few really large ferrocement yachts built by professionals, but they don't look, after five years, nearly as good as a glass or wooden boat of the same age. And I have seen some simply awful unfinished attempts lying in the mud or in the back farmyard . . . .

Whatever, I don't think the novice live-aboard ought to saddle himself with such a problem at this stage of his experience. While I have never seen a ferrocement boat offered for sale (poor souls, not even a market for their exploded dreams), I expect that the "ask" might be tempting. Please resist it, and stay with glass, as something like 95 percent of the southern boatowners do. Believe them: fiberglass—for hulls, topsides, decks, and houses—is the only boat material so far that makes sense in the tropics.

THE HULL ABOVE DECKS

Whatever the configuration—and even if the hull proper is made of wood—the vessel's houses, cabins, trunks, hatches, and other deck protuberances should be of fiberglass or, at least, of fiberglass-covered wood. It is these parts that are subject to rapid and deep rot, far more vulnerable than the hull itself, which for most of its parts is somewhat protected by salt water. The deck accommodations, with its corners and pockets and abutting parts—too frequently unprotected by proper bedding—invite the collection of water . . . fresh, sweet water. And porous paint (all paint becomes porous very shortly under the effects of weather and ultraviolet rays) permits the water to soak into the wood and dry rot soon invades the structure and deterioration sets in.

This is normal, in any climate. However, in the tropics there are two added factors that make dry rot a number-one enemy. First, it is normal, because of daily night-day temperature differences, for rather heavy dews to settle almost every dawn. The boat is almost constantly "wet," and, if not, the second factor makes it so; namely, the live-aboard habit of daily washdowns. Add to this, frequent—almost daily—rains from May until November, and the average live-aboard boat with wooden topsides hasn't much of a chance save by constant attention to those innocent-appearing little flakes of peeling paint or varnish.

Glass-covered wood is the obvious answer, even if the hull is of wood, and many stock boatbuilders do indeed cover horizontal planes with glass, including decks, of course. Decks, to be sure, need antislip features . . . which can be achieved with grid patterns or by covering with teak soles. The glass application to a deck should "turn up" at the juncture with other structures, i.e., at the house or trunk sides, at hatch frames, inside of bulwark and buffalo rails . . . indeed, at every vertical rise from the deck plane. Thus, water will at least be confined and allowed to run off rather than creep or soak in.

Raw glass (as sometimes seen over a natural varnish finish) is subject to rapid deterioration because of exposure to the destructive ultraviolet rays of the tropical (and very hot) sun. It needs the protection of paint, or ray-resistant gel coat(s), or both. Early failure can be noted by peeling gel coat or paint, then small "crazy cracking," and finally failure of the glass as a cover, meaning chipping and separation from the original bonding. Fortunately, glass can be reapplied, rapidly and far less expensively than wood replacement, but it MUST BE DONE, for beneath a glass deck failure, there is wood, and rot is proceeding exactly the same as if the entire structure were wood only.

Older boats, of wood, may be quite handily made "tropic proof" by applications of fiberglass coatings over the wood. It requires expert knowledge and some special grinding tools and techniques and, save for small areas, is nothing for the tyro to tackle. If contemplated, these are the areas to be done, in order of their importance: first, the main deck and all horizontal surfaces—cabin tops, hatches, deck box covers, and cockpit soles. Second, all vertical surfaces (but not hull): cabin sides, bases of spars, hatch frames, bulwarks; possibly the dinghy. Last, the hull itself, including transom, bowsprits, long heads, bumpkins, and swim platforms (unless of teak). There are several standard manuals on general fiberglass techniques available and, even if self-work is not contemplated, it would be wise to consult one if this problem is yours. Probably the most important piece of advice offered by them is this: cut out and destroy *all* dry rot *before* covering any wood with glass coatings; the rot will go on and completely destroy the wood beneath, even if it is covered and sealed.

(See also Chapter 10 for specific treatment of local patches of dry rot.)

The live-aboard boat's above-deck features can be quite standard. It helps much to have extra-large deck bins or other storage facilities, for "junk" does seem to collect when tethered to a dock. Bicycles and scooters need protection; so do outboard motors, scuba gear, water skis, dinghy sail rigs, folded deck furniture. It can improve the quality of life a great deal if there is, in truth, "a place for everything and everything in its place." When you cross tacks with a nifty 50-footer, draped with two bikes lashed to the bow-rail, a motor scooter in the after cockpit, a surfboard atop the dinghy, two pair of water skis stuck in the stack, and four LP gas bottles rolling around the foredeck, you have met a careless skipper, not a careless boat. Most boats will indeed take care of the "extras" you will want to have to enjoy fully the live-aboard life, but you must organize their stowage so they won't become a hazard to life and limb or an outrage to the loveliness of the vessel's concept and design. It's a good trick to do, but it can be done. It is not often found. Hence, be alert to solutions to this problem as you consider an offering.

A good solution to this problem is to have a simple tarpaulin made to cover wooden chocks on an upper deck, or house roof, into which the largest and most unwieldy items may be secured and covered. You thus have protection of the item, reasonable safety, and have preserved appearance and vessel design.

You will do much of your living in the sun, so, properly, your boat should have an area where you can stretch out in a deck chair or on a mat. You will also want and need some shade, and the average "deck house" will serve for this, provided it has some insect protection, a lot of cross-ventilation, and drapes or other means of view screening. This latter is most important, since this is the *living room* of the boat, the space in which you will relax, dine, entertain, and, possibly, with convertibles, sleep as well. It is probably far more important to successful living aboard than the below-decks accommodations, and it should be selected with care. If you cannot visualize happy, relaxed living in the style you wish and are comfortable with, don't buy the boat that does not permit it. (This seems to be a basic trouble of many sailboats: their "living rooms" are below decks, without view, air, or freedom, and soon can become a mere cell in a prison.)

And a last deck feature: the flying bridge. Developed for the sportfisherman, who needed the advantage of an unobstructed view, it rapidly became standard on American yachts—even on silly little 22-footers that, with the addition of that monstrosity, the Bimini top, became higher than long! I suspect that the true reason for the popularity was that capability of riding high, in the position of command and control (some builders even call them "command bridges"), to see—and, more important, to be seen. Whatever—the flying bridge is here to stay. All we need now is to develop a design so that it becomes a part of the vessel design rather than an obvious "extra" stuck on in a unit for anyone who thinks he ought to be seen. Having said which, I hasten to add: on a proper boat (meaning one of at least 36 feet), the flying bridge can become, IN THE TROPICS, a useful and pleasant adjunct to cruising. It does indeed help in navigating shallow waters and in coral heads. It greatly expands the view, so that in certain areas, such as the Georgia marshes, one can see *over* the low growth and out to the sea horizons to the east. It does give a pleasant sense of being outdoors, away from the confines of glass, in the briny breezes, and remote from the din of working machinery. It is, at times, hot and sunny, and it seems to many of us that the cure is to go below and navigate, not raise one of those awnings, or "tops," which utterly destroy whatever symmetry of design a ship might have. Annihilate all the traditions of an honorable art by hoisting for all the world to see a most landlubberly piece of shoreside gear. Did you know that there are vessels that have a flying bridge, with a Bimini top, atop of which is another bridge, with an awning, atop of which is still another control bridge . . . and this, too, may have still another awning, 35 feet high! And the boat may well be only 30 feet long! A possible, and weak, excuse may be fishing, but there is obviously no valid reason for a live-aboard cruising boat to sport such wild contraptions.

If a flying bridge comes under consideration, be very sure that it carries aloft a full set of instruments, plus all controls, which include horn, diesel stops, alarms, lights, etc. There is no real reason to bring electronics aloft. The risk of weathering and extended cabling is not worth the price; just drop below to use a radio. It's that simple . . . and quiet! There should be a well-designed weather cloth that fits over the entire unit from rail to rail, for protection of the rather delicate control instruments. Check, too, for a rail or hand grips from the ladder head to the seating of the bridge—a must in sloppy weather or fast steaming.

Avoid altogether a bridge on a "character" boat, such as a trawler. With the exception of the West Coast tuna boats, they just do *not* belong and are foreign to the design and offensive to the purist . . . of which the Waterway could well do with more.

Far more than in normal summertime cruising, the dinghy will be found a real joy (if not a necessity) in the live-aboard life. By all means, it should be davited. Towed, it is a nuisance and at times the subject of dockmaster disapproval . . . even an extra charge.

It should be davited by a system quick and easy to use (as in an emergency) and harmonious with the architecture of the ship. Usually, the appearance is least affected by carrying the dinghy over the stern, via horn davits, rather than aloft, and it certainly is far simpler to handle manually, no power winches being required. Most cruiser transoms will accommodate a small, 10-foot boat, which is a handy utility size. Anything smaller will not carry a load, nor perform well under outboard power or sail. You will find the "dink" a source of joy if you like to fish, go exploring by motor, or join the many small "dinghy fleets" that are loosely organized into sailing-racer fleets in many winter marinas. For those who regularly anchor out, the dinghy is a must.

It is best to have a glass or aluminum dinghy, with plywood a poor third choice. A wood-planked one will be "open" most of the time under tropical sun and require presoaking before use to swell seams and become tight. Probably the "chine" design, being halfway between a round and a vee

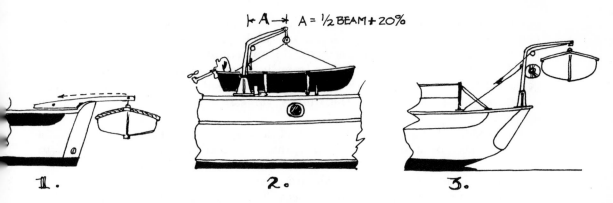

ONE-MAN DINGHY-HANDLING GEAR

(1) Wooden horn davits, popular on medium-size powerboats. The tackle is a single part. There are usually cast-bronze transom steps. (2) Single davit, manual or power, is used for handling a larger or heavier dinghy. Note dinghy fitted to chocks and gripes. Bridle is stainless steel wire and has three parts, with thimble seized at the balancing point. (3) Pair of stern davits, manual or power, is used for a sailboat requiring visibility over the stern, yet still having boom clearance. Horn davits are custom-built and faired into the sheer detail. Metal davits are stock except the vertical riser, which is custom-cut to fit local conditions.

bottom, will suit best, since such a hull will sail well and also carry a heavy load: a true dual-purpose design. Her sail rig should be of the simplest design possible and, via take-apart spars, stow inside the hull length. A centerboard will be required, of course; also an easily shipped rudder and tiller. If the seats can be knocked out when sailing, and the crew can make do on floor mats on the bilges, the boat will handle far better and be far safer. Rather than have numerous, skitterish cylinder fenders, pad the dinghy rail with cotton rope or a modern flexible molding type and save the topsides of all boats concerned.

Unless the dinghy bottom is copper painted, it should be davited most of the time and not left overside. Fouling occurs quickly in tropical salt water. A "spat" of barnacle "seeds" may come in and attach themselves overnight to an unprotected bottom . . . and 24 hours later, nothing short of a machine sanding will dislodge them.

The status of a power dinghy varies with each state. Some allow its registration as part of the "mother ship" at no fee. Others require separate registration (and a fee, of course). If the power is sail or oars alone, there is no registration required. However, check in the port in which you winter; there is some tampering presently going on, and changes may be expected in at least Florida and Georgia. Usually, nobody disturbs you, but there is an awareness of water safety in some state governments, and you may be sure the first step will be to demand a fee of some kind. Fee or not, when in use, the dinghy *must* have a life-preserver of approved design for each person on board and a flashlight for nighttime use.

Last, the dinghy is a running boat, not a lifeboat, and should not be so considered. If you need a lifeboat, or think you will (as you might when planning an extended ocean passage), do not count on the average dinghy. It could not last long in the open sea, even in normal weather. For this purpose, get a rubber inflatable, protect it from the sun and weather, keep it in ever-ready condition, and forget the dinghy (unless, say, it is 16 or 18 feet in length).

The swim platform has arrived—and a very useful device it is. With a transom gate, or a boat ladder, it forms an excellent stage from which to board and leave small running boats, to dive, water ski, and swim. It is a worthy addition indeed to a live-aboard boat.

Also in this area are boarding devices. There are various aluminum ladders available, some that rise and fall with the tide, which make boarding simple and safe. The boat end must be secured; the dock end, usually on rollers or small wheels, is free to move as the boat rolls or water level changes. In areas of high tidal differences, the marinas usually have floating docks, making it unnecessary to climb steep ladders spiked to slippery piles and the like. (Exceptions are: City Marina, Charleston, South Carolina; Oriental, North Carolina; Little River, North Carolina; Bucksport, South Carolina; and most boatyards.) The marina often provides a three-step, movable, wide-based ladder for use on floating docks, in combination with large boats of exceptional topside height. Simplest device of all is a six-foot-long plank with a bearer on the boat end, with tail lashings.

Further considerations of this boat that is to become your vehicle *and* your home, are these: can she do the job, *beyond dockside living,* that you wish her to do? Do you want to cruise during the winter? Where to? For how long? With how many aboard? Do you take her "back home" each spring, and through what waters and sailing conditions? Do you want, mostly, to live at anchor? If so, where? This floating home must also be an able vessel for many live-aboards, so it quite reasonably represents a compromise of principal uses. Example: There is no need at all for a generator on a dockside boat, traveling by marina to and from winter quarters. There is a vital need for one if the accent is on anchoring out most of the time. Example: There is no need at all for a big 60-footer to carry the accommodations as well achieved in a 36-foot houseboat if no open sea navigation is planned. Example: There is no need for high-speed capability (huge horsepower, great tankage, high investment, maintenance, and insurance costs) if the boat is moved only occasionally and for short "afternoon" cruises. (Lots of Florida boats move only twice a year—back and forth from the boatyard for bottom jobs.)

Every marine designer, builder, and writer must eventually take refuge in the universal truth that an ideal live-aboard boat, above all else, must be a reasonable, sane compromise among all the factors required and demanded and affordable by not only the owner but also his wife, his children, and his guests . . . and recognize that he has a very slim chance of achieving perfection. Certainly he can try, and he has tried and succeeded better than any

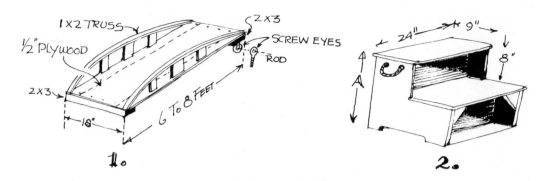

BOARDING DEVICES

While aluminum, self-adjusting boarding steps are available at high prices, many marina dwellers build their own. (1) Used for nonfloating dock. Screw eyes and rod provide a hinge on the boat end. Since this might become steep at times, cover it with carpet or a width of roofing paper. (2) Step unit for floating dock. Measurement "A" should be the distance from dock to boat rail and this is divided into steps about 8 inches high. For a comfortable step, keep riser total plus tread total, in inches to 17 (e.g., 9T + 8R, 6½R + 10½T). This, too, can be carpeted, with a doormat possibly provided at the foot.

planner of human living patterns anywhere. But there is a point beyond which he cannot go; there is a point at which only the users of the boat can determine whether or not the boat is a success. There *must* be some personal adjustments, some give and take, some discipline required to make the whole package "work." All one can do, really, is wisely, unemotionally, utterly realistically select the boat fulfilling the greatest number of the demands, and thereafter make the personal adjustments necessary to achieve a happy, safe, and enjoyable life afloat.

Never . . . never . . . compromise with safety, safety of design and of build; nor with top condition and efficiency of all the separate parts. Never compromise with a factor in the equation without which there would be patent failure. And, above all perhaps, never compromise with cost. If you can't afford it yet you still buy it, you are foredoomed to failure. This is probably the worst reef of all, for those kind gentlemen who "can arrange financing if you'll just sign here" are ever-ready to scatter your wits as you hover between the gleaming beauty of a great cruiser and just a few bucks a month that you know you can't afford. I think that I can state—as a *designer* of boats, a *builder* of boats, and a lifelong *writer* about boats—that budgetary miscalculations . . . plain lack of the wherewithal . . . have ruined more boats and boat people and boat plans than any other cause.

Do, please, get all the subjects of this chapter into proper and realistic focus, and don't move one inch toward ownership until the image is sharp and clear. To do so will truly imperil the entire project and probably forever lose the Waterway brotherhood another convert.

Chapter 9
Accommodations

We cannot possibly investigate fully the subject of "accommodations," so greatly does the matter vary with use, locale, budget, and owner taste. Rather, then, let us accept the subject as most of us know it and discuss accommodations (meaning the tools of on-board living) in the light of using them in tropical climes, during long vacation periods as a live-aboard.

Much as our homes do, the modern live-aboard boat depends upon domestic power—good, 110- or 220-volt alternating current, piped in or made aboard (and sometimes stored aboard in batteries with converters). Without it, we would still be in the age of the coasting schooners, using wood or coal stoves and kerosene lights, augmented by candle "sluts," and the head would be a wooden bucket forward of the knightheads and the shower a plunge into the sea while hanging in the bobstay shrouds.

The live-aboard boat must have an electrically balanced and carefully engineered system, of the best "marine" specifications, with guarded circuitry radiating from a central distribution panel—just like a home ashore, but far, far better insulated and weather protected. The shipboard system must meet the ravages of corrosion, dampness, and vibration. Household wiring is definitely not adequate, and your insurance won't be valid if you have anything less than marine standard, even on a small, low-powered vessel or a simple cruising sloop. If for no other reason, a survey should be ordered. You cannot afford to take a chance with substandard electrical systems.

142

The live-aboard boat—with electric heat, air conditioning, battery charging, cooking, refrigeration, lights, pumps, TV, radios, appliances—needs at least a 50-amp system and could well do with 220-volt service, which is available at modern marinas or from sophisticated generators. The modern boat is an "all-electric" boat, and it's a good trick if you can do it ... or afford it.

Probably most boats, and those you will find in the used-boat marts, will have a combination of power sources, with 110-volt AC for lights, battery charging, and other light demands. Cooking and heating are often by LP (propane) gas or portable fuels (kerosene, alcohol); the air conditioning is a 12-inch fan and an open hatch. There is nothing wrong with such a boat at all, as long as her systems are sound and well maintained.

LP gas, usually stored in 20-pound "bottles," and *always* on deck (even if in a box), is an excellent and inexpensive fuel available in most ports. In 1975 it cost about 15 cents a pound from a filling plant or dealer truck, up to 30 cents a pound at a marina, and about 50 cents a pound in the Bahamas. Sound practice should see a manual shutoff valve *at the tank*, and it should be OFF, except when in use. This obviates a pilot light, and that, too, is as it should be. Liquid petroleum also serves well as a heating fuel, utilizing small cast-iron portable heaters, and as a fuel for combination refrigerators (more on this later). I have seen boats use LP for lighting—fine on a chilly night, for the gaslight creates a good deal of heat, but generally not satisfactory.

Many small cruisers sport small fireplaces or fireplace stoves. These are fine for atmosphere, but not very practical for space heating. The best heating systems are the built-in types, which are fired by diesel oil and cost about a dime an hour to heat a 45-foot boat.

The southern winters start about mid-November and extend to mid-February. The days are 99 percent sunny and warm, with the daytime temperature seldom dropping below 70 degrees. Heat is not often needed. The normal nighttime temperature might drop to the 50s, with a good blanket, or an electric one, adequate. This is the weather that calls for a touch of evening heat ... a portable electric or the romantic fireplace or an iron skillet capsized over two burners of the galley stove. When a norther descends—possible at any time but usually spaced by week-long periods of warm, sunny weather—the central system, ticking over by daylight and fired up in the evening, is called for. It may be called on, in a normal winter, 20 evenings or 10 days. An air conditioner (if you have one) will be used much more than a heating plant.

Reverse-cycle units (combination heaters and air conditioners) are not popular on modern boats, being too bulky and far too shoddy for the necessary exposure (as extending from a bulkhead or sash). The air conditioner must be a marine type, using water and circulating loops to transfer the heat. There are many very complete but custom-designed systems, best installed when the boat is built but possible to install afterward. Most require a 220-volt AC power supply. An insulated boat is a must for both heat and AC systems to function properly ... a practice safe enough on a glass or metal boat, but inviting dead air and rot on wooden boats.

It is by no means necessary to have a lot of fancy gear for happy on-board living in the tropics. Thousands of us deal with the short periods of warmth and "coolth" by direct, low-key methods—such as, when it turns cool, using sweaters, windbreakers, a simple briquette fireplace, or a portable electric. Or we go to the movies. Or, when it turns warm, we open all hatches and ports, plugging in a fan, shedding a few shirts, consuming cool, tall drinks, and jumping off the stern for a swim. Life is not that desperate that we must live as we do ashore; indeed, much of the enjoyment is that we have shed some of the treacherous shore standards and opted for a simpler, less gadget-bound life. And air conditioners, heating systems, multiple push-buttons on a small boat are just that: gadgets that will take charge of your boat, your time, and your pocketbook.

Nevertheless, a 110-volt AC power supply *does* make life easier, and one is recommended. It is free with the dockage charge (in by far *most* marinas), and it gives constant power, either direct or through a convertor, keeping the batteries fully charged automatically and permitting current draw (now 12-volt DC) directly from the battery for use by normal DC shipboard appliances. The boat equipped with a generator may be all electric, but from a practical viewpoint, it is not realistic to suppose that she can always use her generator(s). Marinas forbid it entirely. At an anchorage there will soon be objections, for it is obviously unfair for a single selfish skipper to destroy the peace and quiet for all others. (To stop a generator, swim up to the offender after dark and jam a potato into the exhaust.)

THE GALLEY

The standard galley features are: refrigerator, stove, and sink, plus storage cupboards. At best this is a strictly utilitarian assembly, and the best manner in which to make it presentable and a part of the whole is to screen it and keep it neat and orderly. By its very nature, it is a place where upset, soiled dishes and pots, remains of foods, animal bones, and dead bottles collect. This can't be helped. Why then, do some modern accommodation plans place this galley . . . this place of upset and ugliness . . . in the living area? There could be no worse place for it. These plans frequently place the galley in almost a place of honor: on or abutting the navigation department, the very last place that should be threatened by garbage, disorder, and soiled dinnerware.

The stock excuse is that Ms. Skipper *"won't* be isolated in a hole while everybody else is above decks having a ball." This is utter nonsense. A cruiser of live-aboard dimensions can have a separate, or at least screened, galley with ease, and her people can live in a decent manner. The galley need not be a glory hole; it can be, and usually is on a properly designed vessel, a utilitarian space, quite as efficient as an engine room, or a head—light, airy, and truly a "workshop," for that is what a galley is in truth. Do avoid this stupid plan unless you normally live and navigate and entertain in your kitchen at home. It converts everything on the boat into a kitchen, and you are stuck with it as a way of life. Insofar as this layout (far too standard!) affects the navigating area, it is positively dangerous. How would you like to work out a course on a fluttering chart, in a gale of wind, at night, flanked by a sinkful of dirty dishes or rolling bottles or a neat package of fish bones? Or make a beautiful landfall, in a dramatic sunset, through the fatty haze of a broiling hamburger? (I can get very angry about this, and I have several times refused utterly either to design or build a boat with a deckhouse galley.)

Well, the galley needs a sink, and for a live-aboard boat, this should be a double one with a swing spout. Stainless steel is by far the best material. If it is flanked by a teak counter, rather than a synthetic or plastic one, you have a seagoing setup. The stove should be one that permits freedom in cooking, i.e., with at least three burners and an oven. If there is no oven, install a modern micro-oven in a locker hard by. These are a real boon to the cruiser, saving time and space, and the automatic features permit planning ahead. A stainless steel or baked enamel stove body is best. Iron rusts and aluminum corrodes, needing constant attention.

Cupboards should be on the small side . . . but there should be plenty of them. Keep heavy goods low, light packaged goods high. All working surfaces need fiddles, small rails to keep things from sliding off. Drawers need "stops," devices (available in several designs) to keep the drawer from sliding out in a seaway. Linoleum or vinyl is the easiest floor to maintain; this is no place for carpeting. A galley exhaust blower of some size is necessary in Florida, come a still summer evening.

The refrigerator needs to be large, say, about eight to 12 cubic feet, and if it has a small deep-freeze or holding compartment, so much the better. The door must have a positive latch and a way to secure it at sea. It should be able to turn out ice cubes, probably quite fast. With the ideal combination of 110 AC, 12-volt DC, and LP gas, you can meet any living condition—dockside, at sea, underway, or at anchor. Actually, in the calm Ditch you can steam all day with LP doing the refrigeration. Only if things become rough do you need to switch to 12-volt DC, which is a battery drain if running slow or sailing without power. The boat so equipped does not need a generator, which can't be used in some places and shouldn't be used in others. She can refrigerate, cook, and heat with silent LP gas and be a joy to her owners and her neighbors.

The use of small appliances as adjuncts to the galley is coming into common usage and, dockside, there is nothing at all against it. These may well make a full oven unnecessary. Recently, both washers and dryers have become available in sizes manageable on a boat. While limited to small poundage per washing, they do save trips to the laundromat, and the dryer is useful at all times for bathing suits, towels, and the like. The "high boy" types are generally too tall for a boat. (Maytag makes a marine combination set.)

The galley is a work space and, while it can be a lovely thing of chrome and Formica as well, its primary use should never be forgotten. It is simply a place to prepare food, incidentally to store it, and is in no way a social center. Do avoid overgadgeting it. Keep it simple, clean-cut, easy to work in, light, airy, and fresh—and AWAY FROM THE COMPASS!

Almost part and parcel of the galley is that unique fitment: the dinette. I do recommend one adjacent to the galley and seating at least as many people as the boat will sleep. Recognize that this is quite apt to become a social center, and provide shelves for books, a radio, and pocket "junk" nearby. It, too, should be fitted with fiddles. Very few dinettes, no matter what enthusiastic salesmen say, will "convert" into comfortable double beds; and they should not be counted as part of the permanent sleeping accommodations.

SLEEPING AREAS

Slumber, on shipboard, need not be an invitation to a nightmare. Think of the "bunks" as beds, and treat them as such, giving them proper mattresses, springs, box springs, and bedding—just as you do at home. You are not on a whaler in 1830 but a modern powerboat, with proper ventilation, sanitation, light, heat! Sleep as you like to sleep at home, no matter what the shape of the bed, or where located, or how high or low. Use linen sheets and down pillows and virgin wool blankets . . . why not?

Avoid two things: one, anything but foam rubber (slabs, pellets, wool) for "stuffing" and, two, a covering that does not "breathe." In dry, ventilated quarters, with care via spraying, drying, and cleaning, this floating bedroom can equal the one ashore.

Temperatures in quarters, of a chilly night, will seldom reach "outside" temperatures, because the stateroom is generally at or below the waterline, and the water, only a thin topside plank from your bed, remains substantially at the daytime temperature. You will seldom require really heavy blankets; indeed, a thin blanket with an electric "throw" is generally quite comfortable.

In these areas, too, are the wardrobes, hanging lockers, and other alleged clothing lockers. These ought to be generous, for the very best way to stow all clothing on shipboard is to hang it in an airy locker rather than contain it in tight drawers, luggage, etc. Divide the clothing into dress and work types, and under no circumstances place storm clothing with them; for these, assign a separate "oiler" locker. Every few days, turn a portable fan into these spaces and spray gently with an air freshener and germ killer (such as Lysol).

THE HEAD

In modern boats, the head is generous and well planned. There is no reason for the complexities of an "electric head"; use by landlubber guests and electrolysis will sooner or later do them in. Pump, with a good, quality outfit, and your head problems are much minimized.

The "head" problem today is not in the equipment but in the waste disposal. Certain interests, in the name of preserving the environment, have decreed numerous antipollution doctrines, so along with the 900-foot oil tankers and the commercial despoilers and many a waterside community itself, the yachtsman is now enjoined from adding his bit of pollution to the sea.

Only recently has any sensible and practical approach come for the program, and below are the highlights—applicable to *all* pleasure yachts, from *zero to a million tons*, and certainly to you in whatever boat you live aboard.

1. Whatever you now have aboard in the way of a toilet will be good until at least January 1983. Holding tanks *are* legal. The problem, in the South as elsewhere, is finding a shore discharge station. I can think of fewer than 10 in all of Florida.

2. Available now are legal "flow-through" devices, approved by the U.S. Coast Guard. If installed in a vessel built after January 30, 1975, they are legal indefinitely.

3. Vessels built after January 1, 1977, *must* have Coast Guard approved (legal) flow-through devices installed.

4. These are federal laws. Some states, having lakes entirely contained within the state, require *only* holding tanks and do not now recognize federal jurisdiction over state waters. But they soon will, for there are several challenges in the courts at the moment, and the federal government usually wins such cases if the waters support *any* navigation. This is hardly a problem for the winter cruiser, but he may acquire a vessel subject to such rules.

5. And note the key to the entire matter. Nobody is telling anybody what to install or not to install—wooden buckets, sophisticated toilets, or taut shrouds. The law simply says that nobody may "discharge, spill, leak, pump, pour, emit, empty, or dump" any untreated waste matter into the public waters of the United States. It then recommends, if you choose to install it, an approved "flow-through" device, which treats the waste, so that you then may legally "discharge, spill, leak, etc."

6. Hence, the only legal devices to be permitted as heads on any and all boats after January 1983 are ones of various manufacture bearing the Coast Guard seal of approval or certification.

Complicated it is, but it is as clear as a bell compared to the way it was a year ago!

A shower, usually an alcove off the head, is most desirable in the tropics. It must have a sump, automatic if possible, to carry the waste water to a point above the waterline. A "civilized" shower is a stall shower, a separate compartment; not merely a spray head and a curtain and a soaking for everything else in the "head." The enclosure must be absolutely watertight, of stainless steel, preferably, since leaks, especially between shower stall and exterior planking, are open invitations to wooden hull rot.

Hot water for shower, galley, and other domestic uses comes from a tank and heater, usually of about 20-gallon capacity. Most are electrically fired, from dockside power, and automatic. Some are also heated by the engine cooling water, via a coil transfer, when running, and store hot water behind heavy tank insulation for up to 24 hours. The entire system is under pressure from an automatic pump, activated by demand, and depends upon battery power. A proper supply system will have several hand pumps (in galley and head, on deck), so that water may be drawn even if the automatic system is out of whack.

Potable water tankage should be either stainless steel or Monel, with riveted *and* soldered (welded) seams. There should be generous baffling and adequate clean-outs. Much of the public potable water of the South is heavily chlorinated, and some has marked sulfur content; neither in any way affects the tankage material, but sulfur may, if heavy, affect rubber gaskets (as in the pump) and copper piping.

LIVING AREAS

Day-to-day living on a vessel that is also a winter home varies somewhat from that on a cruiser. It is far more than a shelter from weather; it is the place in which you, your crew, and your guests are going to spend a great many hours of the next winter. It should be a happy place, a place devoted to your indoor hours of leisure, never a stark, Spartan, unplanned area with all the charm of a locker room. It should be—and can be—quite as homey, as comfortable, as inviting and relaxing as its shoreside counterpart, your own living room at home. It's a trick to achieve, but a great many live-aboards have done it.

I expect the secret lies in solid comfort; pleasing decor; ability to heat, cool, and ventilate; capacity to accept the entire ship's company at the same time IN COMFORT and to store, handy and in familiar array, all the tools of leisure living that you need and are used to: books, a desk, radio, a television, favorite pictures and bric-a-brac, a guitar, a slide projector, an organ, whatever you wish. By all means, the boat should be tastefully draped, comfortably carpeted (or fitted with generous-size rugs if engine hatches open into the area, a common layout). Easy chairs, end and coffee tables, sofas—all this gear that you shouldn't carry on a world-girdling cruiser *should* be carried on the live-aboard boat. The chances that such gear will endanger safety are slight: the Waterway is never that rough, and dockside moorings are utterly quiet.

I make no plea for clutter (that will come of itself!), but rather for the careful and thoughtful use of those tools of living that provide comfort and security in your particular way of life. Make these cosmetics your cosmetics— not the stenciled anchors and rubber ducks and violent colors that nautical gift shops think we want. Good, solid, tasteful design and materials—even antiques—just as you would select at home, are the backbone of good decor. Carpeting . . . definitely NOT the indoor-outdoor types of horrible hues . . . lends softness and ties together the whole. Drapes soften the tropical light and, at night, give privacy. Simple design (seldom with flowery motifs), harmonious color schemes, accessories of taste and quality . . . spiced with the tools of leisure; these are the things to start with. If at all possible, create an axis, or center of interest (as a fireplace, a dramatic original oil, a built-in fitment), in the space available, and group the pieces around it. Not all people can achieve this, of course. Women usually can do it better than men. If you can't do it, there are many talented people offering this specialized service in Florida, especially in Miami and Fort Lauderdale. (They usually have a flat fee and often arrange a discount on furniture and accessories purchased for you.) Do not entrust decor to either the architect or the builder; they are definitely not trained, and their only qualification is that they may know more about it than you do, which is nothing.

If the navigating center is also in the "living room," do not permit it to give permanent character to the space. Screen it, cover it, relegate it to a minor place in the overall scheme, or you will live in a machine shop all winter long. This, like the galley in the living area, can ruin the pleasantest of shipboard living rooms.

Now as to shipboard materials:

Carpets are best made of nylon or something similar. Wool and cotton absorb odor and moisture. For padding, use only foam rubber. Do not tack carpets to the deck; rather, fit and bind them so they can be aired and sunned. An excellent way to handle the engine hatches in a carpeted area (rather than binding with chrome strips) is to lay down a short-pile "background" carpet of sober color and patterns; then lay over the hatch(es) several dramatic throw rugs of top quality, covering the hatch seams, of course.

The so-called indoor-outdoor carpets may be all right outdoors and as temporary floor coverings, to be taken up when steaming. Usually they are available only in raw, raucous colors, hardly compatible with quality decor. You should *never* tack them permanently in place, or glue them, especially on a wooden deck—you would be opening the door wide to massive dry rot problems.

Drapery materials may run the gamut of design and color, but they definitely should be of synthetic material. Cotton, wool, or silk simply will not hold up under saltwater conditions and Florida sunshine. Ultraviolet rays, in huge doses there, quickly destroy the synthetics, so drapes *must* be lined, or heavy sash-curtains should also be hung. There is much to be said for loose-weave materials, which, even when drawn, permit the passage of air. Do not use the common weighted tape on the bottom hem: it will surely, one rough day, smash out a window. Rather, use a lower rod and rings or clips; or fit the drapes with tie-backs.

Furniture. A tough one. There are few pieces made exclusively for marine use, and those that are, are more utilitarian (like Castro folding tables) than decorative. Most furniture construction is adequate since the universal use of waterproof glues, but manufacturers still use ferrous hardware, shoddy plywoods, "particle board," and other materials hardly suitable for shipboard use. Probably the best attack is to get the best you can; then protect it wherever possible by back-painting, replacement of vulnerable hardware, and finish protection. Usually this is best done with a washdown with mineral spirits or the like, then a build-up with a dull spar varnish and liberal waxing (paste type). The most common shellac finishes are apt to turn white and spot and are best removed entirely with a paint remover and sanding.

Upholstered furniture is a real problem, mostly in the spring and suspension areas. If it is at all possible, get in and under and, while the springs are still new and unrusted, spray them well with paint, followed by an oil or kerosene spray. Strapped furniture (rather than coil-sprung) should have vinyl suspensions, not webbing or steel. Frequent spraying with deodorants (Lysol is excellent) is necessary, and nothing equals a few sunny hours and a whack or two with a tiller.

The living room on deck is quite a different matter. Here the "yachting" furniture—items of plastic and anodized aluminum tube construction—suits the bill perfectly; indeed, the rattan and bamboo pieces sometimes seen are just the wrong types. The key requirement is the ability to take a wetting, probably of brine, and survive. No shoreside furniture can take this, and the nautical numbers are the only sensible answers. In general, deck furniture is best if it is the folding type, for there are times when clear decks are needed and *any* furniture is a hazard to life, limb, and safety.

Having considered the separate living parts of a cruiser, let us see how these parts fit together and what, really, makes a handy live-aboard layout. The combinations are legion, of course, but there are a few basics that must be kept in mind when selecting a boat on the basis of "layout."

First, it *must* adequately accommodate the group in permanent residence. Each individual needs at least a bed, a wardrobe, and a stowage place for small gear. It should be unnecessary to pass through another sleeping area when using the head, or going on deck—making a very good case for at least two heads on all boats with accommodations for more than two. Sailboats often fail here. Some even have a head tucked under a berth so that its use at night requires the complete upset of the bed and bedding. By far the best cabin arrangement is the "two-cabin" layout, each of which occupies an end of the vessel and each with its own head. Some motorsailers and trawlers have ideal two-cabin arrangements, in the ends, but with a center cockpit and, below decks, a connecting gangway, making it unnecessary to go above decks to reach any part of the ship. ~ *Irwin "37"* ~

Second, the use of temporary beds (convertibles, dinettes, portable cots, wheelhouse settees, etc.) is all right if truly temporary. To sleep so over a long winter, with the vessel in constant clutter, is not a pleasant vacation for anybody. On this basis, some tiny "family cruisers" claim to sleep eight or 10 on a 30-foot length. Possibly fun for a Saturday night—but not for the live-aboard existence. A "big" boat is not one that sleeps 10 people in 30 feet, but one that sleeps two people in 40 feet. Everybody needs and is entitled to reasonable space . . . to live, to rest, to relax, and to *be alone in*. Search for a layout that gives this in as great a measure as possible.

Third, do not select a boat layout on your exclusive terms. Seek a layout of general interest and use—even if it sleeps more than you need to, or has multiple heads, or has more and larger areas than you require—for someday you will sell this boat and you may have a difficult time finding exactly the buyer who wants and needs exactly what you do. A minimal boat would be one with two staterooms, two heads, and temporary sleeping for two more. Your money would be safe and liquid in her. The American family averages two children (for one thing), and most older live-aboards count on having guests, children, and grandchildren "down for the holidays," so they need plenty of room. While *you* may not, the next buyer might.

I was once offered a $60,000 ketch—a lovely Murray Peterson design, almost new—for $20,000. There was absolutely nothing wrong with her, save that her berths all were just 5 feet 9 inches long and her headroom was 5 feet 10 inches. Her poor owner, deluded into thinking he was "saving space," specified these dimensions, against the designer's wishes. But alas, within two years his children had grown beyond the family's stature and could neither stand nor lie in their lovely vessel . . . and she had to be sold. He never did find another short buyer with wife and children guaranteed not to grow, and eventually he had to gut the vessel and rebuild her accommodations.

Pitiful . . . but true . . . and don't let anything like this happen to you, either by design or by purchase. Stick to the popular concept of a live-aboard yacht, and individualize her by cosmetics, decor, and movable features.

Chapter 10
The Techniques of the Live-Aboard

In this, the final chapter, I shall depart from narrative writing and present a potpourri of the many techniques, tricks, and procedures learned by a great many live-aboard sailors. Many will be new to you, some are useful, and all are worthy of remembering as you meet the many, varying conditions of life afloat in the tropics.

TELEVISION

The Southland is flat. Hence TV and radio reception is easy, except in southeastern Florida, where jungles of steel high-rise apartments and condominiums clutter the skyways and blot out even some nearby stations. The only cure is to discover a location along the dock that gives a straight shot to the station, for a tiny antenna 15 feet high has little chance against a steel basket 250 feet high. Under such conditions, opt for a 110-volt set, with outside antenna. Marine antennas are shown in the accompanying illustration. The bat-wing reflector is available for a few dollars at any TV shop. It should be mounted as high as possible (as on a spar), so as to rotate and be aimed directly at the transmitter, found by search. This will bring in quite distant stations of the UHF variety. The "ring" antenna is readily hand-made (and also is for sale in specialty marine shops at $50 and more). It should be placed as high as possible, as on a masthead, and will bring in the local regular stations. Only a few Florida cities have all three networks; it is usually necessary to "reach out" via UHF for at least one of them.

152

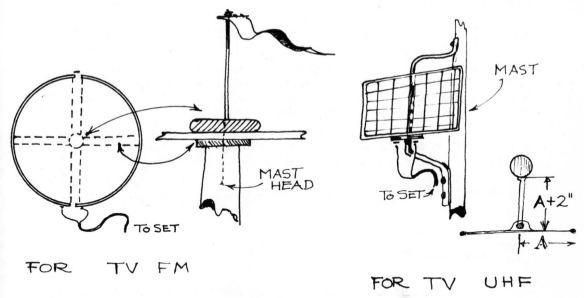

FOR   TV FM

FOR TV   UHF

**TO HELP CURE POOR TV
RECEPTION AT MARINAS**

Use ¼-inch plexiglass spokes and any metal rod or extrusion for the wheel. Rivet or bolt together, making sure halves of the wheel are not electrically connected. Make the wheel about 30 inches diameter for black-and-white 12-inch screens, up to 60 inches diameter for color sets.

Buy a pick-up screen (about 10" x 18", $1.95) at a TV shop and rework the mount on metal bracket affixed to mast. Extend bracket so screen can revolve 360°. Aim it, by hand or boathook (it must be high), directly at transmitting station, using chart and compass. Paint it black.

Many marinas do have cable-television hookups on the docks for boats remaining for long periods. Contracts for service are made directly with the cable company via the dockmaster.

For the boat that anchors out, or depends largely on ship's power, the 12-volt battery TV, in sizes up to 12 inches (diagonal measurement), is not too much drain . . . IF the set is black and white. Color draws far too much amperage for the average cruiser for more than a few hours' operation. (Example: we have a black-and-white, 10-inch screen, a Sony. When it is hooked up to the second, not the starting, battery, we can watch for two or three hours nightly for up to a week without charging. If we are running daily, there is no problem. If not, 15 minutes on the engine puts all the oomph back in the battery.)

Marine electronic service centers will spray any TV (or other electronic unit) to guard against moisture intrusion; or you can do it yourself with a can of CRC or its equivalent. It is a sound practice always, and a necessary practice in the humid summer months.

HI-FI AND AUDIO SYSTEMS

Florida is loaded with excellent FM stations, both "hot" and classical. There is wonderful, day-long, easy-listening music from Coral Gables, Fort Lauderdale, Lehigh Acres, Sarasota, and St. Petersburg that practically covers the state. If you like good music, it is well worthwhile to invest in a good set, with twin speakers, and a tape channel. Records are *out* on shipboard. They will warp almost certainly and, when they are played on a turntable, the pick-up is prone to jump out of the groove if the boat rolls even slightly or is not perfectly level. And not a big, powerful set, please. There is no place for concert-hall volume in either the boat or the marina. (The practice of playing music through the loudhailer so you can hear it on deck, or on the bridge, is frowned upon everywhere; it is forbidden by local ordinance in several Florida cities.)

DOCKSIDE POWER

Marinas above the backriver boatyard class today have quite modern electrical power supply systems . . . and 99 percent of them are standardized as to connecting fittings. Very few permit a boat to plug into their line with a household 15-amp plug . . . nor do you want to, if you value your boat and your health.

The standard equipment is made by the Wiring Device Division of the Harvey Hubbell Corporation, readily recognized by their distinctive, bright-yellow cords, plugs, receptacles, etc. Boatbuilders, too, use the on-board products of this company, and the "shore cord" supplied with the boat is always a "Hubbell." Thus, by the use of adapters, any boat on the Waterway can plug in to any marina dock on the Waterway for 125-volt or 250-volt AC 60-cycle supply.

The Adapter Selection Guide shows the adapters you might require. Most cables are for 125-volt service and of 30-amp capacity, and the popular adapters are listed in the middle group. If you cruise a lot, it would be wise to carry a set and be prepared for any receptacle you may find. If headed for a single berth all winter, wait until you arrive (or write ahead), and pick up the correct adapter then. All marinas have adapters and will lend them to you for short stays, requiring a deposit to ensure return (the adapters cost $10 to $27 each). Polarity checks are not necessary with these modern hookups, assuming that you have (as you surely should!) a grounded system.

ICE ON CRUISE DAYS

Live-aboards making short day cruises, and possibly not equipped to make ice when steaming, have found the use of "eutectic jelly" quite satisfactory, its sole disadvantage being the lack of ice cubes for drinks.

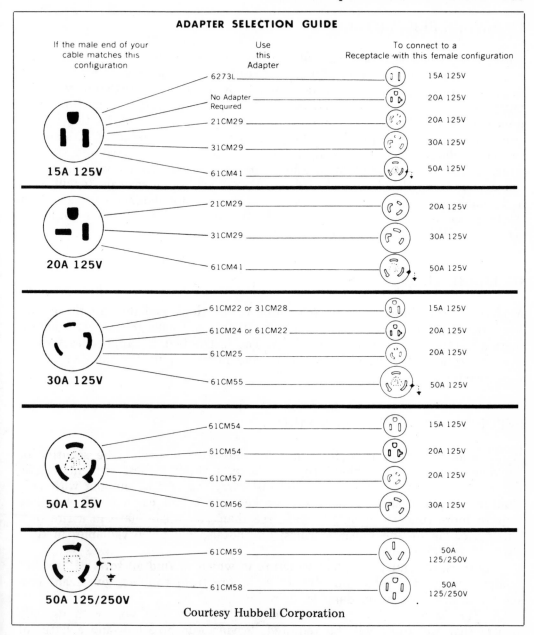

ADAPTER SELECTION GUIDE

Courtesy Hubbell Corporation

For under a dollar, sporting goods stores sell cans of eutectic material about the size of a flat can of paint remover or charcoal lighter. You place from two to six of these in the refrigerator's freezer compartment about 24 hours before use. They freeze solid and will hold, in a cool refrigerator without "current," for up to 36 hours. They can be used over and over and can be stored in any locker at any temperature. The ice-cube problem can be solved by placing the liquor and mixers in the refrigerator along with the "ice cans."

TO SECURE BRIC-A-BRAC

Since the live-aboard boat is apt to have considerably more portable accessories than the weekend cruiser, a tossing can cause havoc. Experienced skippers "stick" all this stuff down, or up, or on with "florist's putty." This putty is used for various purposes by flower arrangers. It is a medium-soft, nontoxic, nonacid putty of about the consistency of peanut butter, and it comes in waxed-paper-protected "tapes." You simply squeeze off a smidgen (which is about the size of a dite) and insert it between stickee and stickor, which may be anything from an ashtray to candlesticks, lamps, wall pictures—indeed, anything that you wish to "stay there" while in a seaway. It will stay, and remain soft and pliable for years, and it does not damage surfaces, even white paint or varnish. It costs about 50 cents a yard . . . and a yard will secure everything needed on a 40-footer.

ON-BOARD TELEPHONES

Modern marinas have dockside telephone connections available for those who need them. A charge is usually made for them, and calls (clearing through a marina central) are usually marked up. The instrument is supplied as well as the connection. The number is the marina number plus the number of the dock occupied.

SECURITY AND SAFES ON BOARD

While some boats do have built-in safes, most do not, and the security of valuables becomes a problem. By and large, I think it best to rent a safe-deposit box in a nearby bank if you must carry this sort of plunder with you. Built-in safes can usually be easily broken adrift and carried off, yet they require more time to open or break free than you might have in a fire or a sinking. Some of the plush marinas, like hotels, will place valuables in their own safes at no charge.

A boat is, of course, an ideal structure in which to find all sorts of "secret" compartments that, while possibly being secure from robbers, give scant protection against fire, water damage, or rodents.

On *Penobscot* we solve the problem in this way: we take with us only papers that we know will be required, leaving our box key and a letter of permission to the bank with a member of the family at home. Then we take a safe-deposit box in a central location in the South, and in it we keep valuables, including jewelry. We open a checking account in two or more banks in areas we plan to visit . . . and use all the credit cards we can. (Master Charge and Bankamericard/Visa, plus oil company cards and a few local merchant charge cards, all work fine.) Sometimes we have trouble raising a dime for a phone call, but we have never lost anything to crime, fire, or the perils of the sea.

COAST GUARD STATIONS
ON VHF—FM RADIO GUARD

Location	Voice Call
Newport News	Group Norfolk
Cape Henry	Group Norfolk
Portsmouth	Group Norfolk
Elizabeth City	Elizabeth City Air Station
Cedar Island Creek	Group Fort Macon
Croatan National Forest	Group Fort Macon
Holly Ridge	Group Fort Macon
Caroline Beach	Group Wrightsville
Myrtle Beach	Group Charleston
Parris Island	Group Charleston
Tybee Island	Tybee Island Station
Jekyll Island	Group Mayport
Jacksonville Beach	Group Mayport
Flagler Beach	Group Mayport
Cape Canaveral	Group Mayport
Fort Pierce	Fort Pierce Station
Jupiter	Lake Worth Inlet Station
Delray Beach	Lake Worth Inlet Station
Miami Beach	Miami Beach Base
Islamorada	Islamorada Station
Marathon	Marathon Station
Key West	Key West Station
Naples .	Ft. Myers Beach Station
Venice	Group St. Petersburg
St. Petersburg Beach	Group St. Petersburg
Tarpon Springs	Group St. Petersburg
Crystal River	Group St. Petersburg

Note: a station is planned for Hobucken, N.C., in 1977-78.

PUBLIC COAST STATIONS—MARINE OPERATORS

If any problem, call operator (or U.S. Coast Guard) on Channel 16.

Location	Channel	Location	Channel
Hampton, Va.	26	Boca Raton	84
(call Norfolk)		Fort Lauderdale	26
Norfolk, Va.	26	Miami	25
Beaufort, N.C.	28	Homestead	27
Wilmington, N.C.	26	Marathon	25
N. Augusta, S.C.	26	Key West	26
Georgetown, S.C.	26	Naples	25
Charleston, S.C.	26	Cape Coral	26
Savannah, Ga.	28	Venice	28
Jacksonville	26	Palmetto	25
Palatka	25	St. Petersburg	27
Cocoa	26	Tampa	26
Vero Beach	27	Clearwater	24
West Palm Beach	28	Crystal River	28
Belle Glade	24		

For those who *must* have a safe, there are several security companies offering small, explosion-proof steel safes that may be bolted into the vessel structure from the interior; they will also float.

SUNSHADES AND AWNINGS

Sunshades are much needed at all times, not for "people shade," but for boat temperature control. While at moorings, such below-decks areas as the foredeck, an uncovered after deck with accommodations below, definitely will be cooler with an awning over them. The southern sun is extremely hot and soon warms all the flat surfaces of the vessel. What is needed is a "light" awning, of white synthetic material, secured in a flat position about four feet above the main deck.

If the awning is flown over a ridgepole (or taut center rope), it will shed dew as well, and possibly allow decks to dry occasionally. Sailing vessels have no problem, since the main boom provides the backbone of a frame. A "fly" of this type is a must in the summer and very desirable in the winter.

Large glass areas, such as a wheelhouse or the forward end of a main cabin, should be protected by a clipped-on cloth cover, especially if the glass area is canted (not plumb). Sunlight streaming through glass creates enormous heat and soon overheats the entire craft.

A much-used method of keeping down heat is to avoid all paint on all flat surfaces except WHITE paint. Sometime rest your palm on a gray or black surface, and then on a nearby white one, and you will understand the difference. At times it is as much as 30 degrees! This is why most southern boats are all-white boats, with only the trim members darker. Even light gray, or Kennebec buff, is frowned upon as a deck paint. The excessive heat of these relatively dark surfaces, plus the effects of ultraviolet rays, soon break down the paint. The seam compounds then dry up and open the surface to dampness and rot.

A gloss paint will "shed" heat more than a semi-gloss and, further, it is a hard, durable surface, easy to keep clean by ordinary swabbing programs. Raw teak, with rubber-based seam compounds, seems to withstand heat best, if a natural deck is wanted. While much hotter than a white deck, teak can take it, especially if it is permitted to bleach into a fairly light tone.

PETS ON BOARD

If you must . . . and a great many people must . . . give some heed to the problems of a pet on shipboard. He's limited in his roving. He has to "unlearn" a great many things that you taught him when living ashore . . . like the difference between a hydrant and a mizzenmast. And he's going to be surrounded by strange smells, strange companions, and an environment of limited exercise and interest.

He is going to be a problem, you may be sure. Dogs . . . even cats . . . do not smell good in the confines of a small cabin, in the still heat of the tropical midday, or when wet or overheated. Neither the marina nor the community is going to allow him to roam the grounds unless leashed. And if you are on the hook, you are going to have to row Fido ashore every few hours or be in even worse trouble. Possibly a small dog, a lap dog, could be happy on a live-aboard boat, but it borders on cruelty to take along a big, freedom-loving family mutt for a winter afloat. Possibly there is some merit in the argument that he's a "watchdog," needed to guard the boat during your absence, but a burglar alarm is better and cheaper.

I am told that cats make far better seamen than dogs, being small, clean, independent, and far more self-sufficient.

All in all, it would appear that the winter vacation would stand a better chance of succeeding without a pet—but if it must be, how about a good, profane green parrot?

DOCKING TIE-UPS

Tie-ups are no great problem if the mooring is composed of a stout harness consisting of bow and stern lines, two spring lines, fenders, and possibly fender boards. One end of the line should be made up into a spliced eye large enough to slip over a 12-inch pile. It is always used as the shore end, so that you can control the boat *from* the boat via the long, cleated end. For a

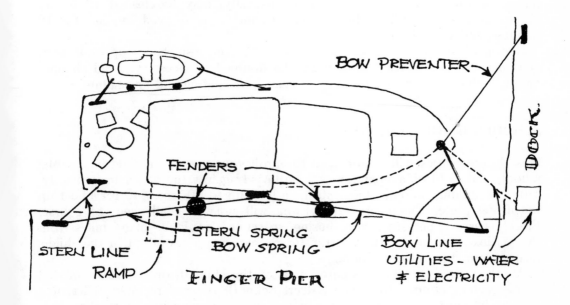

Snugged up at a modern marina.

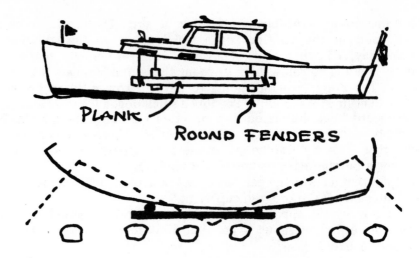

PLANK

ROUND FENDERS

A fender board is necessary when lying against pilings or face dock.

permanent tie-up, slip a split length of old hose over the line in the way of cleats, chocks, or hawse holes.

In some parts of the Ditch, notably from Charleston, South Carolina, to Fernandina, Florida, the tidal rise is as much as nine feet, and all the docks are not floating docks. Lines here must be tended as the tide levels change, since there is little room fore or aft in which to sway on a slack line at high water. Here, too, the fender board serves well against the rather dirty, tarred pilings of the average marina. (Tar, incidentally, may be cleaned off fender boards or fenders with ordinary oven cleaner. It is sprayed on, left for 10 minutes, and then flushed off.)

Half-inch line will serve for boats up to 32 feet, ¾-inch line up to 45 feet, and one-inch line beyond that; it can be doubled if necessary. Lead all lines "clear," which means that there is no chance of chafing and line failure.

SCHOOLING FOR CHILDREN

Most Florida cities will require you to enroll your school-age child in a public school, and a Florida boat tax will be levied against the vessel immediately. This is a nominal amount, like $30 for a boat up to 40 feet, $40 for a boat up to 50 feet, etc. The short-term visitor will not be challenged, of course. Florida has 100-percent school busing, so schools could be many miles from the marina. Prepare for such a transfer by carrying a transcript of the child's record from the previous school.

An alternative to school is enrollment of the child in one of the approved home-teaching courses (like The Calvert School). A strict regimen of learning and study must be instituted. While the parent is usually the teacher, it is possible . . . and probably best . . . to arrange with a school teacher or older

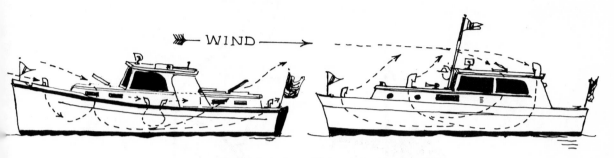

The action of ventilators.

student, or at any rate a stranger, to teach the course. Florida school authorities are familiar with this plan and approve it ... and they may demand proof of results by examination of the student.

Several plush marinas on the Gold Coast offer babysitting services, morning kindergartens, and playgrounds with small pools for children.

HOW TO SET VENTILATORS

See the sketches for positioning ventilators ... remembering that cowls do not scoop *in* the air. Rather, they draw *out* the air (by a process of local vacuum). An open hatch does the same thing, though not quite as efficiently. Vent openings do not *have* to face bow or stern. Rather, they should face the breeze, even if from the beam.

THE WIND SCOOP

Borrowing from the old schooner days, the yacht in southern waters can well use a canvas, Dacron, or vinyl "wind scoop." The throat should be custom-fitted to a forward hatch frame, with a puckering string. The "cowl" needs to be large—about 16 to 24 square feet of scoop area, its wings stretched by lanyards to headstay, shrouds, or temporary standards. On a square hatch frame, it can be faced in any direction desired and, like its smaller counterpart, works best faced *away* from the wind so as to pull, not scoop.

Another, used at the same time on a stern deck hatch or platform hatch, will create a real storm within the boat.

HAND GUNS ABOARD

The question of guns bothers many people in these times. There is no law against having guns aboard, save in Massachusetts (should you come down that

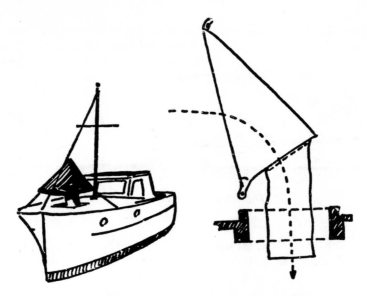

A type of canvas wind scoop for extra ventilation.

way). I daresay most boats can produce a hand gun. I have one. I have never used it ... and I'm very glad that I haven't. But I have heard of a few instances of bad scenes when a gun has settled the matter decisively. I carry one, as I reported, but I really don't know if I'd use it. I am told that unless you know how to use it, you are better off without a gun, for a gun gives you no second chance. By and large, I expect the sane thing to do is *not* to carry a hand weapon ... save, possibly, Mace and/or tear gas. I think 'most any police advice would be the same.

There is no problem in shipping sporting guns, but it is wise to keep them cased and chained to steel eyes in the armory ... and UNLOADED.

POTABLE WATER

Marina-bound, water is no serious problem, save the excessive use of chlorine so common throughout the South. A proper system will have a valved loop that short-circuits the ship's pressure pump and places the service directly on the city mains via a dock hose. Usually a pressure-reducing valve is permanently cut into the line directly after the hose connection. For domestic water service, use a *white* hose; it is cooler and cleaner. Tanked water needs attention in the warm tropics, no matter how pure it is when tanked or how clean tanks and lines are.

To clean tanks and system (pipes, valves, etc.), for each 300 gallons of water, put into the *filled* tank one ounce of hypochlorate of lime. Let stand about 36 hours, then drain and refill. Then, to each 50 gallons of water in the filled tank, add one tablespoon of tincture of iodine. Stir by rolling the boat, surging against the lines, or paddling with a lath through the fillcap. Let stand about 30 minutes before use.

TO PROTECT AGAINST MILDEW

Mildew is an ever-present threat in the Southland, especially during the summer rainy season. It attacks anything that it can cling to: rough or scaly paint or varnish, the vinyls, cloth, canvas, leather . . . oh, especially leather! Mildew is a spore that arrives on the breeze and takes hold in lees, dead-air spaces, sunless areas, and moist areas. Once "landed," it grows, rots, discolors, and smells. It seems worse on a "dead" boat, or one in storage. Here are the ways to combat it:

1. Mix with *all* paint and varnish one of the vials of "mildew preventives" sold by all paint stores in the South for a dollar or so and good for treating up to five gallons of paint. This will in no way discolor paint. It is simply a poison that remains on the surface of the dried paint and prevents mildew spores from growing. It is effective for about two years; after that, it is valueless.

2. Paint or spray *all* surfaces, inside and outside, including surfaces painted more than two years ago, with a colorless germicide. Lysol is excellent and readily obtainable in any supermarket.

If delicate fabrics are not involved, you can spray or sponge with common household bleach (Clorox is fine), diluted about 1:2.

3. To remove "set" mildew, use a 3:1 solution of water and bleach and a stiff brush, and have a can of household cleaner handy for the deep spots and corners. (Comet is best for marine use.) Then spray with Lysol or its equivalent.

4. Effective treatment for a dead boat, or her lockers and crannies at any time, is the use of "gas" bags. These are available at markets and chain outlets in the form of bagged powder or cakes, which slowly evaporate and release poisonous "gases" to prevent mildew spores from setting. A 40-footer would take at least a dozen bags, good for about three months' treatment.

Recently promoted spray treatments promise not only prevention of mildew but its instant removal. The active ingredient is calcium hypochlorite (a strong poison). I have tried only one with dramatic success. It is a Florida product called X-14 Mildew Remover and is available all over Florida and in some marinas. An excellent treatise on the general subject is Home and Garden Bulletin No. 68, *How to Prevent and Remove Mildew.* It is prepared by the U.S. Department of Agriculture and may be obtained for 10 cents (or probably free from your congressman) from the Superintendent of Documents, U.S. Government Printing Office, Washington, D.C. 20402.

DRY ROT

Dry rot is the ever-present threat to boats. Wherever there is wood, even if it is only trim on a glass or metal boat, plus moisture, rot will attack and spread, spread, spread, unless instantly checked. At the very first sign of rot, the attack should begin.

First the dry rot must be discovered. One sure sign is peeling paint or varnish, usually with discoloration (darkening). Clean the surface. Then tap with a small hammer or a marlin spike—anything solid but not too heavy—and listen. Sound wood will sound solid, firm, and even ring slightly. Mushy, rotting wood will sound mushy, soft, and have no ring or bounce.

Dig out, with a chisel, small "carving" gouge, or a sharp knife, all the affected wood. It is usually brown and lifeless, even powderlike if dry. DIG IT ALL OUT, right down to clean, bright wood. It might be easier to remove the entire member.

Then soak the area with copper naphthenate (Cuprinol and other proprietary products) several times, each time drying it under hot, direct sun or a "heat lamp." When thoroughly dry, fill the cavity with an epoxy putty, or a block of new wood set in epoxy glue, or a mixture of epoxy glue and sawdust (or other filler). Keep dry and protect with the appropriate coating as soon as the epoxy has set.

Look for dry rot in the way of fastenings, especially galvanized ones, in corners, in deck pockets that seem to hold water, and between all wood joinings that are neither glued nor bedded. Dry rot never occurs below the waterline (in salt water), but it may attack from the inside, behind refrigerators and tanks and in airless areas like cable lockers, the stem and quarters, and under and around deck leaks.

TO REMOVE BOW WAVE STAIN

The light brown bow stains you see on so many Waterway boats come from the bow wave of a steaming boat. Much of the inland area of the Ditch is fresh swamp water, slightly acid and stained brown by vegetation such as cypress, saw grass, marshlands, and, quite likely these days, by the washings from many pulp mills.

The stain must be scrubbed off with a nonabrasive soap and bleach and a stiff bristle brush, plus HOT water. While an abrasive, as well as some chemicals, will easily remove the stain, this process also removes the paint gloss . . . and the next attack of brown bows will bite deeply into the deglossed paint and perhaps not yield to removal tactics.

TO SHINE BRASS

Regular polishing with a genuine marine polish (Oxford, Brasso) is the only satisfactory attack . . . if you have a crew! Most of us do the brass when it looks so bad that we're ashamed of it.

So, for really needy brass:

1. Wash down with a solution of muriatic acid (about $1.50 a gallon wherever they sell mason's supplies) and water (1:3) and then several polishes, or:

2. Wash off with ordinary Worcestershire sauce; then polish.

3. Bronze wool, fine, will greatly help with stubborn brass. If paint or varnish has slopped over a fitting, remove it with paint remover, a sharp knife, and emery paper.

4. To preserve the shine about 50 percent longer, wax with ordinary exterior (automobile) paste wax.

TO SHINE CHROME

Use the same compound that you use as a cleaner for your automobile (Fuller's Earth in solution), then polish lightly with a marine polish, and, possibly, apply wax.

TO CLEAN SALTED WINDOWS, WINDSCREENS, ETC.

First, wash or sponge with vinegar; then attack with a spray of Windex or something equal . . . and quite "equal" is water and ammonia, in about a 50-50 solution. Newspaper will polish just as well as rags.

TO REMOVE SCRATCHES FROM PLEXIGLASS

Simple . . . polish, polish, and polish plexiglass with a small cloth pad and ordinary toothpaste. Fluoride is not required. Do not even try emery or sandpapers.

TO KEEP THE BILGES CLEAN AND SWEET

In a pumped-out bilge, use boat soap, which is a bottle of commercial-strength detergent (Wisk, Era, Janitor in a Drum), and flood with *fresh* water. Let it slosh around for a week or so, especially when steaming; then pump it overside. If in fresh water (as on the St. Johns River, Lake Okeechobee, the deep Everglades, etc.), add a few pounds of "ice cream" salt to the bilge water after cleaning. I am not above dropping in a dash of pine oil; it all helps.

TO REMOVE OIL SPOTS FROM TEAK DECKS

Cover the oil spot overnight with a smear of asbestos powder (available from heating contractors, hardware stores). Brush it off in the morning; the oil will be with the powder.

This works wonderfully in engine rooms that have picked up oil around the hull parts, especially if helped by a scraper or putty knife.

TO MAKE SOOGEE

Soogee, the Navy standard for deck and exterior washdowns, is made as follows: to 10 quarts (a pailful) of fresh, *hot* water add a cup of commercial-strength detergent (Wisk) and a cup of bleach (Clorox). Apply with a stiff push broom, swab with a cotton swab, and flush with cold, fresh hose water. Comet or another abrasive might help in corners.

CARE OF ELECTRONICS AND ELECTRICAL CIRCUITS

Moisture is a factor to be reckoned with in the South, especially during the humid and rainy months from May to November. Free circulation of dry air is to be sought always by natural ventilation of the hull and, if indicated, the use of portable electric fans in wardrobes, chests of drawers, hanging lockers, and the more remote, lower hull areas, including the engine room.

It is an excellent plan, upon reaching a mooring or dock with the running schedule about to be abandoned for a while, to spray the entire electrical circuitry, both high and low tension, and battery systems as well as shoreside systems, with CRC or its equivalent. This provides a nongreasy, durable moisture barrier for a very few cents; it will prevent those slow power leaks (especially of DC power) and keep the entire system in a "go" condition for months.

Experienced cruisers also run the engines about once a week to combat interior condensation. Run for about 10 minutes, or until the oil has warmed up; this is best achieved rapidly, well strapped in, and thrown into slow forward speed, at about 1200 rpms.

TO DISCOURAGE TEREDOS

If possible, run into and stay in fresh water for 48 hours. Teredos will slow down and possibly back out, since they cannot survive in fresh water for long. This practice also will kill oyster and barnacle "sets," but it will not remove their shells.

TANK VENT CHECKS

All tank vents should be checked regularly for insects building nests in the entrances. This seems a favorite nesting place for several species. It is effective to roll a small piece of copper screening into a pyramidal cylinder and force it into the vent opening. This will at least keep the pests from building deep in the pipe and creating a real problem.

WASTE DISPOSAL

By state law, garbage and dry waste collection centers are part of all marinas. Bag your garbage and take it *daily* to the center for pick-up. Some marinas place garbage cans (or oil drums) at strategic locations along the docks. This practice is all right if the cans are covered and the users keep the covers on. Both types of trash are subject to the depredations of two Florida waterside pests, the raccoon and the palm rat. The 'coon can easily open a can cover, or capsize a can, or open a disposal bag. The rat, present in most stands of palm trees, especially the coconut palm and the sabal palm (both "ornamentals"), is not a city sewer rat but a small, clean animal. But he is a rodent, and dangerous as such. So keep garbage covered and in the specific locations that are protected by poisons and traps.

The disposal of large items (such as old furniture, building materials, etc.) is a problem solved only by calling in a "sanitary contractor," or hiring a cab and disposing of it yourself at a county "land-fill" area. This is simply building land, a controlled garbage dump. A fee is sometimes charged for use by private citizens.

Oil waste (as when changing engine or gear oil) can usually be disposed of at the fuel dock of the marina, where a tank is maintained for just that purpose. Some service stations maintain such tanks also, and they may be used for a small fee; or possibly no fee, if the oil is bought there.

Under no circumstances dispose of anything by casting it into the water. Not only police, but many private citizens, are most environment-conscious, and you will surely be caught (as you should be). The law machinery is readily available to prosecute and penalize you.

If you are off on the anchor, the correct thing to do is to take your litter ashore and *bury* it in some wild place; or carry it with you until public disposal is possible. Much of the tropical water is clear, blue, and almost transparent, so even sunken bottles and cans come back to haunt.

PEST CONTROL AND ERADICATION

Be in no doubt, the Southland is a land of bugs and crawlers. Direct and positive steps must be taken to keep them under control. The "winter months" (December, January, and February) are relatively free of mosquitoes and midges, but after a few warm days, hatches of "blind" mosquitoes, midges, no-see-ums, "love-bugs," and tiny biting flies are apt to descend upon the vessel. The guards against them are these:

1. Complete screening of all openings with at least #18 mesh copper or fiberglass insect screening. This size will not keep midges out, but it will not

keep air out either, so you really can't do much about midges by screening.

2. To keep midges, "no-see-ums," and mosquitoes away, use a spray repellent, usually one with a kerosene base. This also kills. Quite as effective, cheaper, and much longer-lasting are the "punks." These are burners, just like old-fashioned firecracker punk—various shapes of a suffocating powder that drive off these insects. A few up to windward, even on deck of a still night, will keep a fairly large area free. Punks may be burned inside, at night, and will effectively patrol even a large cabin for many hours.

3. To keep flies down, use the above and, in confined spaces, the "insect strips" sold by oil companies. Poisons, such as Paris green, work well, but dead insects then become a problem; they may even be a danger if they fall into food. An old-fashioned flyswatter is a needed weapon in all boat areas and is the only effective control for the big "greenheads" of the swamps and the occasional horsefly.

All the "flyers" can be discouraged by anointing the screens of doors, ports, hatches, and sash with an insect repellent put up in paste form. The most effective one we have found is a compound used against blackflies in the northwoods of Canada and Maine. It used to be known as "lallacapop." It is sold by L. L. Bean, Freeport, Maine 04032. This product is also effective if dabbed on the bill of a cap, the shoe tips, or in the standing rigging of a sailer. It is said that it will discourage anything but a deer or a Frenchman . . . neither of which is a problem of the live-aboard cruiser. (Actually, the odor is not offensive to humans; strange, perhaps, but you *can* live with it.)

4. A pest peculiar to the South is the palmetto bug, sometimes mistakenly called a roach, with all its horrible connotations. He is a flat, winged bug about 2 inches long, and he can squeeze into incredibly tiny places . . . like between your foot and the deck and come out full of vinegar. He loves brown paper bags and cartons and usually rides them from the market to your boat. He is in no way "dirty"; he's a clean bug, just doing what bugs do. He eats only gourmet bug food: draperies, carpets, bookbindings, lamp shades, charts; nothing cheap for this creature.

The palmetto bug is controlled by putting out poison pellets (available at any market or hardware store) and keeping them there, whether or not a bug is seen. You may assume that one will someday appear. Along with red or fire ants, he sometimes boards via the lines and can be trapped readily by wrapping the line, near the wharfside, with a strip of old-fashioned flypaper.

In extreme cases, after periods of long standing during which no control was exercised, Orkin will have to be called in. Orkin is the pest eradicator known all over Florida and the South. He places a tent over your boat, squirts in some magic gas, and things die all over the place . . . rats, mice, bugs, termites. It costs plenty, but it is the only way short of pulling the plug to rid the boat completely of pests.

By and large, it is best to assume the presence of bugs and attack them, even if they are not in evidence. Keep a clean boat and put out the powders, pellets, and pans . . . life in the "buggy" South will not bother you in the least.

HURRICANES

Understand hurricanes. Send to the National Weather Service, Department of Commerce, Washington, D.C., for:

The Hurricane—14 pages, illustrated, 5 cents

Florida Hurricanes—3 pages, 5 cents

Hurricane Tracking Chart—H. M. Gousha Company, San Jose, California, or free from the Shell Oil Co., Tulsa, Oklahoma

Hurricanes are a bugaboo to the northerner, but *only* a mild inconvenience to the southerner. The boater has no choice but to flee from them and, if he is wise, will adopt a plan early in his vacation. The marina will chase him out to save its docks and facilities. The anchored boat usually should not remain in an anchorage, especially if it is also occupied by other boats. The Coast Guard and local marine patrols will help in either situation by offering advice *before* the fact.

We cannot go deeply into hurricane procedures here, but must most emphatically stress the wisdom of preparation very early in the southern exposure period. Life will definitely be better for all hands by reason of a definite plan, educational preparation, and sound command practices that keep the boat ready and operable on short notice at all times of hurricane threat.

FIRE WARP

A dock fire, or another nearby vessel afire, is an ever-present threat. Wise skippers always rig a "fire warp." This is simply a line from the inboard end of the vessel to the extreme head of the dock or pier. In case of fire on board, your boat can be moved *from the dock* into clear water and away

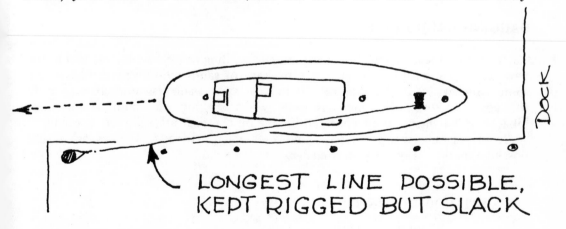

In case of pier or nearby fire, let all docking lines go on the double and haul away, by winch or by hand, on fire warp.

from the dock and other boats. In case of fire on the dock or on a nearby boat, *you* can move your boat into the clear *from your own deck.* Thus, an engine failure, or an engine out of commission (as for an overhaul), or lack of helping hands, need not mean destruction of your boat.

Large vessels (yachts in the 80-foot class, for example) are moved by leading the bitter end of the warp to a deck winch, usually the bow anchor winch.

CAT HARPINGS

When that midnight breeze springs up and the halyards begin to thrum and sleep becomes impossible, rig cat harpings. Only be fore-armed, and rig them when you don't need them. You'll sleep like a baby.

Wind-activated halyards, slapping the mast(s), transmit the thrum through the vessel—and into your ear, so close to the hull itself. The cat harping is any piece of small stuff that breaks the rhythmic halyard slap by holding them off the spar, usually by a lead to a flanking shroud. Sometimes skippers use one of those rubber ropes, with a hook snatched to each end—lubberly but effective.

The hollow spar in which the halyards lead upward is a real problem, for you cannot apply cat harpings to such. By experiment you must select either of the following options, neither of which will be 100 percent effective. (A) Lead the fall to a winch and snug it up so there is no slack. This will last a few minutes or hours only, because the halyard will stretch and slap again. A wire halyard will have a better chance of remaining quiet, since only the short rope and tail can stretch. (B) Slack off and let several bights of line flop into the base of the hollow spar. The halyard may slap a bit, but it will not thrum.

BAGGING BRIQUETTES

To have one mess instead of many when handling stove briquettes, tackle the new paper bag with canvas gloves, a package of sandwich-size plastic bags, and some wire twists. Package about 10 briquettes to each bag and stow them in the coal bunker . . . the mess is gone when stoking the cabin fireplace or hibachi. For lighting, pour charcoal lighter on the coal after slitting the bag.

Avoid burning wood of any kind in a yacht stove; it throws ashes and possibly sparks. Briquettes do neither.

ON A STILL NIGHT ON THE ANCHOR

Plague take the purists . . . carry the anchor cable aft and moor by the stern, on a quarter cleat. You will get much more air and, possibly, lie even better.

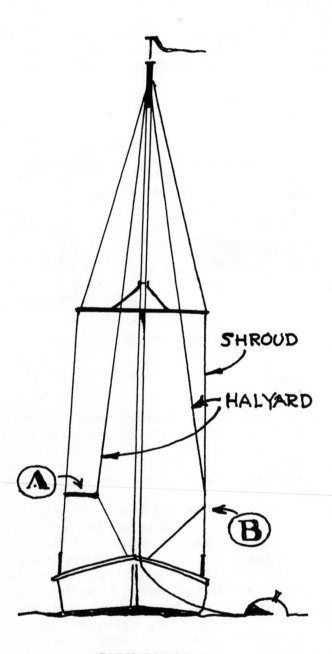

SHROUD

HALYARD

A

B

CAT HARPINGS

To quiet drumming of rigging. (A) Short length of rubber line with hook on each end. (B) Halyard seized to shrouds with small stuff and belayed to usual cleat or fife rail at mast foot. Generally most effective if rigged as high as it is possible to reach.

THE "ASPIRIN HATCH"

There is a unique solution to the problem of the usual fall and spring afternoon showers of the tropics. The "aspirin hatch" is illustrated here. Use any
aspirin tablet and be sure that the first drops picked up by the supporting rod
are guided to the tablet.

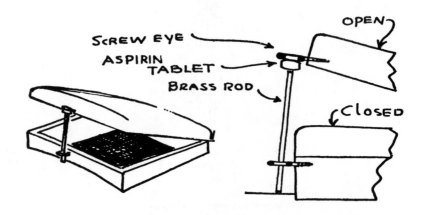

The "aspirin hatch."

WATER CATCHERS

On moorings, or in the offshore islands, you may well need an auxiliary
source of water. The tropical cruiser solves this problem in one of two ways:
   1. By arranging a series of plugs to baffle limbers or scuppers, to trap upper
deck water and lead it into the tank. I once used two of the hollow brass pipe
stanchions common to sundecks, piping them into the tank that happened to
be in the stern.
   2. By rigging a tarp, slack, so that water collects in the center and can be
piped to the tank fill, either by a direct hose link or by a siphon.
   In either case, the deck must be clean (especially of bird droppings) and
free of salt (from spray). Let the first few gallons of a rain shower wash off
the salt; then tank it. A small tarp or deck will collect an amazing amount of
water. In the rainy season in the Bahamas, I have lived several months without
"shore" water, even with washdowns, plenty of showers, and all domestic
uses. I think the tarp is best: cleaner, simpler, and probably more sanitary. A
tarp about eight-by-eight is about right; anything larger will create a support
problem, for a gallon of water weighs about eight pounds, and such a tarp will
readily collect 100 gallons (or 800 pounds).
   Be sure to treat such water as recommended before.

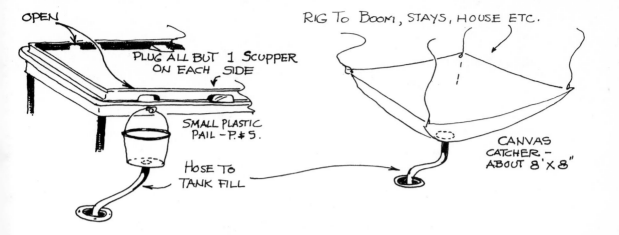

OPEN

PLUG ALL BUT 1 SCUPPER
ON EACH SIDE

SMALL PLASTIC
PAIL – P. # 5.

HOSE TO
TANK FILL

RIG TO BOOM, STAYS, HOUSE ETC.

CANVAS
CATCHER –
ABOUT 8' X 8"

WATER CATCHERS

Left: *Any cabin or house overhead with scuppered hand grip can be utilized as shown.* Right:
*Canvas panel to be rigged to boat parts, spars, shrouds, etc. Hoses in both are simply garden
hose with upper end epoxied in. Basic design will depend upon individual craft.*

SUMMER LAY-UPS

When leaving a boat in Florida, as for the summer or for a visit north, take
her to a covered wet-storage basin. There are many, most of them up fresh or
brackish rivers (which is all to the good). Select a facility with 24-hour
security. All offer two options. Dead storage, after storage battery removal
(which is placed on the line for trickle charge upkeep), includes "keeping an
eye" on the boat against leaks. Service storage means that the boat will be
boarded at least weekly, thoroughly checked, aired, pumped dry (if necessary), and the engines run at idle for about an hour weekly. The first service
cost varies from $1.50 to $2 per foot per month; the second is the same, plus
the charge for labor involved . . . now in the $15 per hour category.

Marinas will not accept dead-storage boats; nor would you want to be in
one unattended for any length of time.

It in no way pays to store a boat outdoors, or on a mooring. The sun
alone—not to mention rain, dew, vandalism, and theft, possibly worms,
barnacles, and grass—will do more damage and cost more than you will save.
Note that the yard *does not* insure your boat for anything; you must still
keep your insurance in force, but it is endorsed at a lesser rate for the
"lay-up" period.

Watch out in these storage yards. Do not let them berth you near a steel
vessel, especially one on which there is welding going on, nor near underwater
cables, bridges, or regular traffic routes. Lock the boat and file the key in the
office. The Florida yards have a long history of service and know a lot more
about caring for your vessel in the South than you do.

Index

174

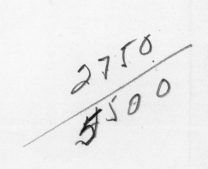

2750.
5500